Tobatí: PARAGUAYAN TOWN

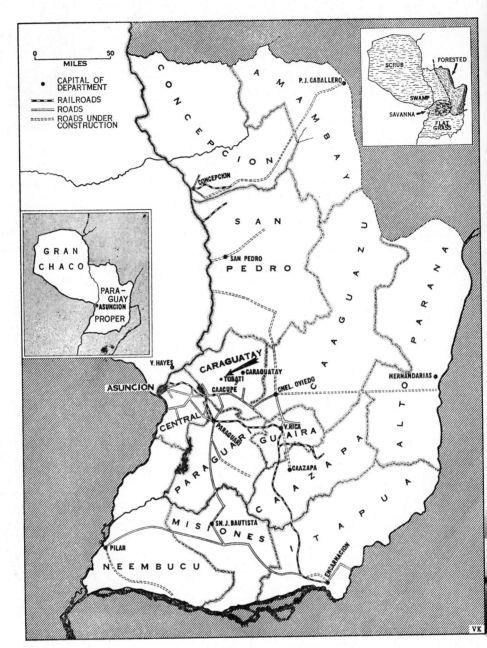

EASTERN PARAGUAY

Tobatí: PARAGUAYAN TOWN

By

ELMAN R. SERVICE

and

HELEN S. SERVICE

THE UNIVERSITY OF CHICAGO PRESS

Library of Congress Catalog Number: 54–11214

THE UNIVERSITY OF CHICAGO PRESS, CHICAGO 37
Cambridge University Press, London, N.W. 1, England
The University of Toronto Press, Toronto 5, Canada

Foreword

The people of Paraguay are among the most interesting and least understood of Latin America. Remote from modern currents of world change, underpopulated, and economically little developed despite considerable potential agricultural wealth, the nation is considered "backward" in most respects. But the significance of this "backwardness" has been badly misinterpreted, owing to inaccurate cultural-historical analysis and wholly inadequate information on the way of life of the modern population. There has developed the unrealistic stereotype that the Paraguayans are essentially a Guaraní Indian people—that the cultural, linguistic, and physical or biological heritage of the modern people is derived from the aboriginal Guaraní Indians. Paraguay is thus thought to be "backward" in having preserved an Indian way of life and in having failed to adopt Hispanic culture. This fanciful idea, which may appropriately be called the "Guaraní myth," has, however, been converted into a national symbol by Paraguayan scholars who extol the virtues of the alleged Guaraní traits. These assertions have been uncritically accepted by scholars elsewhere.

The Guaraní myth is seriously challenged for the first time, and, I think we can say, dispelled, by Dr. and Mrs. Service, who spent a year in Paraguay (1948–49) living with the people, observing and participating in daily family and community activities, recording in detail all aspects of rural culture, and analyzing their findings in the perspective of Paraguay's history. The observations and interpretations recorded in the present volume show the utter lack of evidence for the myth. But if Paraguay loses glamour for not having an Indian heritage, it gains interest for what it really is; and it is certainly much more intelligible in terms of known processes of history and culture change. While

v

the Paraguayans will probably preserve the myth for its symbolic
value, there is no longer any doubt that it does not square with
cultural fact.

The Services present a vivid and detailed picture of life in
Paraguay that will appeal to the general reader and will supply
basic data for social scientists. They explain how the interaction
of Spanish and Indian cultures in the context of a special colonial
setting, a particular geographical situation, and a unique sequence
of historical events has given contemporary Paraguay its distinctive character. They help resolve certain apparent paradoxes: the
rapid change in colonial times from native Guaraní Indian culture to a rather thoroughly Hispanic culture, despite the settlement of the country by only a handful of Spanish men; the series
of violent nationalistic wars carried on by an essentially gentle
people; and the existence of a "nation" in the absence of strong
institutions which are the normal binding forces of a state.

Why the Guaraní myth arose and was perpetuated in Paraguay is worth some consideration. This myth is a stereotype of
the kind found commonly in Latin America. That lower-class or
peasant-like people are widely considered to be "Indian" is the
counterpart of the belief that the upper class is typically Hispanic. The culture of the latter is truly derived from the Spanish
heritage, but it does not exemplify all of it. It consists of patterns
which require comparative wealth and status. It is generally
ascribed the following characteristics: use of material adjuncts
of civilized life, such as shoes, tailored clothes, tiled houses with
glass windows, white bread, wine, and other European foods;
aversion to manual labor; high evaluation of the pursuit of philosophy, literature, poetry, and aesthetic and spiritual values; re-
pudiation of moneygrubbing and deprecation of material values;
practice of warm hospitality and gracious living; use of the Spanish language; literacy; and acceptance of the Catholic religion.
These features best flourish only in the subculture of an economically secure class that has leisure, literacy, education, and
wealth. Anyone living at a bare subsistence level or toiling all
day for meager wages could not support the standards of hospitality and pursue spiritual values in a significant way. Even
orthodox participation in the Catholic church depends upon

opportunity often denied the lower class. It requires the presence of a priest and sufficient funds to pay tithings and to hold church weddings, baptisms, and other rites.

The fact that the lower classes are widely thought to be Indian derives principally from the colonial situation in Mexico and the Andes. In these densely populated areas, the conquistadors came as overlords and exploited the native people, first through encomiendas and *mitayo* or draft labor in the mines and later through privately owned plantations or haciendas. The subcultures of the tribute-payers in the encomiendas and of the agricultural and mine laborers were derived directly from their Indian forebears. The class separation of Spaniard and Indian helped preserve the culture of the latter. The lower-class Indians did not become strongly Hispanicized until they became a plantation or proletariat laboring force. The Indians who remained more or less independent in their own rural villages, especially those who owned land and produced for themselves, were better able to retain their aboriginal heritage. Thus in the early colonial period "peasant farmer" and "lower class" were synonymous with "Indian."

But the preconception that the workers and farmers preserved Indian customs has survived today. That is, failure to share upper-class Hispanic traits is taken to mean an Indian way of life. Even in the various national censuses "Indians" are still defined as persons who do not wear shoes or tailored clothing, who do not eat white bread, who live in various kinds of huts, who speak an aboriginal language, who have a "pagan" religion, and who are illiterate. Most of these are negative characteristics, and none defines subcultures positively in substantive terms.

The tendency to subsume all people lacking upper-class culture as "Indian" has been carried over into cultural studies. One may read accounts, for example, of the Tarascan-speaking "Indian" farmers of highland Mexico or the peasant-like "Indians" of Moche in coastal Peru, but he will search in vain for any substantial evidence of aboriginal culture. Instead of recognizing that such people have a special kind of lower-class Hispanic culture, some anthropologists have attempted to place them in a category of "mestizo culture," which is defined as a kind of mechanical mixture of Hispanic and Indian culture elements rather than a qualitatively distinctive subculture.

This *simpliste* and misleading classification would have been avoided had the nature of these cultures and the processes of historical change been adequately conceived. Hispanic culture was by no means a simple, monolithic entity consisting of a common core of traits shared by all descendants of Spain. Not only did it consist of national institutions, such as the church, state, army, and economic patterns, which affected Spaniards of different classes—and regions—in unlike ways, but Hispanic society comprised at least two principal subcultures which were related to its essentially agrarian foundation. The class of powerful landlords maintained one way of life, the peasant farmers and the agricultural laborers another. In the New World those who were unable to gain sufficient wealth to realize their ambition to maintain an upper-class subculture were no less Hispanic for their comparative poverty and simple life.

Rural subcultures gradually changed during the colonial and republican periods. Whether certain local communities of Indians perpetuated their aboriginal culture or a culture derived from sixteenth-century Spain and whether Indian and white communities developed new patterns depended upon a variety of circumstances. The nature of change was determined by the importance of subsistence farming; the production of cash crops according to environmental potentialities and marketing opportunities; the methods of field production, processing, marketing, and credit support for cash crops; the kinds of political controls exercised by the nation; the amount of education and communications; and other factors, which themselves constantly changed. Thus the emergence of the various subcultures found today in Latin America is a far larger problem than that of tracing individual culture elements to their Hispanic or Indian sources. It is a question of the local area and its productive potentialities, of the cultural-historical factors which have affected the realization of those potentialities, and of the adaptation of certain basic features of the lifeways of the people to geographical, economic, and political factors. The Services have analyzed Paraguayan culture in this larger frame of reference, and in this way they have made it very understandable.

The previous conception of Paraguayan culture illustrates in the extreme how misleading a stereotype can be. Because the basic population of Paraguay is essentially peasant and lacks most of the characteristics thought to typify the Hispanic heritage, it has been considered "Indian." Only Asunción, the country's capital and sole urban center, is Hispanicized and in some degree modernized in response to external industrial influences. Rural Paraguay really constitutes the nation, and it consists of Guaraní-speaking peasants who are devoted largely to subsistence farming, who have an extremely low standard of living, and who possess few of the characteristics of the idealized Hispanic tradition found among the wealthy rural and urban upper classes elsewhere in Latin America. The belief that the Paraguayan peasant is a Guaraní Indian has been fostered by the intellectual and educated Paraguayans, who have made it the principal symbol of a cultural nationalism that, in turn, has been used to further political nationalism. The virtues of the Guaraní language, race, and culture are taught in the schools. Some years ago, when visiting Asunción, I had occasion to observe the intense feeling attached to the Guaraní myth. Certain of Paraguay's leading scholars told me at length of the superior features of the Guaraní culture and language. I was privileged to attend a meeting of one of the country's outstanding scholarly societies, the Academia de la Cultura Guaraní, which is devoted to recording and publicizing the merits of what all leading citizens take to be the basically Guaraní way of life of Paraguay's rural population.

One of the most important substantive contributions that has resulted from the Services' study is the revelation that the Paraguayan people—that is, the people living in the nuclear portion of Paraguay which surrounds Asunción—are thoroughly Hispanic in culture, despite the prevalent use of the Guaraní language and the general absence of many features conventionally regarded as Spanish. There are, however, other cultural groups in this country, for the political boundaries of Paraguay embrace four major areas which are quite unlike. The arid Chaco region of western Paraguay is still inhabited largely by bow-and-arrow Indians who preserve a substantially aboriginal culture. To them, national Paraguay is a country of powerful white men who threaten their existence. The Alto Paraná, in eastern Paraguay, is occupied by recent European immigrants, whose contacts are mainly with Uruguay and Argentina. The southern plains, or pampas, are given over to huge cattle ranches, whose owners are integrated with Paraguayan national institutions and the outside world through specialized production for cash returns but who are numerically less important than the inhabitants of nuclear Paraguay along the upper Paraguay River. These last, the Guaraní-speaking peasant farmers, numbering perhaps one million, are the typical people of Paraguay.

Already well informed on Paraguayan history through extensive research on Spanish colonization and analysis of the distinctive form which the encomienda took in this country, Dr. and Mrs. Service first examined the institutions which give structure to Paraguay as a nation. They found that in comparison with most other Latin-American nations these institutions are weak. Denied access to markets throughout her history, Paraguay has had little stimulus for the production of cash commodities for export and correspondingly little opportunity to import manufactured goods or to establish local industries. Asunción, through which all goods flow, is still somewhat medieval. It lacks wealth to support any considerable middle class of merchants and servicing personnel and has few specialized occupational groups connected with government functions, education, or even religion.

A survey of the peasant farm area disclosed that the absence of a well-developed national economy and strong national institutions is reflected in the predominance of subsistence-and-cash-crop farmers and the absence of large landlords and farms specializing in monocrops. The abundance and natural fertility of the land enables every family to meet its own food needs, although farm methods leave much to be desired, and the diet is by no means perfect. People live in some security so far as minimal needs are concerned, but they do not and cannot aspire to a high standard of living made possible elsewhere by extensive production of a cash crop. The Services found that, while class distinctions are recognized in the rural towns, even the richest families lack the means to support a genuine Hispanic upper-class way of life equivalent to that found among wealthy *hacen-*

dados and planters in other parts of Latin America. Since the absence of agrarian wealth has inhibited the growth of commerce, while manufacturing is virtually unknown, Paraguay also lacks a wealthy urban class of businessmen.

Paraguay's peasant culture has a comparatively limited range of variation. Some persons wear shoes and some do not. Some pride themselves on having been married in a church, while others are content with civil marriage or a consensual union. Some have two- or three-room tile-roofed houses, while others live in one-room thatched huts. A few have been to school in Asunción, but most have attended only a few grades at the local primary school. Status differences are reflected in certain recreational activities, the rich entertaining more lavishly and more exclusively than the poor, but there is no deep chasm which is not crossed from both sides in most daily activities. Social distinctions represent comparatively slight status differences rather than sharply defined classes whose ways of living constitute genuinely different subcultures. It is conceivable that future access to markets and creation of credit facilities will bring about large-scale production for export, which, in turn, will sharpen class lines. At present, there are no large landlords in the nuclear area. The few local manufacturers of commodities for the internal market have difficulty keeping their wage laborers. The peasants satisfy most of their wants by home production and regard a wage job simply as a temporary expediency to acquire cash for some particular and immediate goal.

The culture of the peasant farmers is not Guaraní, and the people are not Guaraní in race. The Guaraní language belongs to the Tupí-Guaraní linguistic stock, which was very widespread south of the Amazon in pre-Columbian times and which was spoken by innumerable tribes having many rather different cultural patterns. There is no Guaraní race; the Guaraní were biologically no different from other American Indians. The present population is a mixture of white, or Caucasian, and native Indian. The culture shows scarcely a trace of Guaraní influence other than language. Many domesticated plants, such as maize, manioc, and peanuts, were native to Paraguay and other parts of America, but these now are cultivated throughout the world, while many Old World domesticated plants and animals are used by the Paraguayan peasants. Houses, beds, utensils, clothing, farm methods, transportational devices, and other features of material culture are overwhelmingly European in origin. Perhaps not over half-a-dozen items, such as the wooden mortar, the children's hammock, and drinking of *mate* can be considered aboriginal.

The Services found that social customs are no less clearly of Spanish origin, although adapted to local circumstances. The family is much like that among most impoverished rural people. Consensual marriage and a fairly frequent change of spouses here, as in many other parts of the New World, are related to the limited amounts of inheritable property and to the absence of state and church reasons for registering civil or ritual unions. A Hispanic feature of the family is the value placed on ritual marriage, but inability to afford church weddings, together with the absence of a local priest in most towns and the comparatively weak emphasis on Catholicism in Paraguay, makes such unions infrequent. The people are Hispanic also in the importance attached to such concepts as *machoismo*, or male virility, and to the *compadrazgo* or coparent relationships. But these, like marriage, are functionally adapted to the nature of the local society and differ in many important respects from their better-known expressions in the Latin-American upper classes. In the latter, masculine virility is part of a larger pattern, which requires premarital chastity and chaperonage of women, idealizes the wife and mother (the "cult of the Virgin"), and gives the double standard special meaning. The Paraguayan male wishes to be very *macho*, but it does not follow that his spouse is a spiritual creature who shuns the earthiness of sex. Instead, she is a lusty sex companion. If men are more promiscuous than women, it is not because culture has prescribed a different standard for each sex. In a society where unions may be dissolved at any time and where children normally remain with the mother, there can only be a single standard, and the family tends to be matrilineal. If a man prefers another woman, he has only to move out rather than engage in clandestine affairs.

Similarly, the Hispanic tradition of the *compadrazgo* or coparent relations, though ideally a feature of church ritual as well as a social practice, has acquired functions in Paraguay specific to the socioeconomic situation. Owing in part to frequent shifts of residence, functioning kinship relations are limited largely to members of the household. Yet there is need for an individual to establish close personal ties with a larger circle of people. This need is met by his becoming godfather to certain children, whose parents become his cofathers or comothers and thereby are closely bound to him. But geographical mobility frequently separates these persons and makes the relationship rather functionless.

It might be expected that, since education and a rational or scientific point of view have made little headway, beliefs regarding natural and biological phenomena would include an appreciable amount of Indian supernaturalism. Surprisingly, this is not the case. The innumerable folk beliefs and practices recorded by the Services, such as the evil eye, the classification of foods as "hot" and "cold," the belief that worms cause sickness, the planting of crops at appropriate phases of the moon, and the like, are all of Spanish origin.

Religious practices, too, are all of European origin, even though they do not conform entirely with orthodox Catholicism. A "cult of the saints"—household, community, and regional saints —with their appropriate brotherhoods, societies, and festivals, rather than Masses, tithings, confessions, baptismals, and church weddings, constitute local religion. As among lower classes of medieval Europe and of much of contemporary Latin America, this kind of Catholicism can be carried on by rural people without the formal church apparatus. It is a community-level rather than a national-level religion, and, as such, it has been adapted to the local peasant subculture in Paraguay as it has been elsewhere.

Much importance has been ascribed to the survival of the Guaraní language in Paraguay. Dr. Service showed, in an earlier historical study,[1] that a relatively small number of male Spanish colonists married polygynously into native Guaraní families.

1. Elman R. Service, *Spanish-Guaraní Relations in Early Colonial Paraguay* ("Anthropological Papers of the Museum of Anthropology, University of Michigan," No. 9 [Ann Arbor, Mich., 1954]).

While they succeeded in Hispanicizing their innumerable wives and progeny, they evidently found it expedient to adopt the language of the latter. Guaraní is Paraguay's national language only in terms of its prevalence among the rural population and its symbolic meaning for nationalism. Most Paraguayans are bilingual, and Spanish is inevitably becoming used for state functions, commerce, and education.

The Services' incisive analysis takes on additional significance when the effect of the Spanish conquest in Paraguay is compared with that in other parts of Latin America. It is clear from their material that the colonial and republican cultures of Paraguay differed very profoundly from those of Mexico and the Andes. The latter areas were densely populated in native times by sedentary, civilized people whose agricultural production was sufficiently effective to support local ruling classes and national political and religious institutions. The conquistadors replaced the native national institutions and rulers with Spanish national institutions and rulers, but they left the local communities fairly intact. The encomienda of the early colonial period was a form of indirect rule intended to facilitate the collection of tribute while protecting the Indians from direct contact with Spaniards. So long as the Indians accepted Spanish sovereignty and the Catholic church and paid their tribute, they were supposed to be left under the authority of their own local rulers. The encomienda survived until property gradually passed into Spanish hands and larger landed estates developed.

In Paraguay the encomienda could not function as a means of indirect rule, because none of the essential conditions was present. The Indians lived on a subsistence basis, meeting their own needs in farm production, housing, clothing, and the like but producing no surplus that could support a ruling class and state institutions. There was no level of sociocultural integration higher than the local community. In fact, the extended patrilineal family formed the basis of society, as among so many of the tropical forest tribes of South America. The Spaniards soon found that they had either to marry into these families and adapt themselves to a very low standard of living or to leave the country. The men who stayed married native women and became the heads of polygynous family units. Within a few generations they had evidently indoctrinated their racially mixed progeny in every feature of the Spanish way of life except language. Instead of a Hispanic upper class and an Indian lower class, Paraguay consisted from the outset of Hispanicized, racially mixed peasants. The family head controlling a group of subsistence farmers cut a very different figure from that of the rich encomendero and *hacendado* of Mexico and Peru.

It was extraordinarily difficult to build a nation on this flimsy economic basis. The Guaraní Indians had achieved no form of state, and Hispanic national institutions are weak to this day. The church has never been strong; political affairs are manipulated by a handful of interested persons but make no great difference to most of the peasants; and industry and trade have scarcely begun to develop.

The modified Hispanic culture is much the same in all the communities of rural nuclear Paraguay, as the Services found by making a survey of the entire area. It is the same because the nature of subsistence farming is similar everywhere and because markets for cash produce are so limited that local specialization has not developed and wealth distinctions have remained comparatively unimportant. For these reasons, the people of nuclear Paraguay have a common cultural core, or list of nationally shared traits, to a degree rarely found in national societies. But the nation is so weakly structured—especially when one considers that the virtually independent Indians of the Chaco and of eastern Paraguay and the European settlers of the Alto Paraná live within its political borders—that nuclear Paraguay might almost be considered a culture area of great homogeneity, a series of similar but fairly independent societies, rather than an integrated nation.

Insights to be drawn from the Paraguayan data are not limited to Latin America. Since the encomienda could not exist in Paraguay as a form of indirect rule, it is obviously not merely a feature of colonial Spanish culture which was imposed everywhere without regard to circumstances. Like the British system of indirect rule, the encomienda required a dense native population, local state organization, a labor supply, and other factors.

Thus, for purposes of ascertaining cross-cultural regularities, "indirect rule" is a broad category of acculturational situations in which native culture is largely preserved while wealth is extracted from the people. Direct exploitation through haciendas, plantations, and mines represents another category in which the native culture seems ultimately destined to be lost when the people are reduced to a wage proletariat. Still another general category might be represented by peasant farmers, which category itself is divisible into several subcategories. Among small farmers who produce subsistence crops and a supplementary cash crop there are differences according to whether the market and credit are controlled from the outside within a colonial context or whether they are geared to local national needs. There are also differences in the survival of native culture and the adaptation of the subculture to the total situation.

In Paraguay, as in much of Brazil, the American Southwest, and the Antilles, the Iberian colonist settled and intermarried with the native population and rapidly Hispanicized it. He converted it into what may be considered a lower-class Iberian subculture, despite a good many local differences.

JULIAN H. STEWARD

UNIVERSITY OF ILLINOIS
URBANA, ILLINOIS

Preface

THE plan for a study of community life in rural Paraguay was conceived in January, 1948. The project began with an intensive analysis of documentary materials which dealt with the period of the social and racial mixture of the native Guaraní with the Spanish colonists during the colonial period. This research continued through the spring and summer of 1948. From October, 1948, until September, 1949, field research in Paraguay was carried on under the auspices of the Social Science Research Council (Area Research Program) and the Columbia University Council for Research in the Social Sciences.

Modern Paraguay, populated for the most part by descendants of the aboriginal Guaraní Indians and the early Spanish settlers, had never been studied by an ethnologist, nor had the rich historical materials ever been used for cultural-historical purposes. It appeared that Paraguay might provide the locus for a study of a mestizo population, which was perhaps mixed in culture as well as in race. In any case, the lack of economic development and the considerable isolation must have preserved relatively intact many elements of the early Spanish colonial culture. Paraguay also seemed to offer an unusual opportunity to supplement the analysis of a modern community with full use of historical information. The country is small and culturally homogeneous and has been subject to rather unusual historical influences since the founding of the colony.

Virtually all the available historical works were read carefully. Special attention was paid to the first hundred years of the Spanish colonial period in order to ascertain the main currents of the Spanish-Guaraní acculturation during this formative epoch. For this latter purpose the famous Manuel E. Gondra collection of copies of Spanish documents at the University of Texas was studied intensively. The basic results of this study were summarized in a recent monograph, *Spanish-Guaraní Relations in Early Colonial Paraguay*, by Elman R. Service.[1]

A large part of the first three months of residence in Paraguay was spent in surveying communities in the non-Chaco half of the country. The aim was to obtain some grasp of the cultural and geographic diversity of Paraguay and eventually to select a community for detailed investigation which would be representative from the point of view of size and economic organization and for its participation in the nation's history and present national life. Some of the time was spent in collecting general information on Paraguay. The most important sources for this sort of data were the Servicio Técnico Interamericano de Cooperación Agrícola (usually called "STICA"), the Servicio Cooperativo Interamericano de Salud Pública ("SCISP"), and the Bank of Paraguay's farm credit program offices.

On the basis of this survey, the town of Tobatí was selected for a seven-month period of intensive study. In terms of the several criteria which we had in mind, Tobatí came the closest to being representative. In the first place, the town itself is an average-sized market town, serving an outlying agricultural population of average density. The area also contains both grazing land and farming land and is thus representative of each of the two major aspects of Paraguay's rural economy. A third important factor to be considered was economic differences between isolated communities and the few towns which, because of better transportation facilities, have participated in the commercial development stimulated by World War II. Tobatí is about intermediate in this respect also. Access to Asunción is not so easy as from some of the towns located near the highway or the railroad, yet Tobatí is not so isolated by transportation difficulties as are many other communities. It was possible to observe in Tobatí the interesting effects of commercial acceleration and at the same time to investigate the large amount of tra-

1. "Anthropological Papers of the Museum of Anthropology, University of Michigan," No. 9 (Ann Arbor, Mich., 1954). See also Elman R. Service, "The Encomienda in Paraguay," *Hispanic American Historical Review*, May, 1951, pp. 230–51.

ditional culture which remains relatively unchanged, preserved from earlier generations.

We find ourselves in general agreement with one of Julian H. Steward's criticisms of modern community studies, which is, briefly, that the methods conventionally used in the study of isolated and homogeneous aboriginal tribes are not entirely adequate for the description of communities which are functionally dependent parts of a larger cultural entity.[2] The constant participation of the community in larger units, such as the economic region and the nation, results in a multitude of cultural features that are observable at the community level but that do not derive from the community itself. Our own work in Paraguay was therefore planned to provide data, when possible, of scope somewhat broader than that of the usual anthropological community study. We could not fulfil this ideal to any great degree, of course, without the co-operation of other specialists, but we were able to accomplish more than we had hoped because Paraguay is such a small country and is so well integrated culturally.

The nature of the Paraguayan rural settlement pattern also required that the field investigation should not be confined to the limits of one town. The agriculturalists do not live in towns but instead usually have their homes near the land they cultivate. The town itself is merely the administrative and market center for a wide agricultural area. The population consists chiefly of store-owners, a few cattlemen, purveyors of various services, politicians, petty manufacturers, and wageworkers. For this reason, even the intensive local aspects of our work resulted in an emphasis closer to a regional study than to a community study, for the market community is merely a dependent, highly specialized part of the whole district or *partido*[3] of Tobatí.

It seemed also that, because this would be the first anthropological field study in a country which is comparatively unknown to the social sciences, we should attempt to provide descriptive material which relates the local culture to its historical past and considers its broader regional relations. The focus

2. Julian H. Steward, *Area Research: Theory and Practice* ("Social Science Research Council Bulletins," No. 63 [Washington, D.C., 1950]).

3. Roughly the equivalent of a county in the United States.

is, of course, still on the local community, for it is chiefly in terms of the detailing of a "pinpoint manifestation" of a culture that anthropology differs in its kind of contribution from other disciplines within social science. In spite of our intentions to broaden the scope of the investigation, it is still more closely allied to the detailed ethnographic study of traditional anthropology than it is to the work of rural sociologists or economists. Such books as Whetten's *Rural Mexico* or Taylor's *Rural Life in Argentina*, Nelson's *Rural Cuba*, and others usually cover a wide area, if not a whole nation, provide a great many statistics, tables, and charts which refer to comparisons between localities, and offer general statistical observations for the whole. The present account, however, attempts to select a representative locality and to describe life in more complete detail for that locality. Such a work is not a substitute for, or "better than," a nation-wide sociological or economic survey; in actuality they should supplement each other. Just such surveys as the above are badly needed for Paraguay.

This book is not complete in certain respects. The historical material, which was such an important aspect of the investigation, is not presented here in great bulk. The most significant part of the historical research, that dealing with the early colonial period, is published elsewhere. There are also many other published works dealing with the more recent history of Paraguay. While they are concerned mainly with the exploits of leaders and with political events rather than with functional culture history, they are an aid to a comprehension of Paraguay's cultural development.[4]

In Part I, the Introduction, we present merely a sketch of the history of the central region of Paraguay, of which Tobatí was always an integrated part. It is intended only as a background description to introduce to the reader the main outlines of Paraguayan history. Historical matters are introduced also in other chapters whenever they seem relevant to a comprehension of the particular subject under discussion.

4. See George Pendle, *Paraguay: A Riverside Nation* (London and New York: Royal Institute of International Affairs, 1954). This work contains the best-chosen modern bibliography on Paraguay and, though very brief, is the most reliable modern description of the nation.

We have tried to include all of our data which have a bearing on the questions which led to our selection of Paraguay for
a field study, a procedure which necessarily precludes an adequate coverage on other topics which may be of interest to certain kinds of specialists in the social sciences. Additionally, our
field study could not aim at completeness, as we had only seven
months in Tobatí and lacked collaborators or assistants. We have
tried, therefore, to be thorough with respect to general social
and economic matters, generally at the expense of psycholog-
ical data, because socioeconomic material is more relevant to
our main interest in Paraguay. We regret that we have very
little material on the local aspects of national politics. While the
peasantry of Paraguay is essentially nonpartisan, many townsmen
take their political loyalties very seriously. Since the recent civil
war, feelings have been greatly intensified, and the situation was
so tense during our stay in Tobatí that we could not interest ourselves in this matter without jeopardizing our other work.

The method we have chosen for organizing the data into chapters is somewhat unorthodox. We tried to use functional rather
than formal criteria in making the divisions, feeling that analysis
was thus made easier. Therefore, we have no single continuous
description of such institutions as the family or the church but
have referred them to particular functional contexts. Certain
economic aspects of the family are discussed in Part II; structural aspects, in Part III; and the ceremonialism of marriage,
funerals, and so on, in chapter xix. The social function of the
church is discussed in chapter xiii, the ideological aspects in
chapter xvii, and some of its ritual in chapter xix.

In one respect the results of our investigation were rather unexpected. The facts that the population of Paraguay is basically
mestizo in race, that the Guaraní language is spoken more widely
than Spanish, and that Paraguayans themselves continually extol
their "Guaraní heritage" seem to have been sufficient evidence
to convince the world that Guaraní *cultural* elements were still
importantly represented. The preliminary analysis of historical
documents seemed to show, however, that the early relations
between Spanish colonists and the Guaraní population were of
such a nature as to tend to erase the aboriginal culture and sub-

stitute the Spanish colonial, on the level of the small community as well as in national institutions.

Our field investigation confirmed this supposition, for we found a striking lack of "Indian" cultural features which could be ranged alongside the racial and linguistic components of the society. The error of assuming that one can infer a population's cultural type from its race or language has been exposed again and again by modern anthropology, but it is apparently necessary to bring up the point once more.

The fact that Paraguayan rural culture appears to be a variant of Spanish colonial culture rather than a direct derivative of Spanish-Indian mixture does not mean that it is not of scientific interest. In certain respects it is quite unusual in Latin America, for local economic and historical reasons. In other respects it is interesting because it is pre-eminently "Spanish-American" in the sense that long-standing isolation and poverty have preserved more of the old Spanish colonial civilization than have many of the communities studied to date. Also of interest is the economic situation of the whole nation and the effects of dependency and semicolonialism on the rural people. Paraguay is so small, and its economic problems are relatively so clear and simple, that one is quickly drawn to a consideration of this aspect of the national life.

Our field methods were, in general, of the sort developed by professional ethnographers. We lived with the people and participated in all possible events, a basic procedure which usually sets off the method of the modern ethnologist from that of other social scientists. We used quantitative methods in the form of a census and questionnaires whenever possible and also conducted intensive interviews with informants. The older, more traditional ethnographic technique of relying on only a few informants is admittedly inadequate for the study of a community which is not the homogeneous tribal culture of primitives. The presence of social and economic classes and of complexities due to the division of labor makes it manifestly impossible for any individual to be familiar with the details of the whole culture. By far the greatest bulk of our information which came from questioning individuals was by means of "indirect interviews" with a great number and variety of people. Informants were never paid directly for work as informants until the final few weeks of our stay, when we collected opinions on each item in our notes to check accuracy and generality. Earlier, we had paid informants indirectly as guides and census helpers.

Because Tobatí is a class-divided community, no person, whether a visitor or a native, can have easy social relations with people of a class other than the one to which he is assigned. We were accepted almost immediately into the upper social level, but, since we were foreigners and had the declared mission of investigating the local customs, we were permitted a considerable social mobility which would be denied a permanent resident. An upper-class person can initiate relations with the lower class, but the lower-class person is usually wary of allowing familiarities to go very far. We had the advantage of the upper-class sort of social mobility, but, additionally, being temporary residents and foreigners, we were, in a sense, outside the social order. A peasant was therefore more free to approach us and even to risk a social error, without fear of permanent disapproval.

We had rented one of the larger, newer, houses in the town. It had a large *sala* with a brick floor, a few chairs of the "porch furniture" type, a smaller bedroom with an iron bed and cotton mattress, an indoor kitchen with a charcoal hearth and a cistern, a small washroom, and a brick outdoor toilet. The house was plastered and whitewashed, roofed with tile instead of thatch, and had plenty of windows, though no glass. We employed a cook but no other servants. This kind of living arrangement was not among the most pretentious in town, but it was clearly an upper-class style of residence. Our clothing and eating habits also conformed generally to upper-class styles.

In general, our greatest difficulty lay in our relations with the peasants. They lived in the more remote areas and often spoke very little Spanish or none at all, and, although they were hospitable and even friendly in a grave sort of way, it was virtually impossible to associate informally and intimately with them in their own households, especially because of the shyness of the women. Our information on the details of their familial life is less complete than that for the town dwellers because we had to rely more on questioning than on participation and close observation.

We would have had a much more difficult time had it not been for the sympathy and understanding of the late Padre Cayetano Cabriza, who, more than any other single individual, held the affection of most of the peasants. Traveling among them under his aegis, and often with him personally, we were able to gain an initial confidence which would probably have been impossible without his so active support. His recent death was a great loss to the countrypeople and townsmen as well, not only because of the great degree of unselfish personal devotion he gave to the community but also because he was no idle sympathizer; he combined a great deal of energy with political acumen and realistic intelligence, to the end of material as well as spiritual improvement.

We shall always be grateful to the many Paraguayans who helped us. We are even more grateful to them for the pleasure we took in sharing the warmth of their friendship and hospitality. To Celia Arias Correa and her family we owe an extraordinary debt. Miss Arias traveled with us, without recompense, for nearly two months during our initial survey of Paraguay, and through her we met friends and relatives of hers whose friendship we shall always treasure: Hector and Carmita Bertoni, the Ramón Martinos, Pedro Muller, the Corваláns, and the José Schmidtbauers.

The people of Tobatí who gave us aid and friendship are too numerous to mention individually. In one way or another, nearly all of them contributed to our work, but we did, inevitably, enlist the aid of certain friends much more continuously than others. Our good companions José and Ramona Finestra and Mariano and María Luisa Finestra were always ready to render any service, and Pedro Rivera, Edmundo Arias, Eminente Gómez, Elsa Cañete, all of the Macchi family, and all of the Cabriza family were particularly helpful.

Our field study was made possible by the financial support of the Social Science Research Council and the Columbia University Council for Research in the Social Sciences. The Social Science Research Council and the Pan American Union were helpful with suggestions for contacts and procedures in Paraguay. The Wenner-Gren Foundation for Anthropological Research provided an excellent camera and a wire recorder. In

Paraguay, Mr. Albion Patterson, director of the Servicio Técnico Interamericano de Cooperación Agrícola, and Dr. Jean
Rogier, director of the Servicio Cooperativo Interamericano de
Salud Pública, were both very generous with their time and
facilities. We thank them for this and for their friendliness. We
were unfortunate in not being able to consult personally with
Miss Emma Reh, who had previously carried on an intensive
diet study in the town of Piribebuý in central Paraguay. However, she supplied us by mail with interesting unpublished notes
for which we are grateful.

We were fortunate in having the advice and encouragement
of Dr. Julian H. Steward during all stages of our work. We
are indebted to him and to Drs. William Duncan Strong and
Charles Wagley for many helpful suggestions. Drs. Conrad Arensberg, George M. Foster, and Morton H. Fried also criticized
parts of the manuscript, and another group of colleagues—Robert A. Manners, Sidney W. Mintz, John V. Murra, and Eric R.
Wolf—who were engaged in field research in Puerto Rico at the
time our study was made, gave us valuable comments based on
their own experiences. Dr. Harry L. Shapiro, of the American
Museum of Natural History, assisted us in planning the anthropometric study and provided the instruments.[5] We are deeply
grateful to all of them.

Linguistic Note.—A small amount of linguistic data was collected in the course of our field work, but it is not included in
this report.

Guaraní is now a written language in Paraguay, and Guaraní
words included in the text have been spelled in the manner
taught in the public schools and used in the newspapers of
Paraguay. There seemed no point in assigning arbitrary spell-
ings to words which have their conventional spelling in Paraguayan literature, inasmuch as we are not attempting any linguistic analysis here.

ELMAN R. SERVICE
HELEN S. SERVICE

ANN ARBOR, MICHIGAN
June 1954

5. The anthropometric data will be published elsewhere.

Table of Contents

xxvii

PART V. CONCLUSIONS

APPENDIXES

BIBLIOGRAPHY

INDEX

List of Illustrations

MAPS

PLATES

(Plates appear between pages 162 and 163)

PART I

Introductory

CHAPTER I

A Town in Paraguay

THE visitor in Paraguay quickly learns that for all practical purposes there are actually two Paraguays. The famous "green hell" of the Gran Chaco, an extensive area on the western side of the Paraguay River, is distinct from what may be considered "Paraguay proper" in geography, economy, and demography. The Chaco is a flat alluvial plain, very sparsely populated and characterized by extensive floods in wet seasons, lack of water at other times, insect plagues, and intense heat. In some parts there is forage for cattle if they are scattered thinly enough, but agriculture is virtually impossible. About the only important economic resource is the quebracho forests which are exploited for tannin.

The third of Paraguay which lies on the eastern side of the river is strikingly different. Here is a landscape of considerable beauty and variation, well watered and drained, with grasslands, forests, springs, and pleasant streams. There is also some degree of regional contrast; some areas are hilly, some are largely plains, and in others mixed hardwood forests cover most of the land. Nearly all of the Paraguayan population lives in this part of the country.

The most populated area lies just below the Tropic of Capricorn, with Asunción almost on the twenty-fifth parallel, so that there is a perceptible change in seasons. The summers are long and hot; midday temperatures are normally over 100° F. in Asunción in December, January, and February. The winters are uncomfortable at times, for the temperature is extremely variable. Paraguay is equally exposed to the bitterly cold winds of central Argentina and to the humid warm winds of central Brazil, so that a mere shift in the direction of the wind causes sudden and drastic temperature changes.

3

Rainfall in central Paraguay is about fifty inches in an average year and is fairly well distributed through the seasons. The climate is thus much more favorable to agriculture than that of the more tropical zones characterized by wet and dry seasons, and yet Paraguay does not suffer the disadvantage of having the dead winter of the temperate zones. Many crops can be grown the year around.

The flora is mostly that of tropical South America. Coconut palms are the most noticeable trees on the landscape. Orange trees, which have grown wild since early colonial times, are also scattered in profusion. Lemon, grapefruit, lime, and tangerine trees also grow well in central Paraguay. The many other fruit trees of tropical America are also common, including banana, mango, papaya, and guava.[1]

Eastern Paraguay's mixed topography of hills and plains, forests and pastures, as well as its position between the tropical forests of Brazil and the pampas of temperate Argentina, apparently provides an environment favorable to a great many different kinds of animal life. One sees the toucans, parrots, hummingbirds, and macaws so characteristic of the jungle but also an impressive number of pampean birds like the rhea, and many kinds of ducks, geese, herons, partridges, grouse, and pheasants. Jaguars, tapirs, boas, monkeys, anteaters, and crocodiles abound in the forests. One of the most common animals, and one of the most curious-looking, is the carpincho (*Hydrochaerus capybaras*), a swamp-dwelling vegetarian about the size of a domestic pig, with three webbed toes, a tapir-like snout, and a gentle disposition.

Asunción, the capital city, lies approximately in the geographic center of the nation, on the eastern side of the Paraguay River, facing the Gran Chaco. Fanning out from Asunción eastward is the economic heart of Paraguay, the central zone, sometimes called the "cordillera," a semiupland consisting of thick woods, or "monte," on the hills, interspersed with broad valleys of grasslands, or "campo." The great bulk of the agriculturalists, and over 60 per cent of the total population of Paraguay, are concentrated in this relatively small area. The few maintained roads and

1. See chap. iv for a fuller description of domesticated plants.

the single railroad pass eastward from Asunción, connecting the capital with some of the small towns which are scattered 10–20 kilometers apart throughout this region. The agriculturalists themselves live scattered on their tiny farms, or *chacras,* in orbits which center on the towns which serve them as local markets and administrative centers.

The mixed campo-monte land of the cordillera is divided in economic usage between agriculture in the monte and cattle-raising in the campo, but agriculture predominates; the scattered valleys support only small numbers of cattle. Proceeding from the central zone to the peripheries of the country, however, especially south and southeast toward Argentina, the plains gradually become more extensive, so that large-scale cattle ranches are the rule and the farming population is negligible. North of the cordillera, grasslands also dominate the monte, but in the extreme north, toward the Brazilian Matto Grosso, extensive jungles and swamps are common. The northern and northeastern forests are even less populated than are the southern plains; there are only a few scattered lumber camps and wandering Indians.

Asunción is pre-eminently the center of Paraguay's economy. All foreign trade passes through its port, and it is also the hub of internal exchange. Goods pass back and forth between the various market towns and Asunción but not between the towns themselves. Consequently, most of the variation in town size and density of the local rural population in central Paraguay is a measure of the degree to which otherwise similar towns are able to participate in the Asunción market.

By and large, it is the difference in transportation facilities which determines the degree of economic importance of some towns over others. There is one antiquated railroad in Paraguay (British-owned) which runs from Asunción to Encarnación, ferries the river Paraná, and thence to Buenos Aires. Towns along the railroad route benefit somewhat from their location. There is one asphalt highway which goes from Asunción as far as Barrero Grande through the cordillera and on to Villarrica as a gravel road. There is one surfaced spur which drops south from this road the short distance to Pariguarí and continues as a rough gravel road as far as San Ignacio in Misiones. The railroad towns, such as Ipacaraí and Coronel Oviedo, have grown in size over a long period, but the recent coming of the highway has contributed more changes than the railroad in a much shorter time. Other roads in Paraguay are merely oxcart tracks, but sometimes trucks can use them. Most towns have no connection with the main road or with Asunción except by such trails.

Tobatí

Tobatí is typical of one of these latter towns. It can be said to be accessible from Asunción by truck, but the service is not regularized for the public, and the route itself is a very difficult one for the last part of the way. The traveler bound for Tobatí from Asunción can expect to find truck transportation almost any day, but he must spend a considerable amount of time and energy ascertaining the departure time and assuring himself of space in the truck, unless he is acquainted with the driver and thus is favored by him. Between Asunción and Caacupé the truck rolls smoothly on the asphalt Central Highway through a hilly landscape of great natural beauty. But the next 19 kilometers from Caacupé to Tobatí are over terrain so difficult that the inexperienced passenger hangs on with both hands, watching the route ahead, hoping to anticipate the next jolt, rather than observing the scenery around him. The truck is usually going so slowly that passengers jump off at their rural destinations and others climb aboard over the tailgate with no signal to the chauffeur.[2]

About a kilometer from Tobatí the truck descends from the low wooded hills into the open, permitting the larger vista of campo, which surrounds the town on three sides. To the left can be seen the thatched huts of Compañía Rosado at the edge of the hills, and to the right the trees and bush of the more distant Colonia 21 de Julio. But looking toward the town, and in a great half-circle around it, the broad grassy plains dotted with small islands of woods dominate the scene, until in the blue haze of the distance they merge with the ranges of hills which seem to surround the whole region like low ramparts. It is in these more dis-

2. A gravel road between Tobatí and Caacupé was completed after our departure.

tant areas of monte that the other *compañías* and *colonias* are
located.

There is very little agriculture near the town, nor does one
notice any scattered habitations in any of the immediately surrounding campo. Small groups of cattle are grazing, and, if it is
late in the afternoon, perhaps an oxcart, an occasional horseman,
and several families on foot may be seen in the distance on their
way home after a day in town.

The first glimpse of Tobatí is of the massive brick tower of
the church, which is situated on the highest ground in the town
(Pl. I). Gradually the thatch and tile roofs of the houses come
into view, and finally the individual houses themselves, some of
whitewashed adobe which contrasts with the predominate green
of the grassy yards, broad streets, and plazas. At a distance these
colors, the tall palms and shade trees, the jasmine and rosebushes
around the homes, and the green spaciousness combine to form
a colorful yet peaceful scene. On entering the town there is
usually but little activity to be seen; a few boys kicking a rag ball
around, two or three burros grazing on the plaza, a horseman
passing, and now and then a barefoot woman with a basket or a
pan balanced on her head going home from one of the small
stores on the plaza.

Tobatí, like other Paraguayan towns, is laid out on the Spanish
colonial rectangular plan, with the large church plaza as the
geographic center. The plaza itself is about 150 meters on a side,
with the church in the center of it. Around it, the houses are ad-
joined in the colonial style, with a narrow veranda and overhanging roof flush to the street. In some of the houses are
the small stores of the merchants, as well as their living quarters,
and in others some families of distinction make their homes. In
other buildings on the plaza are such civil offices as the municipal
headquarters (*municipalidad*), the office of the justice of the
peace and the jail, and the priest's home and office.

Normally in such a town there would also be a subsidiary plaza
surrounding the meat market, an open-sided brick structure
screened by chicken wire to keep out dogs. Tobatí at present has
no functioning central meat market, however, so that purchases
are made from one of several small markets located at the homes

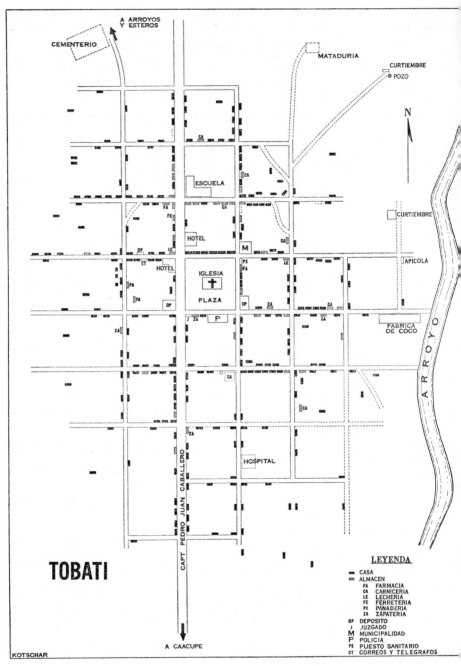

A ARROYOS
Y ESTEROS

CEMENTERIO

MATADURIA

CURTIEMBRE
POZO

N

ESCUELA
CA

FA
FE

HOTEL

CURTIEMBRE

M

APICOLA

DP
LE

CT
HOTEL

PS
FA

LE

PA

IGLESIA

PA

DP
CA

DP

PLAZA

ZA

FABRICA
DE COCO

ZA

J
ZA

P

CA

CA

CA

ARROYO

CA

CA

ZA

HOSPITAL

TOBATI

CAPT PEDRO JUAN CABALLERO

A CAACUPE

LEYENDA

CASA	
ALMACEN	
FA	FARMACIA
CA	CARNICERIA
LE	LECHERIA
FE	FERRETERIA
PA	PANADERIA
ZA	ZAPATERIA
DP	DEPOSITO
J	JUZGADO
M	MUNICIPALIDAD
P	POLICIA
PS	PUESTO SANITARIO
CT	CORREOS Y TELEGRAFOS

KOTSCHAR

TOWN PLAN OF TOBATÍ

of the butchers. A large brick market of the usual sort was begun a few years ago but was never completed.

Paraguayan towns do not have the general market which is so common in Latin America. Purchases and sales of goods other than beef are mostly carried on by the many tiny stores, although occasionally an agriculturalist travels through the town selling his fruit or vegetables from an oxcart. Sometimes manufactured articles or handicrafts are sold from door to door by women called *revendedoras* ("resellers"), who may have purchased a few scarce items in Asunción to sell at a profit in Tobatí.

A recent divergence from the colonial plaza plan is noticeable in those Paraguayan towns like Tobatí whose small middle class has participated in the postwar commercial prosperity. Some of these people, who might otherwise live on or near the plaza, have built brick bungalows on pleasant locations away from the center of town, thus disrupting the old status geography. A few handsome plastered brick, tile-roofed houses with well-kept yards and tile floors and patios may be mingled with the tiny adobe and thatch one-room huts of the very poor who occupy the outskirts of the towns.

Except for the appearance of the buildings on the plaza, the remainder of a Paraguayan town has little similarity to a typical Spanish-American plan. The houses away from the plaza stand alone, dispersed on large plots of ground, set among small manioc and maize gardens and fruit trees. They are usually several meters away from the street and are fenced in to protect the gardens from the cows and very destructive burros which roam the town. The streets are wide and grassy, except for the central ruts caused by oxcarts (Pl. II). More recently, one or two main streets may have been worn free of grass by busses and trucks. During the time we were in Tobatí, an army engineer battalion cleared and graded a few of the main streets with a bulldozer, and side drainage ditches were dug, but no topping was put over the clay. After a couple of heavy rains the streets were more rutted than before, and in dry periods the dust was much worse than when the grass had been permitted to grow. Usually the broad grassy streets are typical in Paraguay and contribute a pleasant, roomy aspect which is distinctly different from most

Spanish, or Spanish-American, rural towns. The grassy streets and plazas serve as pasture and night bedding areas for the large cow and burro population, so that a person abroad at night is always in danger of falling over a recumbent animal in the unlighted streets.

All the land in a circle of 1,000 meters' radius from the church tower is municipal property, and the municipality of Tobatí long ago divided the town into blocks ("manzanas") of 160 varas on a side (151.5 yards). Lots are 10 meters of frontage and 40 of depth on "nonprincipal" streets (east-west) and 10×20 on "principal" streets (north-south). On corners the lots are 20×40 meters, with the 20 meters fronting on the "principal" street. A prospective builder obtains his site by petitioning the municipality. Those who solicit corner lots are under the obligation of building houses of at least two rooms, instead of the more usual one-room thatched "rancho." The law requires that a privy and cooking shed be built behind each house.

The sense of spaciousness in the town is augmented by the presence of a considerable number of vacant lots. These may be used by a neighbor for gardens or pasture if he fences them in. If one intends to build a large house (more than two rooms), he may be granted a double lot. A petitioner has one hundred and eighty days to build on his lot; once he has built the foundations, he acquires title to it. One therefore sees a great many vacant lots with the minimum of foundations on them, built in order to lay claim to the land for later occupancy or for sale.

The streets have official names, but most people do not know them; neither the officer in charge of public works nor the priest and community leader could name more than three streets between them. Directions are given (even to strangers) by saying, "over that way, next to Fulano's house." There are no official or civil "barrios" (wards), although the word is understood and sometimes used loosely to indicate a region of the town. The northeastern section used to be called *barrio húmedo* because it was near the creek, and a small section in the eastern part was once referred to as *barrio caraguatá* because of the many caraguata plants which grew wild there. The closest approach to actual town subdivisions are the four religious societies, each of which is a cult of a particular saint. They are like barrios in that their membership tends to be localized roughly into neighborhoods. The boundaries are indistinct, however, as anyone who has a household image of the saint or whose saint's day is that of one of the four societies may be a member of that society. The functions of these organizations are confined to a religious rather than a civil context, and the use of their names to denote a neighborhood is entirely informal.

The most imposing public buildings are first of all the church and next the school and the *municipalidad*. Most Paraguayan churches were built in colonial times, all of a similar style. They were of adobe, long and low, with a thatched roof overhanging at the sides to form a sort of veranda. As in Tobatí, many towns still have this church but have begun to build a great brick façade and tower at the entrance and have tiled the roof. The *municipalidad*, which is newer, consists of a couple of rooms for offices and an outdoor tiled dance floor. The school, a one-story ell-shaped building, is situated at one corner of its own large plaza. Like the *municipalidad*, it is constructed of whitewashed brick with a tile roof.

There are two small hotels, one belonging to the Romero sisters and the other to the Martínez sisters.[3] Each hotel is partly a small grocery store and restaurant, with a few private rooms and a patio where guests sleep in warm weather. Both have Servel kerosene refrigerators—the only ones in town—which are used exclusively for cooling beer and soft drinks.

Two public springs and the arroyo (creek), all situated on the eastern edge of town, provide most of the water supply. There are a few private wells, but they are either salty or dry most of the time. Two or three of the newest homes and the two hotels have rain-water cisterns, and others of the wealthier families may have water delivered to their homes by boys who make a small business of selling it from oil drums or barrels carried by a burro, but most of the town families transport their own water daily. One of the most memorable scenes of Tobatí life occurs every

3. We have consistently used fictitious names for individuals but have not changed any place names.

day in late afternoon when schoolgirls and women trudge through the east side of town with the heavy clay jars or five-gallon gasoline cans of water balanced on their heads (Pl. III).

Town and Country

The relation of the town of Tobatí to the surrounding rural area is basically the relation of "middle class" to producing class. In the town are concentrated the few *hacendados* (ranchers), the many buyers and sellers, the petty industries, the office-holders, and the few professional people. At the fringes of the town's economy are the numerous poor, who live by part-time wagework or as servants. The town and country form an economic unity with separation of function. Town is where the money is; it is where agricultural produce is sold, where goods are purchased, where political and religious authority is located, where curers, barbers, shoemakers, and carpenters are to be found, and where most fiestas are held. To the townsmen, the country is the location of the bulk of the population, which is to be served or exploited.

Tobatí[4] is actually the name for both the town and the rural area; together, they constitute the *partido* of Tobatí. The *partido*, which is a civil unit, is a subdivision of the Department of Cara-guatay, bearing a relation to it much like a county to a state in the United States of America. Tobatí is of about average size in Paraguay with respect to both the population of the town and the density of the rural population. The town has a population of 1,368, according to a door-to-door census that we supervised in May, 1949. The whole *partido* includes from seven to ten thousand persons.

Within the *partido* are small rural political subdivisions of two types, *compañias*[5] and *colonias*, which are governed by the *junta municipal*, situated in the town. These units have a relation to the *partido* which corresponds in a general way to the more usual Spanish-American *municipio* and rural barrio. The general ap-

4. *Tobatí* is supposed to mean "white" or "white face." It is said that the name is applied to this locality because of the white kaolin which is found in the near-by hills.

5. The use of *compañia* ("company") may be related to the fact that the term was once used by the Jesuits to designate their minor groupings.

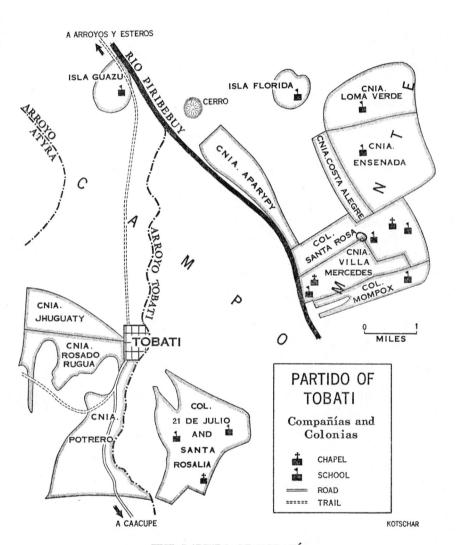

A ARROYOS Y ESTEROS

ISLA GUAZU

RIO PIRIBEBUY

ISLA FLORIDA

CERRO

CNIA.
LOMA VERDE

CNIA.
APARYPY

CNIA. COSTA ALEGRE

CNIA.
ENSENADA

ARROYO ATYRA

C

A

M

P

O

ARROYO TOBATI

COL.
SANTA ROSA

CNIA.
VILLA
MERCEDES

COL.
MOMPOX

N

T

E

M

O

0   1
MILES

CNIA.
JHUGUATY

TOBATI

CNIA.
ROSADO
RUGUA

CNIA.
POTRERO

COL.
21 DE JULIO
AND
SANTA
ROSALIA

**PARTIDO OF
TOBATI**

Companías and
Colonias

✝   CHAPEL

SCHOOL

───   ROAD

=====   TRAIL

A CAACUPE

KOTSCHAR

THE *PARTIDO* OF TOBATÍ

pearance of the country homes is much like that of the ranchos of the town lower class (Pl. II). Usually they are of one small room, with a thatched roof extended over the front to form a shaded area, or "ramada," where much of the family life takes place. The whole impression of the rancho in its setting is a pleasant one. The Paraguayans are clean and keep their houses and the premises free of debris; the ground around the hut is hard-packed and bare and is swept thoroughly every morning and any other time it becomes a little cluttered. Grass is not culti-vated and is discouraged by the sweeping, but most homes are surrounded by the luxuriant plant growth of the semitropical climate. Roses are plentiful and bloom all the year, and hibiscus and several species of jasmine are also very common. Nearly all ranchos have several kinds of fruit trees near by; orange trees are particularly common and are very attractive.

The peasants live on the land they cultivate, so that there is a considerable dispersion in the rural settlement pattern. Certain areas of more fertile soil are more thickly settled than others, however, resulting in a certain amount of clustering. Some of these concentrations of families are served by a one-room school of two grades, perhaps a chapel and a small store or two. The *compañías* tend to correspond roughly to these rural clusterings. The people of a particular *compañía* thus have a certain felt unity due to their contiguity; they are members of a named neighborhood. The *compañías* are also civil administrative units in the sense that each has a local law officer called the *oficial* (his formal title is *sub-comisario*), who serves without pay under the direction of the police *comisario* of Tobatí. The *comisario* ap-points the local *oficial*, with due regard for the opinions of the influential men of the *compañía*.

The *colonias*, which have a similar local unity and an *oficial*, are distinguished from the *compañías* because they were created by a governmental land policy. A great many agriculturalists in Paraguay do not own land, but, on the other hand, there has been a considerable amount of land belonging to the government (*tierra fiscal*) since the demise of the great *hacendados* after 1870. Since about 1928, it has been the occasional policy of the government to redistribute this land to qualified families in lots, normally of 5 hectares (about 12 acres) per family, on an easy-payment plan. A paid administrator, appointed from Asunción, is supposed to look after the colony.

There are eleven subdivisions of the *partido*, three *colonias* and eight *compañías*:

Colonia 21 de Julio	Compañía Jhuguatý
Colonia Santa Rosa	Compañía Potrero
Colonia Mompox	Compañía Rosado Ruguá
Compañía Loma Verde	Compañía Isla Guazú
Compañía Villa Mercedes (also called "Typychatý")	Compañía Aparypý
	Compañía Ensenada

Costa Alegre and Isla Florida are two other named localities which are sometimes referred to as *compañías* and sometimes not. They are small and are less important than those listed above.

All these subdivisions of the *partido* are under the jurisdiction of the *junta municipal* in Tobatí—the governing of the town itself is not distinct from that of the *partido*. In fact, the town itself is rarely thought of as an entity separate from the outlying *compañías* and *colonias*. The name "Tobatí" refers to the *partido* as a whole; if one wishes to refer only to the town it is necessary to say "the pueblo of Tobatí."

According to the national constitution, each *partido* elects its own officers, and the federal government is supposed to have no influence in this choice; but this has rarely been the case in actual practice and is not at present. Since the presidency of Franco in 1936, none of the national governments have allowed local free elections; all officers of the junta are appointed from Asunción.

The most important and powerful local official is the police *comisario*, who, assisted by a squad of youthful army conscripts, directly carries out the orders of the national government and upholds the local laws made by the junta of Tobatí. In Tobatí the *comisario* has at times been a local man, at other times an outsider, but in all cases he is paid by the national government. In times of national political disturbances, the *comisario* may be changed often. In about one month in 1949 the *comisario* of Tobatí was actually changed five times for political reasons. In certain of these changes it was apparent that the local politicians had some influence in the selection of this official.

The junta of municipal officers includes a president and a secretary, who are paid small salaries from local taxes, and five other unpaid members: a vice-president, two members in charge of public works, one treasurer, and one person in charge of public health. There are three alternates to fill any of the posts should they be suddenly vacated. Other local officials of some importance are the administrators of the *colonias*, who serve under the national Department of Lands and Colonies, a director of schools, and a justice of the peace, all representing the national government, though they are natives of Tobatí. The justice performs civil marriages, keeps vital statistics, and also adjudicates local controversies and petty crimes.

Communication and Mobility

Although Paraguay as a nation suffers from isolation, there is a considerable amount of mobility within its boundaries. The technological means of communication by which the people of Tobatí participate in the outside world are slight indeed, but this has not caused village isolation to the degree one might expect.

Until recent years there was no way to reach neighboring towns, except by horseback, oxcart, or walking. Lately it has been possible to reach Caacupé (19 kilometers) and Asunción (62 kilometers) via Caacupé nearly any day by truck. This occurs despite the fact that until 1949 there was nothing between Tobatí and Caacupé which could be called a road.

Barrero Grande, about 25 kilometers to the southeast, is a town about the size of Tobatí. There is no direct means of transportation to it from Tobatí, however, except by horse or on foot. Arroyos y Esteros, a town of about the same size, to the north about 30 kilometers, is somewhat less isolated, as trucks and busses from there occasionally make the rough trip to Asunción via Tobatí and Caacupé. Atyrá, directly west about 10 kilometers, is more handicapped by transportation difficulties, in spite of the shorter distance. Nevertheless, there is a great deal of visiting among the people of these towns.

Other means of communication with Asunción and the world outside are the radio and newspapers. There were twelve radios

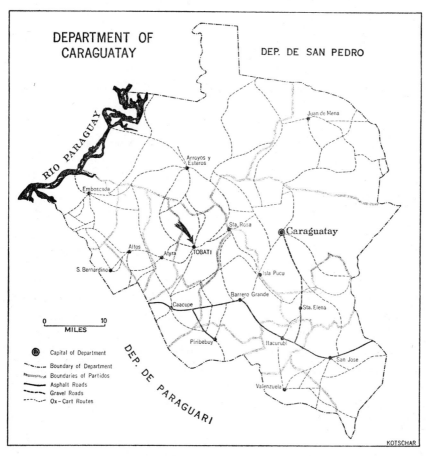

THE DEPARTMENT OF CARAGUATAÝ

in Tobatí in 1948–49, but they are used only rarely in order to conserve the batteries. It is an expensive proposition to ship the batteries to Asunción for charging, as the truck-driver must be paid, as well as the garage which does the work. Several of the radios of our acquaintances remained out of action for long periods of time after the batteries had run down.

Truck-drivers and passengers returning from Asunción often bring one of the small newspapers. These are not read by a great many people, however. Any important news is passed on from the readers to the public by word of mouth, and naturally it becomes greatly distorted by the time most of the people hear of it. In fact, by far the most important means of all news dissemination is rumor. Most notices of public affairs to be held in the town are publicized—and distorted—in this way. Even the important functions of Holy Week become disorganized for this reason. People come at the wrong time, sometimes not at all, because an unfounded rumor of postponement gets around. It is said jokingly that the *radio so'o* ("meat radio") is out of order.

There is no telephone communication from Tobatí. There is a telegraph office, but it was, in our experience, extremely unreliable. The post office, which is run by the telegraph company, receives and distributes mail but has no scales, no stamps, and no information on rates. Stamps must be purchased from Asunción or from one or two individuals in Tobatí who make a small business of reselling stamps purchased in quantity in Asunción. Mail must be registered to have even a remote chance of reaching its destination.

But, in spite of the many communication problems, the foreigner in rural Paraguay is always struck by the amount of traveling which he observes and by the casual familiarity with which many people may display a knowledge of Asunción and other towns, some of them far from the beaten track. The impression he receives contrasts greatly with the localism, the *campanilismo*, of the agricultural communities of much of the world.

The similarity of one town to another in interior Paraguay is immediately striking to the foreigner. The regional distinctions in many other Latin-American countries are not found here to nearly the same degree, and the Paraguayans seem remarkably homogeneous racially and culturally.[6] There may be a variety of factors responsible for this—the nature of the early encomienda, the small size of the country, isolation, wars—but an important additional circumstance could be the impressive amount of population movement.

This mobility is of two distinct kinds: one is basically of townsmen, whose movements are related to the quest for economic opportunities of the commercial and wageworking sort; the other is that of the peasants, who are often searching for better land. The rural mobility, however, is rather localized and fluxlike, whereas the more commercially oriented travel is sporadic rather than constant, depending on variable economic opportunities. Young men travel in search of work wherever they can find it—on ranches, in timber camps, on river boats, and so on. The most consistent movement of this sort is back and forth between the home town and Asunción. It seems that nearly everyone—men, women, children, rich and poor—manages to get to Asunción occasionally for one reason or another. Another factor which influences the movement of at least some townsmen is the political factionalism. In any locality are to be found men who are essentially political refugees. They had once backed the wrong group in their home towns.

Our census and economic questionnaire of the households of the town of Tobatí reveals something of the extent and nature of this movement. Of family heads only, totaling 289, there were 190 who were born in Tobatí and its surrounding *compañías*, while 99 were born outside the *partido*. This seemed to be an astonishing number of outsiders for one small town, but no informants were surprised; they rather seemed to expect it. People who know other towns well did not feel that this situation was unusual, although it was felt that there was probably a degree of difference between towns in this matter, depending on the amount of recent prosperity of the town. Thus Atyrá, more isolated and less prosperous than Tobatí, has contributed more of its population to Tobatí than vice versa.

A breakdown of the localities where the ninety-nine non-

6. William L. Schurz, "Government," in Asher N. Christiansen (ed.), *The Evolution of Latin American Government* (New York, 1951), p. 76.

natives were born shows that, while there was more movement from neighboring towns than from distant ones, many of the people were from widely scattered and distant areas. Atyrá, the nearest town, contributed a total of thirty-three heads of families and was by far the most heavily represented. Altos, about twice as far to the west, contributed ten. Other towns in the Department of Caraguataý which were heavily represented were Barrero Grande, seven; Arroyos y Esteros, six; Caacupé, five; and Caraguataý (about 25 kilometers away), five. Towns outside the department, representing nearly every region of eastern Paraguay, contributed twenty-eight heads of families. These are Asunción, Luque, Emboscada, Trinidad, Carapeguá, Villeta, Areguá, Quiindý, Villarrica, Villa Franca, Sapucay, Capiatá, San Juán Bautista, Coronel Oviedo, Concepción, Pilar, Paraguarí, and Estación Patiño. Six family heads were foreigners, representing Uruguay, Argentina, Czechoslovakia, and Spain.

The above represents only one aspect of the homogenization process—it does not tell us the proportion of people born in Tobatí who have gone elsewhere to live. If not many have done so, we may have merely described an element in the growth of a particular town, rather than a general process. This is, of course, a much more difficult matter on which to get any statistical material from local sources, but a sample of emigration from Tobatí can be described from the ten genealogies which we collected. These genealogies list all relatives of "ego," whether living or dead, present or absent, and include the present location of each relative. Of the living adults listed in the genealogies, 251 were born in Tobatí; but only 143 continue to live in Tobatí, while 108 live permanently elsewhere. Of these 108, 61 live in Asunción and suburbs. Eleven now live outside Paraguay (Argentina, 9; Brazil, 2), and the remainder are scattered in various Paraguayan towns. It does not seem unwarranted to conclude that a large proportion of Tobateños had their origin in many different parts of Paraguay and that possibly an even larger proportion of native Tobateños leave the partido for permanent residence elsewhere. Much of the emigration is directed to Asunción, as one might expect, rather than to other small towns.

Another matter of interest revealed by the genealogies is the extension of kinship ties to wide areas of Paraguay. The ten genealogies of Tobatí native families, chosen to represent the range of income levels, list a total of 356 living adults recognized by the ten "egos" as relatives.[7] One hundred and eighty-one of them—slightly over half—reside in the *partido* of Tobatí; the other 175 live permanently elsewhere. Ninety-four of these 175 live in or near Asunción, while the other 81 are scattered far and wide in nineteen different towns in Paraguay or in Argentina (15 individuals) and Brazil (2). The predominance of Asunción as a location for *émigrés* from Tobatí is undoubtedly due to the much greater economic opportunity for unskilled labor that the capital offers.

Another notable feature of Paraguay is the relative lack of contrast between the capital city and the rural market towns. Asunción is one of the smallest (100,000 plus) and is certainly the least modernized of the South American capitals. It has no public water system, nor is there any public sewage disposal; both private homes and public buildings must have their own wells and cesspools. This creates a very important health problem, for in the poorer sections of the town the people have only the most rudimentary of makeshifts for acquiring water and disposing of waste. To a traveler the city appears rustic, run down, and poor, compared to the resplendent capitals of the neighboring countries.

Because of the normally great contrast in Latin America between rural poverty and backwardness and the large modern capitals which are the focal centers of most of the national wealth and culture, most visitors to Asunción expect that the Paraguayan rural areas must be something terrifyingly primitive, judging from the appearance of the capital city. Many Latin Americans (especially Argentines and Uruguayans) seem to believe that rural Paraguayans must be literally savages, and even the foreign-born entrepreneurs living in Asunción itself also believe it. A visitor who actually travels a little in the interior is a rarity, but, when he does, he is amazed to find that the contrast

7. The reason there are only 251 living adults cited in the sample used in the previous paragraph and 356 in this one is because for this latter problem—the extension of kinship ties—we did not exclude individuals who were born outside Tobatí.

between rural Paraguayans and those he meets in Asunción is not commensurate with what he had been taught. It is a common occurrence for a traveler in any Latin-American country to be warned against the countryfolk; usually the city middle classes have a contemptuous and sometimes fearful attitude toward the peasantry. In Paraguay this attitude seems carried to exceptional lengths.

But the great bulk of the population lives in the rural areas, and it is here that Paraguayan culture (in the anthropological sense of the word) has its real source and where it is perpetuated. The capital city is composed of Paraguayans, most of whom come from the back country or who are at least not much different culturally from the rural people, and of foreign-born entrepreneurs, who are responsible for most of the features of the capital city by which a tourist judges a country—the stores, industries, hotels, bars, restaurants. The rural market towns and the surrounding agricultural areas, which few foreign travelers ever bother to visit, are where the basic Paraguay is to be found.[8]

8. Paraguayan writers, however, are fascinated with the rural scene and with their folk history. The literary and historical works most famous in Paraguay illustrate this very well. See, as examples, Manuel Domínguez, *El Alma de la raza* (Buenos Aires, n.d.); Natalicio González, *Proceso y formación de la cultura guaraní* (Buenos Aires, 1938); Juán E. Bazán, *Del surco guaraní* (Buenos Aires, n.d.).

CHAPTER II

The Nation and Its Heritage

OF THE South American nations, only Ecuador and Uruguay are smaller in area than Paraguay, which covers about 150,000 square miles. Much of this area is either deserted wasteland or very thinly settled, for the population is only slightly over one million. In our hemisphere, only the tiny nations of Costa Rica and Panama have fewer inhabitants. Probably only Bolivia is more geographically isolated than Paraguay. At present the only feasible commercial route for export is the winding, shallow, shifting Paraguay River. Ships which draw over twelve feet of water cannot come upriver as far as Asunción, and the smaller ships which can make the ascent must haul Paraguay's cargoes for nearly a thousand miles to reach the ocean at Buenos Aires. The costs are amazingly high, because cargoes are small and also because an Argentine shipping company enjoys a nearly complete monopoly of the river shipping and is thus able to charge exorbitant rates.

From the point of view of international trade relations, Paraguay is a "debtor nation," whose economy is entirely agricultural and extractive.[1] For example, in the five years between 1943 and 1947, commercial traffic with the principal nations concerned—Argentina, the United Kingdom, the United States, Uruguay, and Brazil—resulted in a total trade deficit of 70,000,000 guaranis. Trade with Uruguay and the United Kingdom was favorable, but the deficiency to Brazil was 49,000,000 guaranis, to Argentina 33,000,000, and to the United States 21,000,000.[2]

1. In the Western Hemisphere, only Haiti has a higher percentage of rural population. See "Pertinent Data on Latin American Countries," in Asher N. Christiansen (ed.), *The Evolution of Latin American Government* (New York, 1951), table on back flyleaf.

2. Silvio Maldonado, *El Paraguay* (Buenos Aires and Mexico: Fondo de Cultura Económica, 1952), pp. 125–26.

Furthermore, the principal extractive industries are mostly foreign-owned and -operated (primarily by Argentines), and, because of this and the uncertain economy and political instability, the result is what might be called a "flight of profits" rather than a normal degree of reinvestment. Also of considerable political importance is the fact that Argentina is by far the most important purchaser of Paraguayan exports. Beef and cattle by-products (mainly hides) were the principal exports, followed by wood products, especially the bark of the quebracho tree, from which a tanning extract is made. From an economic and political point of view, therefore, Paraguay is notable as an archetypical example of the consequences of being a very small, backward, "underdeveloped" nation, striving to maintain itself as an independent entity, when in fact it enjoys only semicolonial status at best.

From a general cultural and historical point of view, Paraguay owes what fame it has to the fact that it is always depicted in travelers' articles or popular books as a repository of old and curious customs, a product of a peculiar and tragic history. Modern Paraguay is always described as an Indian nation, where the cigar-smoking women do all the work, while the men lie in hammocks and strum guitars. Even scholarly works, by foreigners and Paraguayans as well, stress that the population is predominantly Indian in race, the people still speak the Guaraní language, and much of their culture is believed to be Indian in origin.[3]

Paraguay had never actually been studied in an intensive way by a social scientist, however, and one could justifiably wonder whether the "Indian" stereotype might not be overdrawn. Certainly it would be remarkable if the cultural characteristics of a seminomadic forest tribe such as the Guaraní survived to any

3. Julian H. Steward, "The Changing American Indian," in Ralph Linton (ed.), *The Science of Man in the World Crisis* (New York, 1945), p. 298; Alfred Métraux, "The Guaraní," in Julian H. Steward (ed.), *Handbook of South American Indians* (Bureau of American Ethnology Bulletin No. 143 [6 vols.; Washington, D.C., 1946–50]), III (1948), 77; Preston E. James, *Latin America* (New York, 1942), pp. 266–67; Harris G. Warren, *Paraguay: An Informal History* (Norman, Okla., 1949), p. 33 and elsewhere; Natalicio González, *Proceso y formación de la cultura guaraní* (Buenos Aires, 1938); and many others.

great extent in the modern nation. Perhaps the writers of the few sketchy works on Paraguay have accepted too uncritically the native Paraguayans' beliefs about their own cultural heritage. It is possible that the extreme modern nationalism has taken the form of *indigenismo*, an emphasis which glorifies a posited Indian heritage.

But, on the other hand, if it were possible that a strong component of Indian culture could still survive in a modern Latin-American nation, there are many reasons for assuming that it could have happened in Paraguay more easily than almost anywhere else. Paraguay lies in the heart of the South American continent and, like Bolivia, in a landlocked position, isolated to a great degree from modern commercial developments. Such factors as commercial and cultural isolation normally retard culture change and permit the survival of cultural elements of an earlier civilization. Subsistence-oriented peasants make up the great bulk of the population of Paraguay; the middle class is small and largely foreign-born. Modern attitudes and values, which get their greatest impetus from commerce and industry, are consequently slow to develop there.

The whole history of Paraguay has been conducive to the preservation of the colonial way of life into modern times. The outstanding impression forced on the reader by the often peculiar, usually heartbreaking historical fortunes of this small nation is one of continuing isolation from the rest of the world. Throughout most of the colonial period Spain restricted trade from southern South America in favor of the mineral-wealthy northern provinces, and Spanish immigrants were therefore not attracted to Paraguay. Even after independence from Spain was achieved, not only did commerce remain limited because of geographic hindrances, but Paraguay's borders were kept officially closed to foreigners for many years by two of the most fantastic dictatorships in the history of the Western world, those of "El Supremo" Francia and Francisco Solano López. López' reign of terror was ended, and Paraguay's isolation was also ended, by the War of the Triple Alliance of 1865–70, but the country was so devastated by the invasion of Argentina, Uruguay, and Brazil that she has not fully recovered to this day. The Chaco war of the 1930's added to Paraguay's economic woes, and political disruption and sporadic revolutions have kept the country one of the most economically underdeveloped nations in Latin America.

If early cultural patterns are preserved in the modern scene, it becomes necessary to investigate the nature of the early settlement in order to determine, where possible, whether the colonial mode of life indicates the degree of Indian cultural dominance. If Paraguayan culture is in certain ways unique in Latin America, the differences may be due in large part to the extraordinary degree to which early colonial cultural patterns have been preserved into modern times and to the unusual acculturational situation in the early period of adjustment between the Spanish settlers and the Guaraní Indians, which *may* have made something distinctive of that early colonial culture.

Several historians have noted some of the unique institutions of this early period and in some cases have called attention to possible effects on the culture of the modern nation. But none of them has studied the details of early colonial life for the purpose of describing functionally the sort of acculturation which occurred. In addition, it seems that judgments made about early Spanish-Guaraní relations have been biased by the assumption that Guaraní culture actually *has* survived in large part. Thus Arcos says:

> The rule of Irala [the first governor] is significant on account of the relations which he established between the Spaniards and the Indians, which were of such a nature as in a large measure to determine the character of the later population of Paraguay.[4]

And Washburn states:

> It was a constant endeavor of Irala to level all distinctions between the Europeans and Natives, and this he effected in a great measure by encouraging his countrymen to take the brown daughters of the forest for wives, to learn their language and conform to their customs in matters not of essential importance. . . . Thus the government and policy of Irala permanently fixed the character, social and political, of the people.[5]

Foreign writers and the Paraguayans themselves fail to distinguish the racial character of the population from the language

4. Quoted in Bernard Moses, *The Establishment of Spanish Rule in America* (New York, 1892), p. 194.

5. Charles A. Washburn, *The History of Paraguay* (2 vols.; Boston, 1871), I, 57–58.

spoken, and these two from mental habits and attitudes. It seems that inferences as to the culture and "mind" of the Paraguayans are derived from the supposed strong Indian genetic strain in the population. For example, a recent work by a North American historian states:

> Paraguay's economy and society were products of environment and racial hybridization. One may readily see traits that are peculiarly all European or all Indian, as well as others that arose from the mixture of Spanish and Guaraní blood.[6]

Most commonly, cultural elements are posited as "Guaraní" because the Guaraní language is still spoken as a household tongue by Paraguayans. Certainly one of the most striking features of Paraguay is the use of the ancient Indian tongue in the modern context, but to go from this fact to the conclusion that *therefore* the population is largely Guaraní in either race or general culture is completely unwarranted and may result in a false characterization.

The Period of Discovery and Exploration[7]

The original impetus for the exploration of the La Plata area was the false assumption that the land was rich in precious metals. It was for this reason that the great river was misnamed "River of Silver." Rumors of this great source of wealth reached Spain after Sebastian Cabot sailed up the La Plata in 1526, where he found Indians wearing silver ornaments. He was, of course, ignorant of the probability that these ornaments had come from the Andes via aboriginal trade routes.

Reports about this supposedly wealthy region led to the organization of the Mendoza expedition, which sailed to the La Plata from Spain in 1535 and founded its first settlement near the present site of Buenos Aires. This expedition, originally composed of thirteen hundred men, became considerably reduced by starvation and bitter warfare with the nomadic Charrua and Querandí

6. Warren, *op. cit.*, p. 124.

7. The following historical summary is presented with a minimum of footnotes, as it is merely a condensation of parts of the published monograph by Elman R. Service, *Spanish-Guaraní Relations in Early Colonial Paraguay* ("Anthropological Papers of the Museum of Anthropology, University of Michigan," No. 9 [Ann Arbor, Mich., 1954]).

Indians, so that eventually Buenos Aires was abandoned, and Asunción, Paraguay, became the headquarters of the expedition, for here the Guaraní Indians welcomed the Spaniards as allies against the ever pressing raiders of the Chaco. The Guaraní became a source of labor and food supplies to the Spaniards and became auxiliary soldiers, as well.

In the early years of the settlement at Asunción, the Spaniards used the fort merely as a base from which they sallied out in various directions, searching for the legendary sources of great wealth. They made no effort to settle the land or establish encomiendas of Indians for agricultural exploitation, for they were content to obtain aid from the Indians by the simplest and most expedient means, and in such a way that the Guaraní remained willing collaborators. Thus, instead of forcing the Guaraní into a Spanish system such as the encomienda, the Spanish soldiers lived by Indian contributions. It must be noted in this connection that the Guaraní, though horticulturists, were seminomadic and had no large villages, extensive political federation, or hierarchy of officials, so the matter of control over them was a difficult one. There is also evidence that the approximately three hundred and fifty remaining Spaniards were fearful for their own safety, especially when large contingents of soldiers were away for several months on an expedition.

The Spaniards therefore adopted a method for obtaining women, food, and labor which already had its counterpart among the Indians. A Guaraní "chief," the head of a lineage, normally had several wives from families related to him but outside his patrilineal lineage. Women were the horticulturalists in Guaraní society and were thus a source of labor to the chief. The other relatives of his wives customarily supplied labor for the chief at special times. Apparently the military alliance with the Spaniards was consolidated by fitting individual Spaniards into the lineage system with the normal status prerogatives of the chief and war leader. The association of Spaniards with Indians on this kinship-like basis was probably strengthened as the many Indian women began to bear the Spaniards' children. A member of the colony, Diego Téllez de Escobar, described it in this fashion:

It was the custom of the Indians of the land to serve the Christians and give them their daughters or sisters and to come to their houses in a spirit of kinship and friendship. The Christians were thus served because they had many children by the natives, and for this reason the Indians came to aid them as to the homes of kinsmen.[8]

Although the Spaniards expediently adopted a manner of exploitation which was basically a Guaraní type of system rather than a Spanish one, they seem to have enjoyed considerable control over the scattered Indian lineages in the central region, for by 1538, two years after their arrival, they had founded thirteen permanent Indian villages, of which one was Tobatí.[9] These were not yet true encomienda villages, but the Indians were controlled ("reduced") and required to furnish women, food, labor, and auxiliary soldiers to the Spaniards.

In 1556, approximately twenty years after the founding of Asunción, Governor Irala instituted a radical change in the relations of the Spaniards to the local Guaraní by establishing encomiendas. This marked, in effect, the end of the casual, temporary phase of the occupation of the region and began the period of permanent settlement, during which the Indians' labor was now seen to be the major source of wealth; the dreams of great discoveries of mineral wealth were forgotten.

The extensive polygyny of the first twenty years and the fact that the Spaniards and Guaraní regarded each other as kinsmen after the Indian fashion must be regarded as two of the most important of the unusual circumstances which influenced the subsequent cultural developments of colonial Paraguay. The encomienda system which followed was a more characteristic Spanish institution, but the concubinage of Indian women and the kinship-labor pattern were not entirely replaced.

The Encomiendas

The laws of Spain relating to encomiendas were very rigid and detailed, but, inasmuch as they were supposed to apply to all the Spanish colonies, they did not take account of the great native

8. "Relacion de Diego Tellez Descobar a S. M.," in Blas Garay, *Colección de documentos relativos á la historia de América y particularmente á la historia del Paraguay* (Asunción, Paraguay, 1899–1901), p. 270.

9. Félix de Azara, *Viajes por la América Meridional* (2 vols.; Madrid, 1923), II, 129.

cultural differences in the various parts of the New World. They were never entirely enforced in Paraguay, despite attempts by several governors to make the local system conform to Crown intentions. Some of the laws which had grown out of the Crown's experiences in the West Indies, Mexico, and Peru had unforeseen consequences in Paraguay, while others had to be modified or disregarded.

As the system initiated by Irala gradually took form and became adapted to the local Paraguayan situation, two distinct kinds of encomiendas came into being. One, called the *originario* encomienda, consisted of Indians who lived in permanent servitude in the households and estates of their encomenderos. The other, the *mitayo* encomienda, was of outlying villages of Indians who had to give *corvée* labor services (the *mita*) to the Spanish encomenderos for certain periods of the year only; the rest of the time they lived in their own villages and cultivated their own lands. Notable in both systems is the fact that labor services were the rule, in opposition to Crown encomienda laws which required that tribute should be the sole economic requirement. Each system differed in other ways, as well, from the formal encomienda of other parts of Spanish America, especially in violating the Crown laws which were designed to protect the Indians and which, when enforced, had the effect of inhibiting their assimilation into the Spanish way of life.

It should be emphasized that the classic encomienda functioned something like an Indian reservation in North America, in the sense that the protection offered the Indians fostered the retention of much of their culture, whereas the characteristics of the Paraguayan encomienda were quite opposite. The form of this encomienda seemed actually to foster the assimilation of the Indians into the dominant culture.

The *originario* system continued, as its basis, the concubinage of Guaraní women, and Guaraní women also continued to work as horticulturalists. Statements by the most reliable chroniclers of the period from 1579 until about 1630 indicate that in the city of Asunción there were about ten women to every man, and the ordinances of several governors during this period show that Guaraní women were continually taken from the *mitayo* pueblos to augment the *originarios*. Male relatives of these women were also kept by the encomendero in permanent servitude.

It would be difficult to imagine a system of exploitation more conducive to thorough acculturation of the Indians than the Paraguayan *originario*. The Guaraní were completely dominated by the Spaniards, for legal restrictions on their control and exploitation were ineffective. There is evidence, however, that, though laws were not enforced, the possible hardships of the Indians were somewhat moderated by the prevalence of kinship ties between the encomendero and his Indians, so that from the Indians' point of view the situation was not necessarily cruel or unnatural.[10] Additionally, the fact that the Paraguayan situation did not permit a cash-crop plantation system undoubtedly limited the degree of exploitation of the Indians. Nevertheless, it would have been difficult for the Indians to retain much cultural independence in matters incompatible with the encomendero's interests.

One of the important consequences of the *originario* system was the great production of mestizo offspring and the increasingly important role they played in extending Paraguayan dominance to outlying areas. By about 1600 they were already the basic "Spanish" population and had replaced peninsular Spaniards as encomenderos. Santa Fe, for example, was founded by an expedition of nine Spaniards and seventy-five mestizos, and Buenos Aires was re-established in 1588 by ten Spaniards and sixty-three mestizos. The mestizos were also beginning to feel themselves "Paraguayan" and often displayed a very independent attitude toward Spanish authority. Several scattered rebellions in the latter half of the sixteenth century were already called *comunero* movements and presaged the kind of revolts which in later years

10. Francisco de Alfaro, who visited Asunción in 1611 as Crown inspector investigating the failure of the Paraguayans to enforce Crown encomienda laws, was a great opponent of *originario* labor but suggested that there would be difficulty in abolishing it in favor of tribute, "because most of the Indians, in the inspections I have made, especially in the city of Asunción, say they do not want to pay tribute; some . . . because they do not know what it is; others because they say they serve whenever and however they wish and the Spaniards give them gifts; others [say] that they help the Spaniards, not by way of tribute nor servitude, but as relatives" ("Ordenanzas de Alfaro," Article 57, in Pablo Hernández, *Organización social de las doctrinas guaraníes de la Compañía de Jesús* [2 vols.; Barcelona, 1913], Vol. II, Appendix 56).

led to the independence of the various Spanish-American states.

The *mitayo* encomienda was much less important as an acculturative institution than the *originario* system. The *mitayo* Indians, usually located far from Asunción, lived in their own villages and tilled their own lands and thus were more easily able to maintain the integrity of their culture. They were, however, much less protected than the Crown encomienda laws required. The Indians were used as a labor force, instead of paying tribute, and, also contrary to the laws, the villages were ruled by Spanish *pobleros*, or administrators, who actually lived in the villages.

But the *mitayo* encomiendas played a steadily diminishing role in the Paraguayan economy. They were not large at the time of their inception in 1556, when Irala divided twenty thousand Indians among "320 or more" Spaniards[11] (averaging sixty-two Indians per encomienda), and they became even smaller as time went on. The steady drain on their female population to supply women for the *originario* was, of course, of great consequence in limiting the number of Indian births. There are also documentary references to epidemics which killed great numbers of the village Indians. By 1611 many sources stress that the *mitayo* encomiendas often contained less than ten Indians. At any rate, it becomes clear that, by the time the colony was one hundred years old, the basic population of all classes consisted of Spanish-Indian mixtures of various degrees. The *mitayo* encomiendas had become virtually nonfunctional, though many of the villages remained, however, populated by families of Hispanicized mestizos, engaged in a characteristic agricultural subsistence economy.

The earlier symbiosis between Spaniards and Guaraní must have quickly promoted an amalgamation of native and Spanish food crops, agricultural techniques, and modes of food preparation.[12] Paraguay lacked precious metals and, as remarked, early

11. Domingo Martínez de Irala, "Relación breve ... ," in R. de Lafuente Machain, *El Gobernador Domingo Martínez de Irala* (Buenos Aires, 1939), Appendix, pp. 535–46, esp. p. 544.

12. Such important native crops as maize, beans, squash, melons, peanuts, sweet potatoes, and manioc were supplemented by the Spanish sugar cane, citrus fruits, grapes, figs, pomegranates, hemp, flax, ginger, almonds, wheat, and barley. Of great utility were the introduced domestic animals: chickens, pigs, horses, and cattle—goats and sheep. There was an abundance of excellent pasturage, and herding did not crowd the Indians from their agricultural land as it did in the Andean region.

became isolated from outside commerce. The subsistence economy must have fostered acculturation in many ways. It would have had, for example, an important effect in reducing the great gulf which has often separated the attitudes of Europeans and Indians in matters of market, commerce, and money. The Spaniards in Paraguay were, truly enough, the exploiters and the Indians the exploited, but, as this occurred within an economy which was essentially moneyless, it was a situation at least comprehensible to the Indians and possibly even a more acceptable one than it might have been under the conditions imposed by a dominant commercialism.

In addition to economic conditions, the assimilation of Indians and mestizos into a modified Spanish culture was also affected by such factors as the simplicity of Guaraní sociopolitical structure and the lack of large population centers as contrasted with the great native empires of Mexico and Peru. The Spaniards could not simply replace the top-level native rulers and govern through an intermediate class of subsidiary chiefs who controlled a settled and populous class of agriculturalists. Control had to be immediate and specific, reaching down to the individual Indian family.

By the time mestizos became the basic Paraguayan population, a stable colonial culture had been formed. The fact that Spaniards had been so much the dominant group at first suggests that the most important elements in the culture were probably Spanish, but it is possible that for a while several minor Guaraní traits persisted. The large number of mestizo children would have been more often associated with their Guaraní mothers for informal day-to-day education and would have been more isolated from their fathers than if they had been part of a small monogamous family. Elements of Guaraní folklore and superstition were probably passed on in this way. The retention of the Guaraní language was also a consequence of this kind of daily association.

The ambitions of the mestizos, as indicated by their revolts and general intransigence, imply that many purely Spanish attitudes and values were carried over, however, and that, because of the dominant position of the Spaniards, Spanish culture in general carried more prestige than did the Guaraní. There is no evidence from the colonial period that the various political revolts carried overtones of cultural "revivalism" or "nativism" which occurred elsewhere as a result of an incomplete acceptance of natives and mestizos into the dominant civilization.

Thus one of the most important ways in which the development of the Paraguayan colony differed strikingly from the more familiar regions of Spanish America was the early amalgamation of natives and Spaniards into a relatively homogeneous national culture. The unusual form of the association of Guaraní and Spaniards within a predominantly subsistence economy rapidly assimilated the natives into Paraguayan colonial life, and the subsequent mestizo population took a great pride in their local language, territory, and customs. It should be noted again that in Paraguay the Spaniards had *added* to the society such elements of statehood as over-all political, military, economic, and religious institutions rather than *replaced* them at the top level as in Peru and Mexico. This must be considered a very important factor in contributing to the predominant Hispanic cast of the national culture and in the rapidity with which the local Spanish colonial type of culture reached all levels of the society.

The Jesuit Missions

One of the most famous episodes in the colonial period is the founding, flowering, and subsequent decay of the Jesuit colony in the Alto Paraná River Basin. This mission system fostered a radically different kind of acculturation of the Guaraní Indians from that of the encomienda system we have discussed. The Jesuit fathers who ruled this domain of approximately sixty thousand Indians also figured rather prominently in the political history of colonial Paraguay. Although they were located in a wilderness remote from the center of Paraguayan settlement, they were important to the Spanish Crown during the early phase of their existence as a strategic buffer against the expanding Portuguese colony in southern Brazil. The Jesuits were allowed to arm their Indians in order to counter Brazilian raiders, and this military power eventually became influential in Paraguayan political affairs, as the Jesuits thus could hold a balance of power between rival political factions. Their political importance has made the Jesuits the subject of a considerable body of historical literature.

The period of Jesuit power lasted for about one hundred and fifty years. The first missions were established about 1609, and the Jesuits gradually drew Indians to them until, at the height of their influence, they ruled thirty mission towns. Within these towns the Indians were very closely supervised and regimented by the fathers. Religious teachings were naturally emphasized; economic affairs were strictly communal—work in the community fields was a collective enterprise, the herds and granaries belonged to the village, and the products were equally distributed. The Indians all dressed identically and lived in communal dwellings; the only socially distinctive people were the Jesuits themselves, who functioned as teachers and benevolent dictators.

When the Spanish Crown expelled the Jesuits from the New World in 1767, the Paraná mission system fell apart. The region was invaded by unscrupulous traders and by treasure-hunters who believed that the Jesuits had buried great fortunes in gold and silver. The Indians, who had been so closely supervised by the Jesuits in their communal life, were unable to cope with the outside world. Rapid demoralization occurred, and most of the Indians abandoned the mission towns and retreated to the forests.

The so-called "communistic" social order has caused a good deal of controversy, so that many writers have entered the long-standing dispute over the merits or deficiencies of this social scheme. The resulting abundance of recovered source material and secondary works has made this "Jesuit empire" by far the best-known aspect of Paraguayan history; consequently, there is a tendency to overrate its influence as a determinant in the formation of Paraguayan national culture.

The area in which the missions were established was so remote and inaccessible from Asunción that virtually all mission trade was necessarily by river traffic with Buenos Aires. The jealousy of Asunción over the great trade advantages of the Jesuits and the recurrent political strife further served to limit intercourse between Paraguayans and mission Indians, and the Jesuits virtually sealed off their region from contact with outsiders, by force of arms when necessary. The acculturation of Indians by the Jesuits was thereby limited exclusively to the Indians who actually inhabited the mission towns. After the expulsion of the Jesuits, as we have noted, the mission Indians either disappeared into the forests or were forced to adjust to a Paraguayan culture whose essential patterns had long been in existence as a product of a radically different kind of acculturation.[13]

Isolation and Self-sufficiency

The fact that Paraguay was one of the very first of Spain's dependencies to begin and to maintain a serious separatist movement must be tied up with certain salient characteristics of the colonial period. First of all, we must remark the great degree of isolation from the mother-country. This was not merely geographic but was also a result of a Crown policy. From 1535 to 1575, direct trade between Spain and the La Plata region was prohibited, and after Buenos Aires was refounded in 1580 Peru and Panama retained their monopoly on South American trade and were able to convince the Spanish Crown to uphold it at the cost of the development of the port of Buenos Aires. The La Plata region was, until nearly the end of the eighteenth century, almost completely closed to the rest of the world.[14]

Paraguay was also unable to compete for the small amount of internal South American trade. The Jesuits kept the Paraguayans from expanding to the east and also monopolized the minor trade with Buenos Aires and Uruguay. Overland trade with Peru was virtually impossible because of the difficulties presented by the Chaco and Matto Grosso wildernesses. An important political event which further increased Paraguay's isolation was the division of the old province of Río de la Plata into two separate parts in 1617. Buenos Aires became the capital of Río de la Plata and Asunción the capital of Paraguay, a circumstance which en-

13. The most important source for descriptive material on the Jesuit mission system of Paraguay is Pablo Hernández, *op. cit.* See also V. Martin de Moussy, *Mémoire historique sur la décadence et la ruine des missions des Jesuites* ... (Paris, 1864), and Nicolás del Techo, *Historia de la provincia del Paraguay y de la Compañía de Jesús* (Madrid, 1897).

14. Clarence H. Haring, *Trade and Navigation between Spain and the Indies in the time of the Hapsburgs* (Cambridge, Mass., 1918), p. 40.

hanced the importance of Buenos Aires but correspondingly reduced that of Asunción. In Mitre's words, "Paraguay, isolated,
reduced to its own resources, deprived of the vivifying currents
of immigration and the interchange of products, became stagnant
and ceased to be the center of a fruitful and expanding civilization."[15]

The lack of foreign markets reduced the Paraguayan economy
to small-scale subsistence agriculture. Documentary evidence
clearly shows that, while internal development did proceed
slowly, the economy was so lacking in money and commerce
that visitors were struck by this feature during the whole colonial
period. We may here quote a few of their comments in order to
give the flavor of the situation.

López de Velasco, the Spanish royal cosmographer, visited
Paraguay in 1571–74 and made the following comment:

> They have all that which is necessary for sustenance, but no wealth
> in money, for there is none in the land: all their wealth is in the agricul-
> ture of the country. . . . There are no commodities because there are
> no sea ports; everyone puts what he wishes to exchange in the hands of
> a broker in a public house, placed by the city, and those who want to
> trade with others come there; because there is no money except some
> wedges or hatchets of iron.[16]

The famous Ruíz de Montoya, who was in Paraguay in the
early 1600's, said of Asunción, "They have no gold nor silver
mines, and there is no money whatever. Buying and selling is by
the exchange of one thing for another."[17] In 1645, Del Techo
described Asunción and its inhabitants, who "know nothing of
money, but live still by exchange of commodities, after the manner of antiquity."[18] And Acarete du Biscay, a later seventeenth-
century visitor, remarked of the people of Asunción, "Having

15. Quoted in Ricardo Levene, *A History of Argentina* (Chapel Hill, N.C.,
1937), p. 50.

16. Juán López de Velasco, *Geografía y descripción universal de las Indias*
(Madrid, 1894), pp. 551–52.

17. Antonio Ruíz de Montoya, *Conquista espiritual hecha por los religiosos
de la Compañía de Jesús en las provincias del Paraguay, Paraná, Uruguay y
Tapé* (Bilbao, 1892), pp. 16–17.

18. Nicolás del Techo, "The History of the Provinces of Paraguay, Tucumán,
Río de la Plata, Paraná, Guairá, and Urvaica," in Awnsham Churchill, *A Collection of Voyages and Travels* (London, 1746), IV, 15.

plenty of all things good to eat and drink, they give themselves up to Ease and Idleness, and don't much trouble themselves with Trading abroad, nor heaping up Money, which upon that account is very scarce among them."[19]

Even as late as the middle of the eighteenth century, Dobrizhoffer found a similar situation in the capital city: "Money is used very rarely, if at all, its place being supplied by the exchange of commodities, as among the ancients. . . . The want or ignorance of metals may be reckoned amongst the divine blessings and advantages of Paraguay."[20]

After a short period of political anarchy following the independence movements of 1810–12, Paraguay was ruled by the iron hand of the dictator Francia—"El Supremo"—until 1840, and the isolation of the colonial years was continued by political terrorism. The borders were closed to foreign merchants and other visitors, and Francia became famous for his despotic cruelties and the fantastic nature of his foreign policy. This was the period of the famous *caudillos* in South America, an epoch of great anarchy, confusion, and localized civil wars; but Paraguay's Francia created, by his so-called "China policy," a hermit state which contrasted so strongly with the other South American states that it became a great literary topic in Europe.

Francia's successor, Carlos Antonio López, was no less a dictator; but he opened up the country to commerce and built it up internally with the aid of foreign technicians—chiefly English. But the new attempts at world commerce were not entirely successful, because much of the time Paraguay was blockaded by Argentina, especially by the *caudillo* Rosas, and commercial shipping resembled smuggling more than legitimate trade. López did succeed, however, in several projects designed to modernize the nation. He improved transportation and, in fact, installed a short length of railroad—the first in South America. He also built a disciplined army, and, when he bequeathed the nation to his son, Francisco Solano López, he also gave him command of this very dangerous toy, which the youthful dictator decided to use in the

19. *An Account of a Voyage up the River de la Plata, and Thence over Land to Peru* . . . (London, 1698), p. 11.

20. Martin Dobrizhoffer, *An Account of the Abipones, an Equestrian People of Paraguay* (3 vols.; London, 1822), I, 216–18.

game of power politics against Brazil, Uruguay, and Argentina. The new ruler, who took office in 1862, was by late 1864 involved in a war which almost wiped Paraguay off the map.

Paraguay's Wars

During the colonial period Paraguay was in a nearly continual state of alarm because of the many raiding tribes of the Chaco and the sporadic civil wars. Small- and large-scale civil strife still characterizes modern political behavior, but of far more consequence in shaping Paraguay's political and economic destiny have been the two major wars with their neighboring states, the War of the Triple Alliance (1865–70) and the Chaco war (1928–35). The enormous devastation following Paraguay's defeat in the first of these virtually destroyed the small amount of economic progress that had been made since middle-colonial times. The recent Chaco war was not a defeat for Paraguay but was rather inconclusive as to its results; nevertheless, its effect was to perpetuate the economic depression which followed the earlier war.

The catastrophe visited on Paraguay by her preposterous dictator, Francisco Solano López, in the famous War of the Triple Alliance defies description. The iron rule of López and the heroism of his peasant soldiers held off the armies of Argentina, Brazil, and Uruguay for nearly five years. López had invaded both Brazilian and Argentine territory in the first year of the war, but by April, 1866, the armies of the allies were occupying parts of Paraguay, and it should have been clear in that year that López' cause was hopeless. Nevertheless, he never gave up, fighting battles in Paraguayan territory ever closer to Asunción, and even after the capital was captured in January, 1869, López and his few remaining troops fought a guerrilla war against the invaders, until the dictator was killed by a Brazilian soldier on March 1, 1870.

The most striking consequence of Paraguay's overwhelming defeat was the great loss in manpower. It is said that only women, children, and burros survived. Actually, statistics are so unreliable that it is impossible to say what the population of the country was at any time, before or after the war. The modern Paraguayan authorities, González and Ynsfran, say that, of the million prewar inhabitants, only three hundred thousand women and children and old men remained.[21]

Paraguay also lost 55,000 square miles of territory and was occupied by foreign troops for many years. Industry and foreign trade were at a standstill, and the small prewar commercial class virtually disappeared. Petty merchants and peddlers, who were mostly "Turcos" and Italians, followed in the wake of the foreign troops and established themselves in the fashion of the carpetbaggers of the North American Civil War period. Meanwhile, the small class of aristocratic landowners, the native *latifundistas* and *hacendados*, had fled Paraguay, carrying such portable valuables as they could manage. In the confusion of the occupation, government records, including titles to land, were lost, destroyed, or removed from Paraguay. The important landholders never returned to re-establish themselves in their native land, except for a few isolated cases. Even today the relative absence of native middle and upper classes is a striking feature of the social and political aspects of Paraguay's national culture.

The slow and difficult road toward economic recovery was hardly begun before a new period of tension began between Bolivia and Paraguay over claims to the great lowland wilderness, the Gran Chaco, which lies between the two countries. It is difficult to say when the Chaco war actually began, but certainly the drain on the resources of each country was felt long before the war was formally declared in 1933. Both countries began to build forts in the Chaco as early as 1907 and steadily increased their military strength. A series of local skirmishes began in the Chaco in 1928, which grew finally into a full-scale war of such magnitude as would have been thought far beyond the economic capacity of two nations with such limited resources.[22] When the war

21. J. Natalicio González and Pablo Max Ynsfran, *El Paraguay Contemporáneo* (Paris and Asunción, 1929), p. 29. Figures approximate to these have the widest currency, although H. G. Warren may well be closer to the truth when he argues that Paraguay most probably had a prewar population of about 525,000, with 221,079 remaining in the country after the war (*op. cit.*, p. 243).

22. It is generally conceded that both countries received considerable aid from interested foreign groups and nations. It is not relevant to our purpose here, however, to attempt an evaluation of the roles of Chile, Argentina, the United States, England, and various international corporations.

ended in a truce on June 12, 1935, both sides were prostrated economically and very short of manpower. No one won the war in the sense that either nation achieved any apparent benefit.

Since the close of the war, internal strife in Paraguay has been a continuing handicap to recovery. The short-lived governments resorted to increasingly totalitarian methods to perpetuate themselves, but the turnover in presidents was rapid, until Higinio Morínigo took power in 1940. His regime, which became rather famous in North America for its harsh dictatorial methods, lasted until 1948. It is possible that an improvement in Paraguay's economic position due to the boom times of World War II helped solidify the regime, but strife was certainly not absent, for there were various uprisings by discontented elements. Finally, in 1947, an opposition coalition began a real civil war, which lasted for nearly six months. The rebellion almost succeeded, but Morínigo remained in office until June, 1948. For the rest of 1948 and until September, 1949, Paraguay had five different presidents, all representing separate factions of a single political party, the triumphant Colorados. But even with a single party clearly dominant, factional discord and minor civil skirmishes remain characteristic of the political life of the nation.

The Genetic Composition of the Present-Day Population

The aboriginal Guaraní who mixed with the early Spanish settlers are not reliably described in the historical literature, nor are there any anthropometric studies of the modern Guaraní who live in the forests of the northeastern margins of the country. Our own brief observations of them support the contentions frequently found in the historical literature that they were a short-statured, slightly built group, with comparatively light skins and somewhat Caucasoid facial features. We have no assurance, however, that these modern Indians have not mixed with whites or mestizos to a considerable extent.

During the colonial period, there was little immigration from Europe, so there was every probability that the Paraguayan population became largely mestizo. A few Negroes, mostly runaways from Brazil, filtered in but were quickly assimilated. After independence, and especially during the time of the dictators, the borders were closed to both immigration and emigration, and Francia (who was a mestizo) decreed that Spaniards could not marry other whites.[23]

Following the War of the Triple Alliance (1865–70), there was a slight but constant trickle of immigration from Europe, owing to the efforts of the Paraguayan government to increase the population of the country. In the late years of the nineteenth century, about one thousand persons per year came to Paraguay, of whom the largest proportion were Italians. This immigration was largely in connection with the establishment of business enterprises rather than with the founding of agricultural colonies.[24] However, since then some large colonies have been founded by foreign groups, especially Germans. A large part of the immigration of modern times has been religious dissenters, especially Mennonites and Hutterites. Most of these non-Latin immigrants never mixed with the Paraguayans but have maintained their own separate colonies, preserving their genetic and cultural identity, usually in regions remote from Paraguayan settlements. A few so-called "Turcos" (probably mostly Lebanese Syrians and Mediterranean Jews) have come to Paraguay in recent times and have remained relatively aloof as middle-class tradesmen.[25] Italians, Spaniards, and Argentines have come in fewer numbers and have been more disposed to adopt Paraguayan customs and marry into Paraguayan families. This has resulted in a slow but cumulative change in the genetic composition of Paraguayan middle-class townsmen toward Europeanization, while the more purely rural, or peasant, population retains a more Indian physical appearance.

This process may be illustrated by the recent history of Tobatí. This *partido* of seven to ten thousand people contains but seven male foreigners and one foreign woman. Only one, a

23. J. P. and W. P. Robertson, *Four Years in Paraguay* (2 vols.; Philadelphia, 1838), II, 30–31.

24. E. de Bourgade la Dardye, *Paraguay: The Land and the People* . . . (London, 1892), p. 112. He gives the number of immigrants in 1886 as 100; in 1887 as 563; in 1888 as 1,064; in 1889 as 1,914 (no source is cited for these figures).

25. A government decree of 1936 forbids the entrance of Jews of *any nationality*.

Bolivian former prisoner of war, lives in the rural area as an agriculturist, the remainder being engaged in various enterprises in the town. Of these, two are Spaniards, two are Argentines, one is a Czechoslovakian with an Italian wife, and one is a Uruguayan of Swiss descent. All but the Czechoslovakian are married to Paraguayan women.

This proportion of foreigners is small indeed in terms of the total population of the *partido*, but it is significant with respect to the small business class of the town. Apparently there has been a similar small increment of foreigners in previous generations, going back to the years following 1870, for several of the leading families have an Italian or Spanish father or grandfather. For this reason, the small middle class of the town of Tobatí, and of other towns we have visited, tends to be somewhat more European in physical appearance than are the peasants.

These families of partial European descent usually regard themselves as Paraguayans, but in certain conversational contexts they might say that they are really "Spanish" or "Italian." But Paraguayan nationalism is pervasive, and these same individuals would insist on their "Paraguayan-ness" if they were to be compared with foreigners. The rest of the population would likewise consider these people as Paraguayans in such a discussion, but at other times they would not. The age-old hatred, distrust, and envy which peasants hold for commercial people in most of the world is very apparent in Paraguay. The social attitude of the business families toward the ignorant peasants also helps promote a positive cleavage. The peasants thus often refer to the middle-class families in contemptuous terms, chief among them being *gringo-ra'ý* ("sons of foreigners").

Proportion of the Sexes

Paraguayans feel that their country is a "land of women" and often insist that there are two or more times as many women as men. This belief, interestingly enough, began very early in the colonial history and has been continued for so long that it could justly be called a "tradition." That it is traditional does not mean that there is no basis for it, however, for there has been, at various times and for different reasons, a very real shortage of men. This shortage also exists today, but not to the extent that Paraguayans claim. Apparently most foreigners accept the Paraguayan appraisal of this situation, for we have encountered Latin Americans of various countries who describe this Paraguayan anomaly, and most books on Paraguay, both by foreigners and by native Paraguayans, allude to it uncritically.[26]

The imbalance of the sexes began in early colonial times, when the Spaniards acquired "harems" of Guaraní women. There seems to be sufficient evidence that for a long period the women in Asunción outnumbered the men by about ten to one, and chroniclers refer to harems of forty and fifty women.[27] This institution was notorious in Paraguayan history and is the starting point of the traditional notions about the nature of the population. A later historical occurrence which reinforced these beliefs was the tragic War of the Triple Alliance in 1865–70, which was so fantastically costly to the manpower of Paraguay.

Naturally, the normal balance of the sexes in the population would gradually be re-established, but the situation in Paraguay following the war was so famous that the "land of women" epithet became very widely known. Since then, the bloody Chaco war of 1928–35 has cost Paraguay thousands of casualties, and political exile and the emigration of young men to Argentina in search of economic opportunity have played a big part in keeping the male population below normal numbers. Many workers in the Argentine Chaco and on Argentine cattle ranches are Paraguayans; there is a large Paraguayan colony in Buenos Aires, and many border towns in Argentina and Brazil are composed predominantly of Paraguayans.

It seems probable, however, that Paraguayans, and foreigners as well, exaggerate the proportion of women in the population. Women do a great deal of the work in towns and cities, especially work of a petty commercial sort, and are therefore more in evidence than in countries where they are more housebound by tradition. Miss Emma Reh, in her dietary study of Piribebuý,

26. Haiti seems to be similar to Paraguay in the apparent predominance of women and in the traditional beliefs about it. See James G. Leyburn, *The Haitian People* (New Haven, 1941), p. 193.

27. See E. R. Service, *op. cit.*

found 33 per cent of the homes in the town headed by women but felt that in the rural *compañías* the balance of the sexes was more nearly equal because of the economic disadvantage single women would encounter in agricultural work as opposed to life in town and city, where servants and laundresses would be more in demand.[28] Our census data from Tobatí and incomplete data from the *Censo de agricultura del Paraguay*[29] support the above suggestion.

In the town of Tobatí we found that up to ten years of age boys slightly outnumbered girls (233 boys, 213 girls) and that thereafter the sexes were about equal in numbers, until the age of eighteen. The male proportion of adults, however, then sharply decreased. Of persons over eighteen years of age, only 265 were males, while 425 were females. Nearly one-half of all the households in Tobatí were headed by women (140 with female heads to 153 with male heads). But STICA files on 529 agriculturalists outside the town in the Tobatí *partido* listed only 36 female heads of families, about 7 per cent. Of the total of 94,433 working agriculturalists in all of Paraguay for whom the STICA had data, 9,611 were females, or slightly over 10 per cent. These figures show that the famous predominance of women in Paraguay is largely a feature of town life. An independent economic existence for women is rare in agriculture.

28. Emma Reh, *Paraguayan Rural Life* (Washington, D.C.: Institute of Inter-American Affairs, Food Supply Division, 1946), pp. 16–23.

29. Prepared by the Servicio Técnico Interamericano de Cooperación Agrícola, 1942–44, and published by the Bureau of the Census, Washington, D.C., 1948.

PART II

Economy

CHAPTER III

Land Tenure

In TOBATÍ, and in Paraguay as a whole, we find the rural poverty, underproduction, and peasant backwardness that are so familiar in many of the world's underdeveloped or semicolonial areas; but there are several other characteristics, chiefly in regard to rural land tenure, which are quite unexpected. First of all, we must note that direct exploitation of the peasants by means of the agricultural hacienda is virtually nonexistent. Large landholdings exist surely enough, but they are not agricultural. Nor are plantations—single-crop agricultural industries employing wage labor—either numerous or large enough in size to be an important influence in the agricultural zones. The independent peasant *chacras* of family size are by far the predominant economic mode of Paraguay. Yet, curiously enough, the majority of these peasants do not own the land they cultivate, a feature usually, in other regions, associated with absentee landlordism and land scarcity.

Most of the Paraguayan agriculturalists are actually "landless" only in the sense that they lack legal title to the land they occupy —there is no real scarcity of fertile land. Paraguay is a relatively underpopulated country. More than any other Latin-American nation, the Paraguayan government has striven to encourage immigration, because of the often-expressed belief that the poverty and general lack of development must be related to the scarcity of people rather than to the scarcity of land.[1] The population

1. Nevertheless, even at the height of this policy, from 1920–40, Paraguay was, along with Chile, the least favored by immigration of the ABC countries (César R. Acosta, "La Población rural del Paraguay," in *Materiales para el estudio de la clase media en la América Latina*, III [Washington, D.C.: Unión Panamericana, 1950], 95–106, esp. p. 96).

density in 1946 was only three persons per square kilometer,[2] and, according to the STICA agricultural census, the fertile eastern (non-Chaco) part of Paraguay had only 3,425 square kilometers under cultivation in 1942–43 out of 160,000—slightly over 2 per cent.

The latifundia of Paraguay consist most importantly of foreign-owned tracts of forest and jungle in the Gran Chaco and in the northern and northeastern borders of Paraguay's eastern zone. These areas are exploited for timber and quebracho extract. They are nearly completely unpopulated, except for the scattered camps of workers and a few wandering Indians. Great cattle ranches (also often foreign-owned) exist in the Chaco and in the great plains of Misiones in southern Paraguay. This latter region is especially suited for agriculture, but it is only thinly populated.

In Tobatí there are private landholdings of fair size, but they do not conflict importantly with the interests of the peasants. The cattle ranges of the Rizzi family and the smaller *hacendados* are not desirable (or desired) for agricultural exploitation. The rice plantations are few in number (eight) and not large in size, except for the 95 hectares of the Rizzis. These do not occupy good agricultural land because they are sandy campo soil, located in the flat lowlands because of the irrigation problem.

A few of these *hacendados* also own some scattered areas which are suitable for agriculture and which are occupied sporadically by squatters or renters. The best of this land is rented, on the average, for 10 guaranis annually per hectare[3] (about three American dollars at the very low official rate of exchange or about one dollar at the free market rate in 1949). Most of this privately owned land, however, is occupied by families who pay nothing and who are likely to move at any time. Padre Pedro Martínez, the local priest, who owns some of this land, explained that he had no use for the land himself and that, furthermore, to eject the squatters would involve a long and expensive legal process and would create ill-will. Such owners feel

2. *Dirección general de Estadística del Paraguay* (Asunción, 1946).

3. The owner of rented land pays a municipal tax of 1 guarani annually per hectare.

that the possession of large amounts of agricultural land is profit-
less, as no tenant can make enough money to pay a worth-while
rent. The peasant, with luck, can only cultivate enough land to
meet his normal subsistence needs, with but little left over for
the necessities he must purchase.

There is possibly an additional reason why landholders do not
try to eject squatters. Many of these landowners "own" the
land only customarily, in terms of a public opinion kind of consent, rather than in any legally approved way, and therefore do
not dare to use the courts. As we have shown earlier, many of
the titles to larger holdings were lost after 1870. We must also
note that primogeniture has never been practiced in Paraguay,
so that inheritance divisions for a long time have tended to decrease the size of privately owned rural holdings. A universal
complaint of landholders is that for many generations people
have not dared to probate wills even when a title was available
because "lawyers and courts get all the money." As a consequence, ownership often became anything but clear.

To some degree, the landowner may profit from the presence
of squatters on his land, even in the absence of formalized rent
or produce-sharing arrangements. If he is a rancher, the squatters apparently are under more obligation than other workers to
work at low wages during the busy seasons of roundup and
branding. Tenants also may bring part of a good crop as a
"gift" to the patrón, especially at his birthday or some such special occasion, and are ordinarily willing to do some small labor
as a favor to the owner. Normally, these relationships are
ephemeral and informal because of the peasant nomadism, but,
in the rare cases where they become more permanent, a more
structured complex of mutual personal obligations tends to come
about, approaching the patrón-peón relations of a hacienda
system. Most often the mechanism of this formalization is the
compadre system. As we shall see, however, such situations are
rare, and the landowner has no regular means to enforce them.

The STICA agricultural census of 1942–43 reveals that over
three-fourths of all the Paraguayan agriculturalists were without
property in land. Only about 5 per cent paid something in
money or products as rent, while the great remaining bulk of

them were simply squatters on privately owned or government land. In Tobatí, of the 529 families sampled in the STICA census, only 36 owned the land they worked—less than 7 per cent. Thirty-two paid a small rent, while 437 were simply squatters. The remaining 24 held their land in combinations of the above three methods. We also find that in Tobatí nearly all the *chacras* were very small (3–7½ hectares) and that the area actually under cultivation averaged only 2 hectares per family.

An interesting fact related to the above situation is that the yearly estimated incomes of the peasants sampled do not vary directly with the type of tenure. In Tobatí, as in other parts of Paraguay, all the above types of occupancy are represented at all the income levels; a relatively successful peasant or a particularly poor one might own his land, rent it, or merely occupy it as a squatter. This is particularly noteworthy when compared with data from recent reports on Mexico, for example, where, even among peasants, owners are nearly always in a higher income bracket than nonowners.[4]

Land values are not particularly high in Paraguay. One hectare of good *tierra colorada* in the monte, purchased from a private person, costs about 20–30 guaranis, according to several informants, and sometimes a little more if it is close to the town. Government-owned land is sold in Colonia 21 de Julio on an easy-payment plan for 30 guaranis per hectare. The government has also made available a credit plan to enable peasants to own the land they cultivate, but in Tobatí very few people have taken advantage of it. As we have noted, much of the agricultural land owned by townsmen lies vacant or is occupied by squatters who pay no rent. And in the *colonias*, peasants have settled on the government land, originally understanding that

4. See, for example, Nathan L. Whetten, *Rural Mexico* (Chicago, 1948); Ralph L. Beals, *Cherán: A Sierra Tarascan Village* ("Publications of the Smithsonian Institution, Institute of Social Anthropology," No. 2 [Washington, D.C., 1946]); George M. Foster, *Empire's Children: The People of Tzintzuntzan* ("Publications of the Smithsonian Institution, Institute of Social Anthropology," No. 6 [Washington, D.C., 1948]); Julio de la Fuente, *Yalalag: una villa Zapoteca Serrana* (Mexico: Museo Nacional de Antropología, 1949); Oscar Lewis, *Life in a Mexican Village* (Urbana, Ill., 1951).

they were to pay each year until they became private owners, but most of them seem to remain squatters.[5]

The many peasants interviewed do not seem to regard owner- ship as especially desirable or important. According to two for- mer government administrators of this project, even the govern- ment does not press for these payments. The administrators have been changed often, in conformity with national political fac- tional shifts, and as of 1949 no government collector had made an appearance for several years.

This lack of interest in ownership per se does not mean that the Paraguayan peasant is communalistic or lacks a comprehen- sion of private property. It seems to be, rather, that there is a realization that ownership of agricultural land confers no direct financial advantage in itself—*chacra* ownership is not seen in a profit-and-loss context. The general orientation toward the land appears to be that it is necessary for subsistence and that no one should be expelled from it or kept from access to otherwise unused land.

Certainly an important reason for the peasant's lack of interest in owning a plot of land is the habit which we have called "agri- cultural nomadism." The great majority of the peasants frequent- ly move from one location to a presumably better one. The search is always for what they call "virgin land," which is usual- ly not actually virgin but has been uncultivated for several years.

There are differences in the degree of nomadism from area to area, depending on the relative fertility of the soil. The monte land at the crests of the low wooded hills is the best land, and the occupants stay on their plots for several years at a time, even after productivity has fallen off considerably, because it is not easy to find a location of equivalent fertility. This restrict- ed area verges off into the hillside land, which is lighter, more eroded, and thus more quickly exhausted by the crude farming techniques. Valleys, slopes, and *islas* (small wooded areas in the campos) are tilled by the majority of peasants, who move often- er than the more fortunate peasants of the hilltops. There is ap- parently a degree of difference in relative prosperity—the peasants

5. According to STICA data on 529 *chacras*, 291 of them are settled on government-owned land.

on poorer soil move oftener and are poorer than those on better soil, other things being equal—but there seems to be no consistent difference in type of tenancy. In fact, there are a few more owner-peasants in the *colonias*, which are of poorer soil, than at Villa Mercedes, which is the richest area.

In general, the primitive conditions of production so restrict the amount of land a peasant can cultivate alone that he is barely able to feed his family. Additionally, it has been the continuous experience of the peasant and of his ancestors that added production for sale on the market brings in very little money for the effort expended. In no case has the production ever been great enough to create *capital*, which could then be invested in equipment, land, and labor further to increase production.

The demographic pattern of the whole nation is interesting because it provides an illustration on a large scale of the difference between peasant agriculture and true farming. Although the greatest proportion of the agricultural population of Paraguay, and over 60 per cent of the total population, has been concentrated in the relatively small central zone since the earliest colonial times, this region is not the best agricultural land in Paraguay. The great plains of southern Paraguay, especially Misiones, are much better for field agriculture, but very few agriculturalists live there, nearly all the land being given over to cattle ranches. Misiones is much like Iowa in soil type, with the same thick turf which must be broken by plow and the black fertile soil running to a great depth. The lighter soil of the northern campos and the looser soil of the wooded montes were much easier for the early digging stick and the later hoe. The government has made repeated attempts to resettle agriculturalists from the central zone in *colonias* in Misiones but has so far not been particularly successful. What is missing, of course, is the stable market for agricultural produce and a market orientation on the part of the peasants. Plow-and-field agriculture in Paraguay implies *farming*, with its capitalization and profit-taking possibility and motive. If farming, rather than peasant subsistence agriculture, were a practical mode in Paraguay, there is no doubt that the fertile plains of Misiones would be broken by the plow as rapidly as were the great prairies of North America.

The Rizzi Acquisition: A Case History

All of the six most powerful families in Tobatí owe their position to wealth in land inherited from the original acquisition of the Rizzi brothers. The story of the origin and development of the Rizzi fortune is thus the story of the creation of the new group of *hacendados* who have become the dominant economic and social group in Tobatí since the disappearance of the former landholders in the War of the Triple Alliance. We have information that the story to be related has its counterpart in so many other areas of Paraguay that it is, in broad outline at least, rather typical. Aside from its typicalness, it is hoped that the details will also reveal something of the nature of the economic groupings in Tobatí, especially the contrast between the large capitalist-oriented tenures and the more typical peasant subsistence orientation. The story of the Rizzis was related to us by one of the inheritors, an intelligent and trustworthy informant, and was checked independently in detail by two other members of the group who are well qualified to know the story.

The present Rizzi holdings include (in 1949) pastures of 14,000–15,000 hectares, supporting five thousand head of cattle; an irrigated rice plantation of about 95 hectares; and several less important sections of land, some of which are suitable for agriculture. The main income is from the sale of rice and cattle. Most of the land is held and operated in common by five of the six separate families who have inherited shares in it. Such an inheritance is often held undivided in Paraguay to avoid an inheritance tax of 25 per cent and expensive court costs. If the heirs can be held together by a leader, the working operations may also be much more efficient. Among the Rizzi heirs there has been some talk of ultimate division because of various familial rivalries, but it is understood that division would result in eventual financial losses through inefficiency in the subsequent operation.

Arturo Rizzi, the grandfather of the present proprietors, came to Tobatí in 1869, near the end of the War of the Triple Alliance, following the Brazilian army, which overran that area. He was at that time an itinerant peddler, not long from his native Italy. He suffered great privations in order to save enough money to begin the production of *caña* (a crude rum) on a small scale. He eventually operated his small distillery profitably, probably because of the ready market for cheap liquor among the Brazilian occupation troops. This distillery is considered by the present descendants to be the enterprise which was the basis of the later fortune. Today the brand of the Rizzi cattle is a barrel, symbol of the *fábrica de caña*.

Several peasants informed us that the Rizzis got their start by finding a hidden treasure and that the cattle brand stands for the keg in which the valuable jewels were buried. The Rizzis (who can document their story of the distillery) described this latter tale as an example of the peasants' obsession with treature-hunting. They explained that the Paraguayans have no conception of enterprise and hard work as a means of improving their estate; success can only be achieved by a stroke of luck, such as discovery of a treasure cache, or by political means.

Arturo Rizzi finally moved into the town to live, bringing with him his two little girls, who had been abandoned by his Paraguayan mistress. In Tobatí he opened a small store and another small *caña* distillery. After these enterprises began to make profits for him, he invested his savings in a small piece of campo, where he kept a few head of cattle. Through the next few years he added to the land, hectare by hectare, whenever he could save the money. In those days commerce was virtually at a standstill, and Arturo had to work very hard to save even a little money.

At some point during these years, Arturo was joined by his brother, who arrived from Italy with his small son, Fidel. Arturo and his brother "never spent a cent on themselves" and never gave credit or used credit. The expansion of their business was slow but steady, "but the family continued to live a life of privation in order to save and save."[6]

When the young Fidel grew to manhood, he married one of Arturo's daughters, his first cousin, thus consolidating the in-

6. Such statements as this were repeatedly emphasized by our informants, who feel somewhat bitter about the Paraguayans' attitude toward the Rizzis' ancestors. It is apparent that the general feeling was that the "gringos" cheated the peasants.

heritance, and took an increasingly active part in the operation of the family business. His role becomes especially noteworthy because he initiated a successful pattern of credit manipulation. The subsequent great expansion of the landholdings of the Rizzis then conformed to the pattern of land acquisition very common in Paraguay before the turn of the century.

The original lands of the aristocracy had been left vacant following the war, and the national government expropriated them and also the large holdings of the church.[7] The government was desperate for money at this time and started selling small plots of this land to individuals at a very low price.[8] Much of the land was campo, not the most suitable for agriculture and not appropriate for stock-raising, so long as it remained in small parcels. The Rizzis lent money at high interest rates to many of the peasants who had bought such plots, taking as security the forthcoming harvests or the land titles. The local peasants were not accustomed to borrowing at interest or to the advantages and dangers of credit usage in general and were thus easily dispossessed of their land. Usually the peasant borrowed before a harvest, when he was most deprived and when prices were high, and then, when he went to sell his tobacco or cotton, he found to his consternation that many other peasants were selling, too, and prices were much lower. He could not pay back the entire loan and thereafter fell deeper and deeper into debt, as the monthly interest rate of 20–30 per cent mounted faster than he had ever dreamed. In short order, he found he could do nothing but give up title to his land. It is possible, too, that, then as now, the mere title to land did not seem particularly important to the peasant, especially if it were campo. Our informants find this a congenial theory, of course, but other indirect information, as well as the present attitude of the peasants, makes it seem convincing to us.

The Rizzis also bought outright as much land as they could.

7. Much of the campo around Tobatí belonged to the church. It was called "land of the Virgin (of Tobatí)."

8. We have been told that the government sold the land for 2 pesos the cuerda (71.93 meters a side). The peso has been superseded by a 100-peso unit, the guarani, in recent years, because of great inflation.

They eventually acquired not only most of the campo surrounding the town but also the land comprising the present Colonia 21 de Julio. This was an old settlement, however, and the residents refused to move, declaring that the land belonged to the Virgin of Tobatí and did not, could not, belong to Rizzi. Eventually this particular tract was bought from the Rizzi estate by the government and made into a *colonia*.

The present Rizzi holdings are much smaller than the total acquired by Fidel. It is said that nearly half was lost to the inheritors because no legal transfer of titles had accompanied many of the original acquisitions. Today most of the extensive campo lands are still in the hands of the Rizzi heirs, but the agricultural land is occupied by squatters. The form of enterprise of the post-1870 *hacendados* in Paraguay is characteristically cattle ranching and the very recent capitalist large-scale field agriculture of the sort exemplified by the Rizzi rice plantation. The fact that they have allowed their cultivable land to go to squatters almost by default should be sufficient evidence of the state of the Paraguayan market for agricultural products.

CHAPTER IV

The Peasant Economy

As WE have noted earlier, there is a generalized state of rural poverty in Paraguay, despite the great natural bounty of the land. The lack of export markets, combined with high transportation costs, lack of capital and credit facilities, and the very small size of the internal market, results, on the local rural level, in an absence of modern tools and techniques, uneconomic marketing methods, nomadism, and a noncommercial attitude. In the market sense of the word, agriculture "doesn't pay," even though the majority of the population must engage in it to live.

The average peasant over most of Paraguay is described by several widely traveled informants as being able to cultivate only about one and a half to two hectares in any one season because of the lack of implements and oxen. This conforms closely to the average found in Tobatí by the STICA census. It is said that weeding is the most costly aspect of the work and the item which, in effect, limits the amount of land under cultivation. Even should the peasant possess resources sufficient to rent a plow and oxen for more extensive planting, he cannot accomplish the required weeding with his limited tools and customary work habits. Oxen are of no help in this work; there is only one ox-drawn mechanical weeder in the whole *partido*. The few wealthier agriculturalists, who plant four or five hectares, normally are in possession of more fertile land and are therefore able to hire occasional help for the weeding.

The basic food crop is manioc, which is served at every meal. Next in importance are maize, which is usually planted in the same field as the manioc, and cowpeas and peanuts. Cotton and tobacco are the most usual crops grown for the market, with cotton probably the most prevalent because it can be grown on poorer land. The peasant does not plant a European-style vegetable garden, although the women raise small amounts of such items as onions, garlic, watermelons, and squash. Only a few of the most sophisticated townsmen care for vegetables like tomatoes, lettuce, carrots, peas, and radishes. In general, the rural population has no taste for them.

There is quite a variety of additional field and garden crops which are commonly known, but they are planted more rarely than the basic crops (see Tables 1 and 2). A fairly complete list of recognized plants in the region of Tobatí includes the following:

CULTIVATED CROPS

maize (*maíz*)
manioc (*mandioca* or *mandió*)
cowpeas (*porotos*)
peanuts (*manís*)
sweet potatoes (*batatas*)
watermelons (*sandías*)
sugar cane (*caña de azúcar*)
coffee (*café*)
cotton (*algodón*)
tobacco (*tabaco*)
onions (*cebollas*)
garlic (*ajo*)
cabbages (*repollos*)
alfalfa (*alfalfa*)
lima beans (*mantecas*)

rice (*arroz*)
soybeans (*soyas*)
navy beans (*habas*)
mate (*yerba mate* [*Ilex paraguayensis*])
lentils (*lentejas*)
peppers (*pimientos*)
lettuce (*lechuga*)
squashes (*zapallos*)
peas (*arvejas*)
string beans (*chauchas*)
radishes (*rábanos*)
tomatoes (*tomates*)
gourds (*calabazos*)
carrots (*zanahorias*)

FRUITS

grapes (*uvas*)
oranges (*naranjas*)
bitter oranges (*naranjas agrias*)
bananas (*bananas*)
lemons (*limones*)
limes (*limas*)
guavas (*guayabas*)
coconuts (*cocos*)
pineapples (*piñas* or *ananá* [Guaraní])

cantaloupes (*melones*)
mangoes (*mangos*)
avocados (*aguacates*)
grapefruits (*pomelos*)
cherimoyas (*chirimoyas*)
castor beans (*tártagos*)
apricots (*duraznos*)
tangerines (*mandarinas*)
papayas (*mamones*)

NATIVE WILD OR SEMIDOMESTICATED FRUITS

yvapurú
yvapuró
pakuri
pakuri guazú

guavirá
guavirú
guavirami
ñandypá

The productivity of Paraguayan fields is described by agricultural experts as much lower than it need be, because of antiquated methods and failure to use fertilizer, insecticides, and proper crop rotation and seed selection. Fertilizer is used only on seedlings of bananas or tobacco, which are replanted later. Cow manure or grass, weeds, and brush cutting are put on the seedlings. Similar fertilizer may be used in vegetable gardens in town after seeding.

Several pests persecute the peasants. Probably the foremost is the occasional plague of locusts which sweeps up from the Argentine plains, laying waste the country. Another is devil grass, called *pasto gringo* because it was said to have been introduced by English engineers who planted it to secure the soil on railroad embankments. From there it rapidly spread over the whole country. Ants are particularly destructive in some localities. Many peasants know of no weapon against them, but a few have tried Paris green or sulphur. Probably the habit of burning over new land is the most effective means of pest control used, although this is not its direct purpose.

Crop rotation is a recognized technique. That is to say, crops are customarily changed from one harvest to the next, as it is realized that the same crop in one field year after year exhausts the soil more rapidly than if crops are changed. This does not mean, however, that the order of rotation from one crop to another is done in accordance with the best agricultural practice. Most often a new field is first planted in cotton, a cash crop. After the cotton is picked, the field is usually planted to *porotos* (cowpeas), which nitrogenate the soil. After the *porotos* are harvested, manioc or maize is planted, often both together in the same plot. If maize is planted alone, it is usually followed by a peanut crop. But if manioc is planted with the maize, the field must be left unplanted after the maize harvest, as the manioc lasts from one to three years, depending on the amount used. Following the peanuts or manioc, the field is left to "rest" and grow brush and weeds.

This fairly typical rotation is described by government agricultural experts as poorly or ignorantly planned, especially since it is tobacco which needs the most fertile land, while cotton can be grown on poor land. A rotation described as more advantageous consists of tobacco as the first crop in new land, which is then left fallow for nearly a year. Peanuts are then planted, followed by cotton, cowpeas, and finally maize. Manioc can be planted with the maize because the field will be left fallow following the maize harvest, and the manioc can be dug as needed over a long period. The field is then left idle for several years. It is said that ten or twelve years are necessary before the land is fully replenished, but it often will be used again before that time.

The time of planting and harvesting throughout the year seems due partly to tradition and partly to experience with the varying rainfall and temperature of the four seasons. The seasonal variation, though noticeable, is not so clear cut as in a temperate zone or even in a tropical zone of true wet and dry seasons. Consequently, certain crops may be planted at two different times of the year. The agricultural year begins in April and May, when the intense heat of summer lessens and rainfall is somewhat more abundant. Most fruit trees are planted in this season, especially bananas, which are the most important fully domesticated fruit. Tobacco is planted in seedling plots (*almástigo*), and the rare garden vegetables, such as lettuce, tomatoes, cabbage, squash, and peas, may then be planted. The most common variety of cowpeas (*porotos San Francisco*) are harvested in this season. Peanuts are also often ready for harvest at this time. The cotton and tobacco harvest may be continuous from late summer. Oranges, grapefruit, lemons, and limes are beginning to ripen.

In June, July, and August, the land from which the *porotos* were harvested is plowed and planted to maize and manioc. Cowpeas are sometimes planted again if there is a plot ready for them in the normal rotation. New fields are cleared to receive the tobacco or cotton plants. The citrus fruits and bananas are plentiful and ripe.

Tobacco and cotton may be planted in these fields all spring (September, October, November). Peanuts may be planted also at this time, as may such fruits as cantaloupe and watermelons.

Full summer (December, January, February) is dominated by harvesting activities. Only two special crops may be planted in this season: the above-mentioned variety of cowpeas (*porotos San Francisco* or *porotos tupí*) and a variety of maize (*tupí pytá*). The fruit harvest is variegated, mangoes, watermelons, cantaloupe, pineapples, and guava being the most common. The tobacco and cotton harvest is beginning and will last for several months from place to place. Maize is ripening, and fresh corn (*choclo*) is a common dish. Peanuts and some cowpeas may also be ripe.

The tools and equipment used in general agriculture are few and primitive, consisting generally of hoes, axes, machetes, and shovels. Because of the general poverty, however, not all people own all these implements. The commonest items are the two indispensables for Paraguayan farm work, the machete and the hoe (*azada*). A comparatively prosperous peasant may also own a pick and shovel, ax, sickle, rake, and wheelbarrow. Oxen are owned by only the most prosperous, but they are sometimes rented to other farmers.

The plow is most usually a homemade old-Spanish wooden plow with an iron point, which plows only a very shallow furrow. In the last few years there has been some interest in the modern steel plow, mostly because of government propaganda in its favor. The average older man seems still to prefer the implement of his fathers, and most others, however favorably inclined, do not have the money to buy a steel plow. It is reported that some of the poorest peasants in the recent past had to use a digging stick because of lack of plows or hoes, but this would be uncommon now. Ordinarily, a hoe would be used in planting if a plow were lacking or if the land were new and full of stumps.

The hoe and the machete are used for weeding a clearing. The hoe blade is a heavy piece of iron somewhat larger than a North American garden hoe. It is attached to a heavy wooden shaft which is often crude and homemade. The machete is the common Latin-American size, but the extreme end is curved or hooked backward away from the cutting edge. There is a so-called "North American" type being sold, which has the point curved the opposite way, making a sort of hooked knife at the end. This is the kind of machete used in cane-cutting in some parts of Latin America. Paraguayans do not like this hook and usually cut it off, leaving the machete straight-edged.

The oxcart (*carreta*) is the most indispensable kind of farm transport. It varies in size, but the tracks are always a foot or two wider than those made by automobiles. The body of the cart may be square or up to half again as long as it is wide. The cart rests directly on the axle, which, of course, is in the middle of the cart. The two wheels are large in proportion to the size of the cart, often five or six feet in diameter, and are spoked rather than solid. The cart in daily use is not usually covered, but for long trips it is often sheltered by a cover of cowhides, burlap bags, or some such material.

Most of the tools and technical knowledge used in agriculture, except for the general ones mentioned above, are specialized in terms of particular crops. As we discuss these methods, crop by crop, we shall try to give an estimate of the labor costs involved in planting, weeding, and harvesting, so that, as these costs are compared to the market prices for each crop, some understanding of the difficulties faced by the Paraguayans may be obtained. The peasant, normally illiterate, or at best semiliterate, and sometimes speaking no Spanish, is not conversant with cost-accounting methods of any kind, nor is his judgment of income reliable. Our figures on these matters had to be compiled indirectly by observing the process of production many times and by questioning informants on small specific points. It was found that, while different informants might be wildly divergent at guessing the labor cost of weeding a whole hectare of maize, they might agree on the time involved in hoeing one row. Figures on total costs and income also were made by adding up specific small bits of information. The following material is thus an estimate and therefore unreliable as data, but it is probably accurate enough to be suggestive of the economic problem. These calculations do not take account of such tribulations as dry spells, plagues, and accidents which cut actual production to a much lower average.

Manioc

Nearly all families plant manioc; even many town dwellers have small plots of it. The STICA census showed that, of the 529 rural families reported, 525 produced manioc. Of these, the amount of land given over to its cultivation averaged about 0.67 hectare per *chacra*. The average production per hectare was 12.3

toneladas (one tonelada = 1,000 kilograms). (See Table 1 for additional information.)

The plant in use in Paraguay is the "sweet" variety, not the "bitter," poisonous type. Paraguayans seem to believe, however, that their manioc is somewhat poisonous, for they peel the thin brown skin and carefully scrape off the inner layer of white pulp. The boiling process is supposed to expel the acid from the rest

TABLE 1

BASICALLY SUBSISTENCE ITEMS (1942–43
STICA CENSUS)

Item	Percentage of *Chacras* Which Raise Item	Total Amount of Land in *Partido* Devoted to Crop (Hectares)
Crops:		
Manioc	99	351.4
Maize	95	335.4
Cowpeas	84	135.4
Oranges	61	....
Peanuts	58	96.7
Bananas	39	....
Sweet potatoes	38	50.5
*Domestic animals:**		
Chickens, ducks, geese	96	15.781 (total number of animals)
Horses	53	929
Milk cows	43	862
Pigs	39	515
Oxen	23	363

* The figures for domestic animals, especially horses, are probably actually lower in 1949 than the numbers given here because of confiscations during the civil war of 1947–48.

of the root. Dogs, chickens, and pigs eat the discarded skin and pulp without harm, however.

Manioc planting usually takes place in July or August, and, under good conditions, some of the plants will be ready for eating the following March or April. In dry land the crop can stay in the ground for as much as four or five years. In low land, it often begins to rot after about a year. Worms and locusts are the greatest enemies of the manioc, and there are no methods for fighting them.

It is believed that manioc should be planted in the new moon for best results. It is planted from cuttings about "five or ten fingers" long, taken from the stalk of a parent-plant. Usually two cuttings are placed two or three centimeters apart in a hole seven or eight centimeters deep. The rows are between one and two meters apart and the plants a similar distance from each other in the row. When planted with maize, three rows of manioc are customarily planted between two rows of maize, because "maize is hot" and would harm the manioc if the proportion of maize were greater.

When possible, five people are used in the planting. Two men are kept busy making holes with a hoe or shovel, beginning at opposite ends of the row and approaching each other. A third person is in another field, making cuttings from mature plants, while the two others do the actual planting, one laying the cuttings in the holes, the other covering them over with his foot and tamping them down. In actual practice, of course, a field is planted by whatever number of people is available. If, as occasionally happens, the cuttings are planted in plowed furrows, three is the ideal number of people for planting, as there is no need for the hole-diggers.

Weeding the plot is laborious and must be done completely three or more times a year. This is usually done with the hoe or, less often and less easily, with the machete. Little attempt is actually made to dig out the roots of the weeds.

Harvesting is a simple matter. The plant is simply pulled out of the ground, or, if the ground is hard and the root is long and deep, a machete is used to loosen it. Ordinarily, a woman digs only one day's supply, because it tastes better fresh and because it does not keep well. The day's supply is usually boiled the first thing in the morning, drained, and hung up in a basket ready for use.

If a surplus of manioc is grown, it may be ground up into a dried flour for later use or for sale. In this process, the manioc is peeled, washed, and soaked, and ground up into a juicy mass. It is then worked through a homemade fine sieve through which only the milky fluid passes. After this fluid is evaporated, the fine flour which remains (*almidón*) can be used in many favorite dishes. The coarser, fibrous part left in the sieve is molded into balls about the size of baseballs and dried in the sun. This *typyratý* is used in place of bread or fresh manioc when these items are unobtainable. It is considered hard to digest and probably is.

The manioc-grinder is usually a large wheel set into a plank which is elevated waist high on four legs. The wheel turns by a rude hand crank, and the flat outer surface, covered with tin perforated with nail holes, grinds the manioc, which is held against it by hand on the plank table. The ground pulp falls into a container. One arroba (10 kilograms) of manioc will give about 2 kilograms of *almidón* and 1½ kilograms of *typyratý*. The grinding is about half a day's work. The accompanying tabulation shows labor costs and cash return for one hectare of manioc.

LABOR COSTS

Planting	15 man-days
Weeding	20 man-days
Harvesting and preparation of *almidón* and *typyratý*	615 man-days
Total	650 man-days
Cost of transportation to market (estimated average)	15 guaranis

CASH RETURN

2,460 kilograms of *almidón* (at 0.90 guarani per kilogram)	2,214 guaranis
1,845 kilograms of *typyratý* (at 0.20 guarani per kilogram)	369 guaranis
Total	2,583 guaranis
Less transportation cost	15 guaranis
Net return in cash	2,568 guaranis

A farmer raising manioc completely as a cash crop—which is never done, of course—thus spends 650 man-days to realize a cash return of 2,568 guaranis, or 3.95 guaranis per man-day of labor. His labor on manioc is thus worth considerably more than the value of hired day labor (1.50 guaranis). It should be remembered, however, that manioc is even less usually a cash crop than is maize. Both are normally raised only for food, and costs are not calculated.

Maize

Like manioc, maize is a staple in the Paraguayan diet and is grown by virtually all peasants (Table 1). Production was calculated by STICA at 107.2 arrobas of maize per hectare, and the average family plants slightly less than two-thirds of a hectare.

There are two basic varieties of maize, *maíz tupí* and *maíz blanco*. *Maíz blanco* is a soft-shelled type most commonly used for human consumption. It is said that it is not good for animals and that horses do not like it. After it is pounded in a wooden mortar, the coarse flour is used in a great variety of dishes, many of them baked. *Maíz tupí* is given to horses, fowl, and pigs, especially for fattening. It is a much harder corn than *maíz blanco* and consequently difficult to prepare as food. About the only culinary use is in two special dishes, *locro* (a soup) and *masamorra* (a kind of sweet pudding). Although *blanco* is usually yellow and *tupí* usually white, either type may appear occasionally in other colors. For example, *tupí* may be flame-colored and very hard and is called *maíz tupí pytá*. This is a late type and is often planted in October. Popcorn is known but not used much in the country. About the only other variety of maize is a newcomer, *maíz brasiliero*, which, though useful for animal forage, is still quite rare.[1]

Both the main types of maize may be planted in the winter (July and August, especially), and green ears (*choclo*) are ready for eating in December and January. *Tupí* can be planted later, in September if desirable. Both should be planted in the waning moon. Mature ears to be dried and stored are usually ready by the next March.

The planting usually involves three people; two make the holes with hoes, and the third follows, dropping the grains and covering them and tamping the earth with his foot. If a plow is used, one man may do the planting alone. Some people have the custom of putting three grains in one hole and two in the next, alternating. Other farmers say that they always put three grains in each

---

1. Our nomenclature for maize may not be accurate for other areas of Paraguay, for we find that it does not agree in all respects with that presented by Bourgade la Dardye, who seemed to have made a wide study. He names the four varieties as follows: (1) white maize, called *abatí morotí*, is *Zea mais vulgaris aestiva* and is used for *chipa* and roasting; (2) hard maize, called *abatí atá* or *abatí tupí* (*Zea mais autumna*), is used for animal food, *locro*, and *masamorra;* (3) red maize, called *abatí pytá* or "Brazilian maize"; (4) popcorn, called *abatí pichingá* (E. de Bourgade la Dardye, *Paraguay: The Land and the People* [London, 1892], pp. 163–64).

hole. Some people who have cows plant four seeds in each hole, and, when the plants are half-grown, they take out one of the plants for fodder.

The plantings are made about a meter apart, usually phrased as *cinco cuartos* (five handspreads), and the rows are also about the same distance apart, unless manioc has been planted with the maize, in which case more space is left between rows to give more "air" to the manioc.

The field must be weeded a month or so after planting, and, if manioc has been planted, the whole thing must be hoed two or three times again before harvest time; otherwise one or two weedings is all the field will usually get. Ants are very troublesome, and there is also a green worm which eats the leaves. Birds come when the corn is small, and in this period the farmer often camps in his field to scare them away. After harvest, weevils give a great deal of trouble. Some people put the grain in the sun; others keep it closed in large pottery jars, and some have tried covering the corn with sawdust. Ears for seed are hung up in the smoke of the cooking fire, but eating ears are not, as the smoke harms the taste. Probably the majority of the people leave the ears hung up on poles and wires outside in the sun. The husk is usually left on the *tupí*, while the *blanco* is husked before it is hung up.

Harvesting of mature ears may begin in December and last through March, with the greatest amount of activity occurring in January and February. The harvester walks along the rows breaking off ears and throwing them ahead of him into a pile. When he is abreast of the pile, he stops picking and goes down the row to a point as far from the pile as he can throw and works back toward it. Later, he will pick up the heaps of ears in a cart or in bags. After the maize is picked, the green leaves of the plant are cut for fodder. The stalks are usually left in the field.

Some people leave the biggest and healthiest ears for seed, but this is about as far as seed selection is carried. Maize for immediate use is shelled by hand as it is needed, and seed corn is left on the ears. Cobs are given to pigs and chickens to work over, and some are saved for the outhouse.

Wooden mortars are used for grinding corn. They are made

in various sizes, the most usual being about waist high to an average woman. They are carved out of very hard wood (lapacho or *yvyrápytá*). They are round, hollowed on the top, and end in a very heavy flat base. The corn, usually about a liter at a time, is pounded by a hard pestle, about the size and weight of a baseball bat. The maize flour of the *blanco* variety is usually made into various kinds of unleavened cakes, and especially into *chipa* and *sopa paraguaya* (which is not soup but resembles corn bread or johnnycake, with cheese and onions added).

Like manioc, maize is not normally planted as a cash crop, although many peasants sell small amounts from time to time. The people of the town are such a small proportion of the total population of the *partido* that the local market is thus easily supplied. The accompanying tabulation shows costs and cash return for one hectare of maize.

LABOR COSTS

Planting	6 man-days
Weeding	8 man-days
Harvesting, shucking	15 man-days
Marketing	1 man-day
Total	30 man-days

CASH COSTS

Plowing (hired)	20.00 guaranis
Seed	2.40 guaranis
Transportation to market	4.50 guaranis
Plow cultivation (hired)	10.00 guaranis
Total	36.90 guaranis

CASH RETURN

107.2 arrobas of *maíz tupí* (at 1.80 guaranis per arroba)	192.96 guaranis
Less cash costs	36.90 guaranis
Total	156.06 guaranis

Thus a peasant cultivating one hectare of maize for sale at (March, 1949) market prices in Tobatí could value his own labor at 5.20 guaranis per day, which is considerably above the prevailing day wage for agricultural labor. In terms of this calculation it would be profitable to expand the production of maize as much as possible. The calculation does not include costs of tools, however, or of storage, meals for hired labor, and the possible (but not usual) costs of land, or rent. The average peasant does not have money at hand to pay the labor costs of expanding production, nor can he count on the above market price not being cut in half by the time he is ready to market his next crop. Most important of all is the factor which renders our calculation somewhat irrelevant for actual conditions; the peasant does not plant as much as one hectare of maize and does not plan to market it. If he sells any, it is typically an arroba at a time, marketed not when the price is high but when he needs money for a family exigency.

"Porotos" (Cowpeas)

This third most common crop in Tobatí, after manioc and maize, was planted by 84 per cent of all the agriculturalists. (Table 1). There are several subvarieties of *porotos*, the basic difference apparently being in the color. The two commonest are a reddish kind, called *porotos San Francisco*, and a type resembling black-eyed peas, called *porotos señorita*. Others are *porotos blanco, porotos negro,* and *porotos blanco pequeño*.

They are usually planted on "tired" land, the exact time of the year depending somewhat on the availability of the proper field, but the preferred time is from October through December. The planting usually involves two people, one who makes the small excavations sixty to seventy centimeters apart and another (often a child) who drops in six or seven seeds and covers them over with his foot.

The whole field must be weeded at least once, usually about one and one-half to two months after planting. In three or four months the crop is ready for the laborious harvest. It would take one man alone about a month to harvest one hectare, but, as the harvest must be gotten over quickly because of the possibility of rain spoiling the crop, all members of the family are used, and a labor exchange (the *minga*) may be arranged with neighbors.

After the pods are picked, they are scattered in the sun to dry for two days. They are threshed by beating them with a stick on a hard floor. The peas come loose very easily, but small, light pieces of husk remain mixed with the peas and must be separated. This is often done by spreading the peas thinly in a shallow basket and blowing the husks away, either with the mouth alone or with a tube of leather fitted out with a wooden mouthpiece.

Lima beans (*mantecas*) are the most common legumes other than *porotos*. They may be grown in fields but often are found in the house yards, where they may produce most of the year. English peas and a type of navy bean are also known but are quite uncommon in Tobatí. The accompanying tabulation shows labor costs and cash return for one hectare of *porotos*.

LABOR COSTS

Planting	8 man-days
Weeding	7 man-days
Harvesting	30 man-days
Total	45 man-days

CASH RETURN

916 kilograms (at 0.25 guarani per kilogram)	229.00 guaranis
Less transportation costs	4.50 guaranis
Total return	224.50 guaranis

The value of the average peasant's labor in producing *porotos* is thus 4.98 guaranis per day. Like manioc, however, this crop is grown for consumption rather than for sale.

Peanuts ("*Manís*")

Like *porotos*, maize, and manioc, peanuts have always been an important native subsistence item (Table 1). They may be sold for cash, as there is some demand by peanut-oil manufacturers in Asunción, but no one plants in large quantities in Tobatí. As food, peanuts are often toasted, mashed, and eaten with honey or cane-sugar syrup for an evening meal or for breakfast. Peanut meal may be used to make cakes and sweets, and it is mixed with corn meal for a special *chipa* for Holy Week.

There are two basic varieties. *Maní colorado* is bigger, better looking, and usually preferred. *Maní negro* is small, but the shells are fuller of nut. Peanuts are usually planted in October and sometimes may be mixed with manioc if there is no maize with the latter. Harvest can begin after three or four months, so two or three plantings a year are possible.

Because the plants are close together, plowing is most desirable before planting; otherwise, much time is lost in digging so many holes. Three seed nuts are placed together, about seven or eight centimeters deep, with the plants separated by about twenty-five centimeters from each other, just enough distance for a hoe to pass easily between them in weeding. No fertilizer is used, and the old vines are not left in the fields but instead are used for animal fodder.

Weeding is exceptionally laborious because the plants are so close together. The field should be hoed completely at least once and preferably twice before the harvest. In harvesting, the vines are cut and hung in large bunches over a pole, so that the air and sun can reach them for thorough drying. This may take eight to ten days. After drying, the nuts must be separated from the vine. This may be done by hand alone or with the help of a tight wire stretched waist high between two stakes. A handful of vines are struck against this wire with an underhand motion, and the nuts fly off and pile up on the ground against a wall which is behind the wire. The nuts may be roasted with the shells on, but oftener they are shucked first by hand.

We did not observe any of the actual planting and harvesting of peanuts, so we made no attempt to calculate labor costs.

Miscellaneous Subsistence Items

Onions (*cebollas*) are the most nearly ubiquitous kitchen-garden crop. They are eaten whole as young plants, and the mature bulbs are used in the form of garnish. Sometimes the green leaves are cooked separately in soups or stews. Garlic, squash, and sweet potatoes are the other vegetables commonly used in the rural areas.

Sweet potatoes (*batatas*) are boiled or roasted for eating and are sometimes substituted for manioc. They are planted in any season and ripen in two or three months. Squash is used in *locro* (the maize soup), in stew, as a dessert called *kiveve* (Guaraní), and the seeds are used to make a tea which is a common remedy against fever. Squash is believed to be a "cold" food, so it is commonly used when it is felt that something is needed to "refresh" a meal.

The coco palm (*cocotero*), which is scattered in nearly all the peasants' fields, has a variety of uses. The fronds are gathered for fodder, the fibers are used to make twine, the wood is used for house rafters, and the shells sometimes serve as fuel. It is also thought of as an important reserve in times of food shortage. The heart is especially prized if the tree is young, and may be merely boiled and eaten or, more usually, ground up like manioc and made into *almidón*. The *almidón* serves as flour, and the fibrous residue (*afrecho*) is sieved into fine and crude parts. The crude part is fed to farm animals, and the fine may be mixed with *almidón* and made into a *torta*, something like a heavy un-leavened bread.

Fruit is a very important element in the diet of the population and can be had for very little work. The trees are virtually un-cared for—no insecticides or fertilizers are used; pruning is not practiced, nor are seed selection and grafting. The orange is probably the most characteristic fruit, and nearly every home has a few orange trees growing near by. They are always eaten by peeling the orange part way through the skin spirally but not down to the pulp. Then a cap is cut off the peeled end, and the juice is sucked out. When a person is offered oranges, he is ex-pected to do away with five to ten at a sitting. The orange starts to ripen about March and lasts through August.

Other, less common citrus fruits are mandarines and limes, and grapefruit, which is a recent introduction in Paraguay. Man-darines and grapefruit are ripe only for a comparatively short time, but limes bear the year around.

The mango is the most characteristic Paraguayan fruit, next to the orange. Mangoes and a small papaya (*mamón*) are ripe in December and January, though a few papayas may continue to ripen until winter sets in, in June. The banana is a year-around fruit. The various common wild fruits listed earlier in this chap-ter become ripe at varying times of the year, but primarily dur-ing the hot months.

Commercial Crops

There are several kinds of crops which could be called "cash crops" in the most general sense of the word: cotton, tobacco, bitter orange, *yerba*, rice, and sugar cane being the most important (Table 2). It is necessary at this point, however, to make an important distinction among them. It is only cotton and tobacco which are of any general importance among the peasants: many people grow small quantities of these crops to get a little money for the household, whereas bitter-orange trees, *yerba* trees, rice, and sugar cane are grown by only a few town-dwelling business-men, and on a much larger scale of investment. Cotton and to-bacco belong in our consideration of the peasant farmer, but the others are really specialized agricultural "industries" and will be discussed in chapter vi, "Commerce and Industry."

TABLE 2

BASICALLY CASH CROPS (1942–43)

Item	Percentage of *Chacras* Which Grow Crop	Total Amount of Land in *Partido* Devoted to Crop (Hectares)
Cotton...............	59	188.4
Tobacco..............	39	69.5
Sugar cane...........	16	28.4
Yerba mate...........	2.3	....
Rice.................	1	130.5

Cotton is the most common of the purely cash crops. All peasants seem to know how to grow it, and probably all have grown it at one time or another. Of the 529 *chacras* in the STICA sample, 312 of them grew cotton, each averaging about six-tenths of a hectare. The common varieties grown in Tobatí are called *algodón estranjero* ("foreign cotton"), which has fibers attached to the seeds; *algodón paraguayo;* and *algodón colorado*, which is a reddish-hued fiber used in embroidery designs.

Planting occurs from September through November. Before the planting, the seeds are soaked for most of a day in water mixed with wood ashes. Two people usually do the planting, one hoeing shallow holes, the other dropping four or five seeds in each hole, tamping the dirt over them with his foot as he goes. The harvest takes place about six months later, when all hands, including small children, are put to work. The cotton is spread out to dry in the sun, and then the complete bolls, seeds and all, are put in bags for sale.

Production in Tobatí averaged 722 kilograms per hectare, and in May, 1949, it was being purchased by middlemen for 4.50 guaranis per arroba. The costs of production are estimated as shown in the accompanying tabulation.

LABOR COSTS

Planting	8 man-days
Hoeing (three times)	27 man-days
Harvesting	9 man-days
Drying and packing	6 man-days
Total	50 man-days

CASH RETURN

722 kilograms (at 0.45 guarani per kilogram)	324.90 guaranis
Cash costs (plowing)	20.00 guaranis
Total	304.90 guaranis

The value of one man's labor in growing cotton for sale is calculated at 6.09 guaranis per day.

Tobacco was planted by 39 per cent of the agriculturalists. The seeds are first planted in small fertilized garden plots (*almástigo*) in March or April, and in two to four months, when the plants are about twenty-five centimeters high, they are transplanted. There is a strong belief that the tobacco will fare better if planted on Good Friday or, second best, on the eve of the Día de la Cruz. The *almástigo* plot is fenced against chickens and pigs and watered during dry spells.

The transplanting is a laborious process, and the whole family is enlisted for the task. Each person has a stick with which he makes small holes for his resetting. The plant is set carefully about one meter from the next plant and the dirt pressed around it with the hands.

The harvest usually begins in February and continues slowly for about three months. The peasant goes to the field every few days, depending on the weather, and breaks off the ripest leaves from each plant. Five to ten leaves are tied together at the stems with homemade twine, and these are then tied to a horizontal pole and hung in the sun to dry. These poles are brought under the ramada when it is rainy. Ten to fifteen days of drying in the sun is usually sufficient. After the harvest the old plants are chopped down. If this is done properly, the trunk will produce another plant, but most people do not try this, as they say the new plant always has worms.

People who have been working with tobacco should not wash themselves afterward, because tobacco is exceptionally "hot," and one can sicken from subsequent contact with water (which is always "cold," even if it has been warmed).

Domestic Animals

Stock-raising is a very important economic enterprise from the point of view of the economy of the nation. Townsmen regard beef as virtually the staff of life. There is a great deal of nonagricultural land in Paraguay, particularly in the Chaco and in Misiones, where huge herds are maintained.

The *partido* of Tobatí, like many others, has extensive pasture land which is not used for agriculture. It is owned and stocked with cattle by a few of the wealthier upper-class families of the town. A few peasants own milk cows, oxen, and horses, and others have worked for wages on the cattle *estancias* at one time or another. In 1943, less than one-half of all *chacras* had any kind of cattle at all, and less than a quarter had oxen.[2] Of those who own cattle today, it is most commonly one milk cow per family.

Most cows give only one or two liters of milk a day, but better ones may give from three to five. The milking is done early in the morning by the woman of the house, who prepares to milk by tying the cow's head tightly to a tree or post and tethering the calf close by and within view of the cow. Fresh warm milk is highly prized as a breakfast drink. People who can afford it give special rations to the cow, such as palm fronds, manioc, or maize, thus augmenting the milk production somewhat; but, in general, cows are merely pastured and are not separated from the calves.

2. *Censo de agricultura del Paraguay, 1942–1943 y 1943–1944* (Washington, D.C.: Bureau of the Census, 1948), pp. 194–96, Tables 76–78. Out of 529 farms cited, 231 had cattle of some sort, 228 had milk cows, and only 121 had oxen. The revolution of 1948 reduced the number still further. (See Table 1 for further information.)

There are no veterinarians; each owner tends to the ills of his own animals. Hoof-and-mouth disease is common, and the animals also suffer from the discomfort of large lumps under the skin caused by collections of larvae from eggs laid by a kind of fly (*ura*). These, if tended at all, are cut open and washed out. No attention is paid to selective breeding.

Draft cattle (*bueyes*) are usually, though not always, castrated. At about three years of age an ox is broken for work by putting him in the yoke with another one which is already well trained. It takes about a month to break him properly. Commands and methods used in governing the oxen are the usual Spanish and South American ones.

The few townspeople who specialize in cattle-raising are the wealthiest people in the vicinity. On these larger-scale ranches cattle are run and cared for much as they were in North America before the introduction of scientific breeding and modern veterinary methods. There is no aid in the calving of the cattle or in the foaling of horses. One rancher has introduced a few zebu bulls from Brazil to his herd, but that has been the only local attempt to improve the quality of the herds, which are the native South American *criollo* mixed breed. This does not mean that these cattlemen have not heard of better breeds or of breeding methods, but so far the market does not make the demands of quality, nor is beef graded, so there is no sufficient incentive to change the methods. The roundups (rodeos) for branding and castration are the same as those that are familiar in North America. Cattle are not specially fed for the market. In Paraguay, slaughtering is done at the big slaughter-houses in Asunción by first stabbing the animal between the shoulders, cutting the spinal nerve, after which the throat is cut. In smaller-scale operations, as in the municipal slaughter-house in Tobatí, the animal's head is tied to a post; he is then thrown, and his throat cut.

About half the farms in the department have one or more horses. They are *criollo* animals of poor conformation and are small in size. Paraguayans take pleasure in horses, which are a part of the traditional way of life, and consequently there is considerable pride in their ownership. There are many sports involving horses, the commonest being Sunday and holiday races. Horses ordinarily are not used for traction but only for riding.

Horses are cared for in a fairly sophisticated manner. Various illnesses are recognized and treated "scientifically" (as opposed to supernaturally), though the means are often traditional folk remedies. In case of open wounds, creosote is applied. Of the many remedies for colds, the commonest is to burn sulfur where the horse will inhale it. Certain native herbs are also used in this way. A sulfur and salt mixture is given by mouth for colds and any general kind of disorder. Rain water is given to a wind-broken horse to drink and is also used to bathe his chest and shoulders. Saddle sores are usually treated by an application of ashes of alligator skin or the carbon deposit from the outside of cooking jars. *Caña* is given for stomach ailments, and washing in water is believed efficacious for hoof-and-mouth disease. When a horse dies, its carcass is not sold; even the hide has little value.

A horse may be trained at various ages, but two to three years is considered the best age, when the horse is "broken" in a literal sense, most violently. Geldings are preferred to stallions because they are tamer. Mares are not regarded as fit for riding except by women, and a man who has to use one through necessity feels ashamed. Horses live mostly on pasture, but, if a horse is working hard or being readied for a race, it is given special feed to the extent that the owner can afford it. Maize (*tupí*), raw peeled manioc, coco palm fronds, and *afrecho* (the roughage left from making *almidón* of either palm hearts or manioc) are the most usual supplementary foods. Maize is considered best, and alfalfa is also good, but very little of it is grown in the region.

Burros are very common, especially among the people who cannot afford horses or oxen. They are used in various petty tasks and are also ridden by women and children. They cost very little, and the upkeep is negligible, as they eat anything. There is no pride in possession, and the burros ordinarily are not even named. They may be castrated but usually are not, as it is felt that they are stronger if "complete."

There are a few mules in use. They are not liked so well as horses because of their intractable dispositions, but most people admit that they are better than horses for many purposes because they are much more durable and have a more comfortable gait for long rides. They are not so intelligent or so fast as horses, of course.

Sheep and goats are kept by very few farmers, chiefly because of the difficulty and expense in fencing to keep them out of the crop land. Ranchers customarily have a few, however. A small operator is more likely to have goats than to have sheep. The goat meat is used for food, and the skin with the wool on it can bring a small price for use as a saddle cover. Sheep are castrated and their tails cut when they are about forty to sixty days old. The wool is sold (unwashed) in Asunción. The meat is not sold in local markets but is occasionally used for barbecues.

Between one-third and one-half of the farmers had pigs in 1943,[3] but there is no regular market for them. In town as in the country, a person slaughters his own pig and sells the meat to friends and neighbors. Boars are castrated for fattening, and, if a sow is to be slaughtered, she is made pregnant first and slaughtered after about one and a half months. Pigs are fed any kind of garbage. Maize is known to be best, but most people cannot afford this expense. Beef entrails are often purchased from the butcher by townsmen as cheap pig feed. Pork ribs are the most prized parts for eating; all the rest of the meat is ground up for sausage.

Chickens are owned by nearly all rural families, along with occasional ducks and guinea hens. The chickens are a nondescript small breed of a variety of colors and shapes. Little or no care is given them, and egg production is poor. A few people have built rude chicken-houses, but in general the chickens roost in the back-yard trees. By day they wander the neighborhood scratching for food, as they are rarely purposely fed. There is, on the average, one rooster for eight to twelve hens. It is said that if a rooster is absent the hens will not lay and also that a rooster will not accept new hens into his flock, so a new rooster must be raised for each new group of young hens.

Dogs and cats are common household pets. Paraguayans do not treat them kindly, however, and they are usually on the verge of starvation. Strange dogs are regarded with fear or cau-

3. STICA census.

tion, probably with justification, as the dogs have no reason to act friendly. Even if one feeds his dog, it is considered bad to give him raw meat, as it supposedly makes him fierce. Cats, too, are seldom trustworthy, as they are always afraid of a blow.

Hunting and Fishing

Probably the animal most commonly hunted is the carpincho ("water hog"), a semiaquatic mammal about the size of a small pig. Dogs are used to scare up the animal, which seeks cover under water. The hunter waits with a spear or a firearm and kills the animal when he detects the movement of the water. The flesh has a musky odor, and some people will not eat it. Others say that there are methods for slaughtering and cooking which destroy this odor so that the flesh is good to eat. The fat from the animal is rubbed on the chest as a cure for tuberculosis.

Deer are hunted near Compañía Rosado in the near-by hills, but this is not a common activity. The deer are usually hunted with rifles, but the bent-sapling noose snare is known.

There are some fair-sized catfish in the arroyos, but fishing is not widely practiced in the district, and some people have never tasted fish. There is no prejudice against the eating of fish, however, and in towns along a river fish can be bought in the market during the winter months.

The collection of wild honey has been practiced in Paraguay since preconquest times. Bees' honey is highly regarded for its medicinal value more than for its use as food and is avidly collected when the opportunity presents itself. Men watch for bees until they see where a hive is located. Then they make a smudge and chop away the tree to expose the honey. No protection is used other than the smoke, and the men do not seem afraid of the bees, which are small and rather peaceful. Sometimes a farmer may semidomesticate a swarm of bees by preparing a box with molasses or sugar in it and attracting a swarm to it by beating on a tin plate. One man in the town of Tobatí has thirty-six hives of domesticated bees, which he exploits commercially. These are called "German bees" because German immigrants were the first to introduce beekeeping to Paraguay. Honey is sold in strained, pure form, not by the comb.

Monkeys and parrots are sometimes trapped for sale as pets.

One Tobatí family specializes in trapping them for a dealer in Asunción who exports them to Europe. Parrots are caught by the birdlime trick. A very gummy tree sap is put on some sticks about twenty-five centimeters long which are loosely planted upright in the ground and then tied together and to a tree. A tame parrot is used to decoy the wild birds, who alight and become entangled. Monkeys are trapped by mixing *caña* and molasses in a two-to-one proportion. The trapper tastes from the bowl by dipping in it with his hands and licking them off. The monkeys, who have supposedly observed this, later come down and imitate him. They love the taste and get drunk, and are then easily caught.

Monkeys are also trapped because they are such a plague to the farmers. One informant described the following method used to get rid of them: One monkey is caught by the Mickey Finn trick described above, dressed in a red coat of tough material securely sewed on so that he cannot get it off, and released to join his band. His fellows are exceedingly frightened of him and immediately leave the region. This is supposedly the only way in which monkeys can be frightened away from a farm.

CHAPTER V

Specializations

As IN all societies, the most basic division of labor is that delineated by sex and age distinctions, with the activities of male adults
regarded as the most important. Only men act as barbers, carpenters, charcoal-burners, musicians, hunters and fishers, and train-
ers of horses and oxen. They kill and butcher all animals except
barnyard fowl, build houses, make bricks, and in general are in
charge of all important economic activities which cannot be defined as household tasks. Important economic transactions, too,
which are above the level of household economics are normally
done by men. All political activity is the concern of men only.
Around the house a man makes repairs and may help in some
of the heavier work like chopping wood, but typically he dis-
dains housework. He never markets, carries water or packages,
cooks, sews, or launders clothing.

A woman's work is not so clearly defined. If she is independent,
she may undertake certain of the normal male activities without
censure, but many of the specializations mentioned above are
forbidden. A lone woman works for wages at tasks which are
essentially specializations of household activities, such as cooking, laundering, general service, cigar-making, weaving, lacemaking, and sewing. If she lives with a man in a complete household,
she undertakes, in addition to the care of the family and house,
the care of the domestic "barnyard" animals, fruit trees and gardens, marketing, and small-scale buying and selling. During the
"all-hands" harvesting of cotton, women are considered better
than men at the painstaking and grueling task. While women play
no part in politics, they may be quite important members of reli-

83

gious societies and committees. Women are often officers of societies, though such a post as president usually goes to a man.

Economic activity among children begins at about six or seven years of age, consisting of such simple tasks as running errands and taking messages. Grownups of either sex never do these things if there is a child to send. This is not an unimportant activity, for a great deal of communication between households is done using children as messengers. Distances are not inconsiderable either, as the peasants are not clustered in villages. The custom of purchasing only very small quantities of goods also necessitates a great deal of errand-running. Girls have a daily water-carrying task, and both boys and girls may be used indiscriminately around the house, although there is a general tendency of leniency toward the boys. It is often said that the parents "spoil" the boys and use only girls for various tasks when a choice is possible. This corresponds to our own observations of family life. Girls care for a younger sister or brother like "little mothers," but boys are not expected to do this sort of thing. At about ten or twelve years of age the sex division is more complete, and the boys begin to help their fathers with minor tasks in the fields, while the girls stay home with their mothers. Girls seem eager to work around the house and are usually in good humor about it, while boys are often disgruntled, even at a rather early age.

Professional Specialties

The occupational specialties of Tobatí are numerous if one includes the part-time occupations of people who are basically engaged in agriculture (Table 3). True professions, however, are rare from the point of view both of numbers of kinds of professions and of numbers of people practicing them. There is no professional doctor or dentist, nor is there a lawyer. Even such officials as the justice of the peace and the police *comisario* are not well paid, do not stay in office very long, and, consequently, do not consider their jobs as other than temporary posts.

In the person of the "Pa'i" (familiar diminutive of "padre"), Pedro Martínez, the priesthood in Tobatí is easily the occupation of greatest power and highest status. We feel that this is, however, a result of the personality and accomplishments of this particular man rather than of the prestige inherent in the office. Generally, the priesthood does not carry much weight in Paraguay, and many towns do not even have a resident priest. The priesthood and the political offices of the *municipalidad* do not

TABLE 3

OCCUPATIONS AND PROFESSIONS IN THE TOWN OF TOBATÍ

Male	No.	Female	No.
Hacendados	17	*Hacendadas*	1
Buyers and sellers:		Buyers and sellers:	
Store-owners	18	Store-owners	17
Resellers	2	Resellers	5
Industries:		Professions:	
Brick factories (owners)	18	Farmers	18
Tanneries (owners)	2	Day laborers	9
Professions:		Teachers	19
Farmers*	69	Butchers	1
Day laborers	38	Weavers	7
Housebuilders and bricklayers	26	Seamstresses and needlework-	
Public employees (other than		ers	111
teachers)	14	Laundresses	25
Carpenters	13	Cooks	21
Butchers	11	Bakers	1
Chauffeurs	6	Potters	4
Barbers	4	Cigar-makers	3
Cattle drovers	4	Milk-sellers	3
Shoemakers	4	Midwives and curers	4
Stableboys	4	*Santo*-makers	1
Tailors	3		
Harness-makers	3		
Curers	1		
Druggists	2		
Truck "guards"	2		
Bakers	1		
Beekeepers	1		
Oxcart-drivers	1		
Blacksmiths	1		
Santo-makers	1		

* Only four or five male farmers live in town and actively engage in full-scale farming. Many of those listed are old and retired or are living in town because they have no work. To a lesser extent this is true of all the professions. The numbers listed do not mean that that many people are actually engaged in working in their professions at any given time.

pay much salary, but the padre and the officers are all *hacendados* to some degree.

Schoolteaching ranks high in social esteem, although, as in most public posts, the wages are very low. There are nineteen teachers in the town, all of them women. Most of them are young, and none is the sole support of a family.

There are two druggists in town. They are the closest thing to doctors in the modern sense, although there is a first-aid post, *puesto sanitario*, maintained by the national government's Department of Public Health. A young man trained in first aid and tooth-pulling is retained there, but most of the countrypeople do not trust his methods.

The people seem to be "legal-minded," and the country is very much inclined toward red tape in conducting its affairs. The peasants usually go to some respected literate townsman for legal advice and letter-writing. There used to be a professional *escribano público*, who wrote letters and gave advice for a fee, but this profession seems to have disappeared, except for one man who charges a small fee for advice but does not get much business.

Housebuilders, who are also bricklayers, are the most successful and numerous of the skilled workers. A few of them work as contractors and hire labor. Bricklayers (*albañiles*) receive 3.50 guaranis daily, which is at least 1.50 guaranis above the normal pay for unskilled labor. They were particularly successful in 1949 because of the recent popularity of "California"-style brick houses and the spurt in business prosperity which has resulted in more of these houses being built than in any previous year. A good *albañil* in such times can be fairly certain of a full year's work. A contractor-*albañil* naturally hopes to earn considerably more than the worker he hires, but his calculations are often awry. One of our acquaintances reported, however, that he averaged 7.00 guaranis per day on his last job.

The thirteen *carpinteros* were also riding the wave of building prosperity in 1949. There are no professional painters or any other kind of professional workers concerned with housebuilding. The *albañil* usually does the whitewashing. Woodwork and doors are not painted but are merely oiled.

Butchering is regarded as a skilled profession in Tobatí, but it looks as though anyone could hack up meat just as well. The only "cut" is the *lomo*, or tenderloin muscle, which is removed in one piece and sold at a higher price. The rest of the beef is simply cut up in chunks and all sold at the same price, except for the fat, entrails, and head, which are sold separately and more cheaply. Normally a meat-seller buys from the owner or reseller who has already killed the animal. He may help with the killing and in turn be helped in the initial butchering of the animal into its large parts. He pays 0.50 guaranis per kilogram for the beef and usually 6.00 guaranis for the head and viscera together. He will sell the meat for 0.55, and the *lomo*, which is ordinarily sold in one piece, for 0.60 guaranis per kilogram. He sells the head complete for 2.00 and the large intestine for 1.50 guaranis, while the liver and other viscera will bring about 6.00 guaranis. In one case which we followed through with the butcher, he bought 190 kilograms of meat and realized a profit the same day of 14.90 guaranis, having sold everything. He cannot, of course, always count on selling all he buys, and he tends to practice his profession only intermittently, as there are eleven butchers but only two or three beeves killed on any given day.

Two butcher-slaughterers tend to specialize more or less as middlemen in the process, by purchasing the live cattle and doing the slaughtering and then selling the large parts to the butcher-sellers. One of our acquaintances usually sells the slaughtered animal to a butcher for about 25 guaranis over the price he paid the *estanciero*. Out of this, he pays a total of about 17 guaranis to the municipality for the slaughtering fee and various minor taxes.[1] He is the owner of the hide, which, if it is a good one, he may sell to the tanner for between 20 and 30 guaranis. These two men seem especially favored economically, for only two or three hours of work (before dawn) thus often bring over a 30-guarani return. The licensing of individuals for this occupation may be a sort of political favor, but we do not have definite evidence for this.

There are six men who consider themselves to be professional truck-drivers, but only two of them work regularly. They also have to double as mechanics, with responsibility for making minor repairs. One chauffeur earned 120 guaranis per month, which included about twenty-four working days. Nearly 50

1. He must pay (guaranis) 10.20 as *impuesto municipal* for each animal; *impuesto interno* (registration), 10 yearly; a *patento* of 12 yearly; *patente de balance*, 4. Simple butchers must pay a municipal tax of 8 guaranis semi-annually. *Zapateros* (7 guaranis semiannually), *carpinteros* (4 guaranis semi-annually), and pharmacists (15 guaranis semiannually) are the only other occupations regarded by the municipality as "professions" of enough importance to be taxed.

guaranis of this, however, had to be spent on meals in Asunción restaurants, where prices are much higher than in Tobatí. Driving trucks from Tobatí to Asunción is very taxing physically, as there is no road to Caacupé and the trucks are not usually in good shape. Heavily loaded trucks are often bogged down in sand or mud, and mechanical breakdowns are so common that a chauffeur is sometimes as much as twenty-four hours on the road for a single one-way trip.

Four men list themselves as barbers, but there are actually many more who cut hair when they get an opportunity. The only equipment needed consists of a razor and a strop, a pair of scissors, and a comb. There is only one barber who has a place of business, an ordinary wooden chair in the front room of a house on the school plaza. The others go where they are called for a job. Haircuts cost 0.50 guarani and are not badly done. Men ordinarily shave themselves, although a man may come to the barber for both a haircut and a shave on a fiesta day.

There are four shoemakers, who also do repairs. The majority of the people have no shoes, and most of those who do have them wear them only for dressup occasions, such as a wedding or a dance, or to attend church or on exceptionally cold winter days when there is a hoarfrost on the ground in the early morning. It is a common sight to see people walking to a dance carrying their shoes in their hands until they arrive. This is said to be done for comfort as well as for economy. The shoemakers, therefore, do not have a great deal of business. Their only customers are the wealthier people of the town, and many of them, of course, purchase their shoes or boots in Asunción. A pair of locally made work shoes costs about 15 and men's dress shoes 20–25 guaranis.

The three full-time tailors make fairly good profits when they have work. The customer supplies his own cloth, while the tailor furnishes the thread and buttons. A pair of pants costs about 15 guaranis and amounts to one and one-half days' work for the tailor. A pair of bombachas (bloomer-like "gaucho pants") costs 20 guaranis and are about two days' work. A full suit (coat and pants) costs 50 guaranis and takes about a week to make. Most of this income is profit for the tailor, but work is obtained very irregularly.

Other specializations among the male Tobatí population are minor in number of people involved (see Table 3 for listing). Employment is intermittent, and mostly these specialists make a living by other means or are not entirely self-supporting.

Thirty-eight males classify themselves as day laborers, but their work is better called "odd jobs." About seventeen grown males work at the *fábrica de coco*, but not steadily, and the turn-over there is great. Some of the laborers help out on the cattle ranches at roundup time or by driving cattle to market. Others may be employed from time to time in one of the brick factories or as labor at harvest time on one of the larger farms. Now and then a man works around one of the richer Tobatí homes, cleaning up a garden or taking care of horses. Some unskilled labor is used in housebuilding from time to time. Wages average 2 guaranis per day in town, with perhaps one meal. Wage labor is so unrewarding and so inconstant that it is impossible to maintain a family by this means. The day laborers are mostly young men who are not self-supporting. Many take such work only when they have some pressing need for cash for some special purpose.

"Las Mujeres"

One of the aspects of Paraguayan life so often publicized is the economic role of women. Basically, the prominence of women in economic activities in the town is due to the great proportion of single women who must support themselves and their children, but many married women also contribute to the support of the household. Women are especially in evidence in the economic life of the town because of their activities of a petty commercial nature, particularly as store operators and re-sellers. Seventeen stores in the town are owned and managed by women, and, of the other eighteen, nearly all are tended by women most of the time.[2]

The greatest number of women (one hundred and eleven), both single and married, consider themselves seamstresses and needleworkers. Only a few of these, however, have sufficient employment to support themselves. Seamstresses work on order

2. Retail economics is discussed in chap. vi, "Commerce and Industry."

only, under the same conditions as tailors, but they charge much less, and there is great competition among them.

Paraguayan women are famous for their excellent fancy needlework, especially for lacemaking and hand embroidering on homespun, hand-woven cotton (called *a'po'i*). The making of the very fine "spider-web" lace—*ñanduti*—is an old enterprise in Paraguay and is famous among foreigners for its quality. *Ñanduti* is a specialty of the town of Itaguá near Asunción and is less commonly made in other areas. Atyrá, near Tobatí, is also famous for lacemaking of the type called *encaje-yú* and for embroidery. In Tobatí very little *ñanduti* is made, but several women specialize in making homespun tablecloths and blouses and in crocheting bedspreads and doilies. These women work on order, but they often prepare some work for sale from house to house or for sale to a reseller who markets it in Asunción. The return for a day's labor is only about 2 guaranis at best—the same as for unskilled male labor—but this is usually spare-time work and merely an addition to the family income. In a few rare cases a whole household of women is self-supporting by this work.

Twenty-five women say they make their living as laundresses, but many more will undertake this work when the opportunity presents itself. A laundress will wash clothes for 1 guarani per dozen "pieces" (a handkerchief or napkin may count as one-half piece and a sheet as two pieces). The customer furnishes the soap and bluing. Three dozen "pieces" is a full day's work, as the laundress must call for the laundry, go to the creek for the laborious hand washing, take the clothes home for drying and ironing, and then return the laundry to the customer after the ironing on the second day. Some laundresses charge less but tend to do an inferior job. Two to 3 guaranis is the most a laundress is capable of making in a day. Competition is very stiff, and many of these women find work only once or twice a week.

Cooks work in the two inns or for the wealthier townspeople. A real professional, such as the hotel cook, might get 30 guaranis per month plus at least two meals per day, but household cooks get only half that at the most. Normally, however, a household cook gets food and lodging for herself and often for one or more children as well. The children act as servants and errand-runners.

There are only four women who consider themselves professional curers and midwives, although many older women are certainly part-time practitioners. No information is available on the profitability of this kind of work.

There are three full-time cigar-makers, but, inasmuch as nearly all women know how to roll cigars, if only for their own use, many resort to this work whenever sales are possible. The more professionally inclined purchase the tobacco from a farmer or wholesaler and roll cigars for sale in quantity to the stores. It is possible, by working hard, to roll six hundred small cigars in one day, which may be sold to a store for 1 cent each. The tobacco costs about 4 guaranis. The day's labor thus brings in about 2 guaranis. Some storekeepers purchase the tobacco and pay the women 0.50 guarani per hundred to roll the cigars. Large and medium as well as small cigars are made by such an arrangement, however, so the output in a day is considerably less than six hundred.

Part-Time Specializations among Peasants

All the peasant specializations are truly subsidiary. No other occupation or wage labor can ever take the place of the basic agricultural production—either in the conceptions of the people themselves or, probably, in actuality. Those who live on the better land or who are more productive because of the possession of such equipment as oxen and plows are less likely to have subsidiary occupations. Compañía Villa Mercedes, for example, has the best land and consequently fewer minor activities, with the exceptions of woodcutting and charcoal-burning, which are localized there because this *compañía* also has the most timber. Colonia 21 de Julio, on the other hand, has the poorest land of the populated areas, and here there is more subsidiary activity of the handicraft sort.

Of all the various nonagricultural activities, the care of domestic animals is easily the most important. The economic value of ownership of a yoke of oxen for plowing has already been described. To this should be added the fact that the same oxen yoked to a *carreta* (two-wheeled cart) is an item of considerable economic importance. A *carreta*-owner may charge as much as

5 guaranis to freight a load of farm products a distance of only three or four kilometers. Fodder for the animals is not expensive in the country, due to the abundance of relatively free pastures and the plentitude of palm fronds, which are a favored fodder. A yoke of oxen and a *carreta* and plow, however, represent a considerable initial investment, and this is the reason that only a small minority of families own them. An ordinary pair of working oxen cost 250–300 guaranis. A steel plow costs about 60 guaranis, a wooden plow much less, as it is usually homemade. A *carreta* will cost about 300–600 guaranis, depending on the size.

Cattle are not raised for beef by the peasants, as they cannot compete with the *hacendados*, who own the great herds and the extensive campos. Milk cows, however, were owned by 43 per cent of the farmers of Tobatí in 1942–43, normally only one or two per owning family. Again, it is in Villa Mercedes, the richer *compañía*, that there are the most, while the people of 21 de Julio have the fewest.

A cow without a calf costs from 100 to 200 guaranis, and a good milk cow with calf costs about 50 guaranis more. An ordinary cow with calf gives only from 1 to 2 liters of milk a day, though some exceptional ones give from 3 to 5 liters. Milk sells for 0.25 guarani per liter, but few people in the country sell milk, as one or two cows ordinarily give only enough for the family. These few who do make more of a business of it sometimes augment the cow's diet with maize and manioc and may occasionally get as much as 7 or 8 liters a day. Once the cow's (or ox's) usefulness declines, it can be sold to a butcher. No distinction is made between "prime" or "young" beef and old worn-out cattle; the only variable is the quality of the hide, as all beef sells at the same price. Consequently, the disposal of a useless cow or ox to the butcher is of considerable economic importance to the owner, as he may receive as much as 100 guaranis for it, depending on the estimated weight. There is always a danger, of course, that the butcher may not buy it at all if it is too skinny and the hide poor.

Horses and mules are not of great direct economic utility, as the Paraguayan sees it, but are a great convenience, and ownership of horses, especially, is a source of pride and pleasure. Fifty-three per cent of the peasants owned horses in 1942–43, but probably many fewer in 1949 because of the intervening civil war. Mules were owned by very few people. Horses are extremely variable in price, and their use is so indirectly economic that it is impossible to estimate their value. The ubiquitous burros are likewise difficult to assess. They are plentiful, cheap (10 guaranis), and cost nothing to maintain, but Paraguayans disdain them, although women and children are constantly using them for directly economic purposes.

Sheep and goats are kept by only a few families, but most ranchers will have a small herd. Peasants feel that it is a lot of trouble to provide pasture for them, and they seem to be forever devastating the gardens. A female sheep costs only about 10 guaranis, but the meat is not sold, and wool production and weaving of wool cloth are not so common a tradition in the central region as they are in Misiones. A sheep is sometimes used in a local *asado* (barbecue fiesta) but is more often donated than sold.

Pigs and barnyard fowl (chickens, most commonly) are important supplementary foods. They are usually raised for home consumption and not for sale, although in the case of full-grown pigs extra meat is sold or exchanged with neighbors. A large fattened pig is worth from 150 to 200 guaranis in town and, presumably, a little less in the countryside.

Handicrafts are important supplementary sources of income among some peasants. Colonia 21 de Julio is best known for its straw hats, a specialization which seems to be rather localized there. The hats are entirely handmade; the only tools necessary are a knife and a homemade bone awl. The material is strips of fiber cut from the leaves of the caranday (copernicia palm). The leaves must be kept damp to reduce their brittleness, so work on hats usually takes place in the shade during the siesta, on rainy days, and on moonlit nights. A man gets 1.50 guaranis for a finished hat which takes him a total of about six hours of work.

Pots are made by a few women in the *colonia*, if they have access to the proper kind of black clay. The usual simple cantaro, slipped but unpainted, takes about two hours of work, not counting drying and baking time, and sells for 0.70 guarani to a reseller. Pottery-making is thus fairly well-paid work, but the market is unsteady. Simple hammocks, which sell for about 3.00 guaranis on the spot, are also made from time to time by a few individuals. Candlemaking is a common leisure-time occupation among many women. Beef fat is bought in town for 1.00 guarani per kilogram. This will make about fifty medium-sized candles, which may sell for about 0.05 guarani each. The tin molds are bought in Asunción for 3.00 guaranis for a six-mold piece, if simple homemade wooden molds are not used. Weaving and lacemaking and general needlework are occupations known to most older women. There is a tendency for lone women to specialize in this work, however, so that most of the practitioners are more or less "professionally" occupied and tend to live in the town itself, where the market is better.

Charcoal-burning and woodcutting are largely concentrated in the Compañía Villa Mercedes, though there is some in various other scattered localities. A hardwood called "curupay" (a *Piptadenia*) is generally used in charcoal-burning. In the instances observed, the *carboneros* paid half their profit to the owner of the wood lot. It takes an average of about seventeen days to burn 150 arrobas of charcoal. If purchased directly without calculating transportation, the charcoal sells for 0.40 guarani per arroba. The net return is thus 60.00 guaranis, or 30.00 guaranis to the worker for seventeen days of labor. Except for the cutting, the work is not hard. The fire needs constant attention, but various members of the family may share this work.

Sawyers cut logs into planks for sale to town carpenters. Two men work on a long saw, one in a pit beneath the log and the other on top of the log (Pl. X). Two kinds of wood are favored, *yvyrápytá* (*Peltophorum*) and lapacho (*Tabebuia*). Calculations by the sawyers indicate that they make a profit of about 7 guaranis a day each. This calculation is based on actual sawing time alone; but there is also great labor in hoisting the log about and loading the planks on the cart. Most of this wood is sold to housebuilders in Tobatí and Caacupé.

Part-time musicians, usually guitarists, pick up some money at odd times, but this is not an important specialization, as so many men are adept at guitar-playing. In general, if a specialist is very good or if his specialty is important, he lives in town, as he can serve more people and more nearly approach full-time professional status. Thus curers, midwives, carpenters, and housebuilders concentrate in the town.

Similarly, agricultural specializations which need considerable capital to begin with are usually part-time interests, or investments, of wealthy town families. The few *yerba* and rice plantations, cattle ranches, and petitgrain distilleries which are found in the country are owned and operated by townsmen.

CHAPTER VI

Commerce and Industry

THE most typical commercial enterprise in the town is the small store (*almacén*), which carries a supply of daily household necessities and which often buys small amounts of farm products for resale. There are about thirty-five of them scattered around town, and occasionally there is a small one located in one of the rural hamlets. Nearly half of them are owned and operated by widows or spinsters. The others are typically attended by the wives and daughters of the owner. In fact, nearly all the small-scale commercial enterprises of whatever kind are run by women.

There is considerable difference in size and income among the various *almacenes* and, among the larger ones, some differences in kinds of goods sold. Two of the large ones on the main plaza have a considerable dry-goods stock, as well as the usual complement of notions and small food stocks. Two others sell more pottery than anything else, while a third carries quantities of pots, pans, candles, rope, spurs, and hardware but no groceries. Several others have so little capital that their complete stock could be put in a large trunk. Notions and comestibles are the main stock in such cases. Hardware (especially tools) and dry goods make the greatest profits but take the most capital investment; hence these items are largely handled only by the most successful stores.

There is no clear distinction between wholesale and retail purchases, although informal allowances are made for quantity buying. Normally an *almacén* owner has an arrangement with a *patrón*, a store-owner in Asunción, who sells him goods at a discount because of the quantity purchases and because of the consistent relationship. Business relationships of this kind are quite personal in form, as though it were a case of friendly mutual aid. Only one man in Tobatí is close to being a distributor and wholesaler. His main capital is a truck which he uses to bring purchases from Asunción for sale to *almacenes* in Tobatí. He also buys farm products in Tobatí and sells them in Asunción. However, he often sells the same goods, when he has time, to individuals at the same price at which he sells them to the *almacenes*. This particularly infuriates a local storekeeper, a Spaniard, who is more accustomed to the strict observance of wholesale-retail distinctions.

Because of the lack of large distributors and the failure of supply and demand as an effective regulator, there are considerable differences in the prices of the same items from store to store, a situation, incidentally, which is true to a degree even among the large stores in Asunción. Despite these differences, however, the people of Tobatí are not "shoppers" to any extent but tend to go consistently to a particular store for certain items. Friendly relations are set up, and one becomes duty-bound to continue trade with the friend, *compadre*, or relative who runs the store.

The *almacén* owner must labor diligently, waiting on a great number of people, in order to dispose of his small stock, for the people buy only very small quantities at a time. This is true even of such staples as salt or sugar. In addition, children are sent to buy an article only as the immediate need arises, so that the same child may make repeated trips to the store for one or two items each time. There are almost no storage facilities in the kitchens of the houses; most families have only the simple outdoor cooking shed or lean-to, with hooks for hanging meat, corn, onions, and cooking pots. Even in more elaborate kitchens shelves and containers are notably absent.

A description of the transactions in one hour in Francisco Morales' *almacén* may be illustrative. Most of the marketing, like all work, is done in the morning ("dinner" is at noon); thus the hour observed, 10:30–11:30 on a Monday morning, may be considered a fairly busy time:

1. Woman buys a needle .... 5 centimos
2. Child buys *galletas* (small hard biscuits) 10
3. Child buys *galletas* 5

4. Child buys salt 15
5. Child buys soap 25
6. Child buys *yerba mate* 16
7. Child buys matches 15
8. Child buys candy 5
9. Child buys noodles 30

Because most of the *almacenes* of Tobatí must purchase from retail stores in Asunción and then add transportation costs and taxes[1] and their own small markup, it is generally much cheaper for an individual to purchase goods in Asunción, especially if they are fairly expensive, like lamps, clothing or dry goods, shoes, or imported items, including imported foodstuffs. Any person making a visit to Asunción shops for his friends and relatives and usually returns quite burdened. Another method is to give an order and money to a truck-driver, who will make the purchases and deliver them in return for a small tip.

In the *compañías* the *almacenes* are few, scattered, and very small. They tend to concentrate on only the most immediate household necessities, for generally the peasants do their buying in Tobatí. Prices in these little country stores are much higher because of transportation costs. Trucks cannot get into the *compañías,* so the storekeeper must get his goods from town by ox-cart or on horseback. As an example of the difficulties caused by lack of transport, a small *almacén* deep in one of the *colonias* is run by a lone woman who supports herself by selling *galletas* (small unleavened biscuits), sugar, salt, *yerba mate*, cigarettes, and matches. She must buy these articles from a larger *almacén* in a near-by *compañía* of the *partido* of Barrero Grande, which purchases from another in the town of Barrero Grande, which, in turn, buys from a store in Asunción.

In the largest and wealthiest *compañía,* Villa Mercedes, the largest *almacén* carried the following items: a few bottles of *caña* and sweet vermouth to be sold by the glass, beer (sometimes), *galletas*, sugar, salt, *yerba mate*, cigarettes, matches, four small cans of meat, three combs, a few school notebooks and pencils, kerosene, a five-gallon can of lard, and a jar of hard

---

1. There is a national tax on business firms (*registro de firma*) of 10.00 guaranis yearly. The *almacén* must also pay a local tax of 4.50 guaranis semiannually; 1.00 guarani yearly to have scales checked; and, if liquor is sold, an *expendio* of 6.00 guaranis semiannually.

candies. The equipment in the room consisted of a rude table, three chairs, scales, and a Coleman lamp. The family members sleep in the room at night and cook and eat in the shack behind.

Occasionally a peasant, usually one with no family, will keep a few bottles of *caña*, which he sells by the glass. In such cases, and sometimes in the case of the *almacén* owners, the enterprise is distinctly subsidiary to their agricultural work.

Revendedoras ("resellers") are variable in number, for this kind of commerce is usually a part-time activity undertaken as a favorable occasion presents itself. Seven people of the town population, five women and two men, describe themselves as professional resellers, but many others, especially women, do it when they have time or when a disparity of prices makes it especially profitable. It is normally done in this way: a woman in Tobatí buys some products which are scarce in Asunción and takes all she can carry to the market or to some store in Asunción, where she trades them for something which is scarce or expensive in Tobatí. She may sell this in Tobatí to people who come to her house, or she may go from door to door. The disparity in prices between Asunción and Tobatí, less the bus transportation, is her margin of profit. Her labor, time, and discomfort are, of course, considerable. Because of personal friendships and special knowledge, she may make quite a profit, however, in times of real scarcity of certain items. For example, a single woman of our acquaintance is a very keen businesswoman. She makes frequent trips to Asunción with about thirty cheeses or ten chickens to sell in the farmers' market and returns with soap, perfume, and face powder to sell among the upper-class families in town. In June and July of 1949, rum disappeared from the free market in Asunción and could not be obtained in Tobatí. At this time of year milk products were in short supply everywhere, so she was able to make a black-market contact for rum in Asunción in exchange for cheese, which she obtained from rural relatives near Tobatí. She was realizing a tidy profit at this time and traveling nearly continuously between Tobatí and Asunción. Other items frequently sold in this way are eggs at times of short supply, maize in some years of poor crop, and nearly all lace, homespun, and embroidered products.

Many single women are not normally classed as *revendedoras* but are always alert to purchase a load of bananas or oranges cheap from some peasant who is not so sophisticated about current prices as she is. She will then sell them from door to door in very small quantities. The grower cannot afford to take the time to sell in this way, and stores ordinarily do not buy a whole *carreta* full of any one item, for fear of spoilage. Many town dwellers have some fruit trees of their own or small vegetable gardens. The market is thus so restricted and scattered that no one but poor *revendedoras* will take the trouble to cast about for purchasers.

Town Industries

Industry in the town of Tobatí consists of the small brick and tile factory, the several family-operated kilns, and two small tanneries. Brick and tile manufacture is essentially a modern development; Paraguayan houses are traditionally adobe and thatch, but in recent years new houses of the wealthier people and public buildings have been made of brick and tile. Tobatí has a low area of black clay just on the east side of town which makes excellent tiles, so that there is some export to the neighboring towns. Tobatí thus has more people engaged in this particular industry than do most other towns of the vicinity.

There are eighteen small kilns on the eastern outskirts of the town, and one larger enterprise. The methods used in all of them are identical, except that in the large one there is a greater specialization of labor, a sort of production line, and a motor-driven clay-mixer. Each of the eighteen small factories is typically owned and operated by a family. Two or three male members of the family work the factory, or, in some cases, a small boy is hired at low wages. All the factories sell at the same price and work on order. The layout consists of a homemade mixer, an open-sided low-roofed drying shed, and one or two small kilns.

The clay is dug up with shovels and hauled by oxcart, or by wheelbarrow if the factory is close, and deposited near the mixing spot. The clay is combined with one-third sand and a little water and is then shoveled into the mixer. The mixer is a tall, slender, upright cylinder of staves bound together with wire. Inside is an upright log with short pegs or spokes arranged spirally, so that, as the log is revolved by ox power, the mud is mixed and at the same time forced down from the top of the mixer and out at the bottom.

The drying shed is really only a roof. It is usually about 15 × 30 meters in size, with the roof sloping to within about a meter of the ground at the two sides. Thus the bricks are protected from rain, but the open sides permit circulation of air. The mixed mud is brought in by wheelbarrow and deposited in the center of the shed, where the bricks and tiles are shaped in wooden forms. Usually two people are working at the table, while another gingerly carries the bricks to pile them systematically, beginning at the edges of the shed. They dry in three to ten days, depending on the temperature, the humidity, and the amount of wind.

The kiln is composed of bricks piled about 6–10 feet high and 10–20 feet on a side, usually with three fireholes. Anywhere from thirty-six hours to three days may be used in the firing.

The single large establishment was originally an investment of a financial group in Asunción. It was supposed to house a motor-driven coconut crusher, but it has since been used as a tile factory, with the motor used to power the mixer and a modest assembly-line belt. The factory owns a truck for out-of-town deliveries. The *fábrica de coco,* as it is always called, employs about forty people when it is working at capacity. In the spring of 1949 nine of the employees were women and fourteen were children. The pay is 0.50 guarani per hour for a man, 0.33 for a woman, and 0.28 for a child. These wages are above the town average, but the factory has to conform to national labor laws because it is incorporated. In spite of these wages, however, there is considerable turnover in personnel. It is said that the wages are not really very satisfactory, because the machinery often breaks down and the workers are not paid during the long waiting periods.

The other eighteen factories are nearly exactly alike, so we may take one as closely representative of the rest. The kiln run by the Pérez family represents a capital investment of 4,390 guaranis (at 1949 prices) for the shed, mixer, kiln, wooden forms, yoke of good oxen, *carreta,* shovels and wheelbarrow, taxes and registration fee. This particular kiln holds five thousand tiles, five thousand regular bricks, and twenty-five hundred of the thin flooring bricks, which is the proportion normally burned at one time. From digging up the clay, through the mixing, shaping, and burning, the process costs about 280 man-days of labor in good weather, plus a cash outlay of about 50 guaranis for firewood. The family realized from this work a net income of 725 guaranis, or 2.40 guaranis per man-day of labor. Not all this labor is hard work, however, and a large part of it may be done by children. The family is accustomed to thinking of this profit not in terms of man-days of labor but as profit to the family. In this case, considering the occasional labor of children, the income to the family is about 10 guaranis per day. Not all the brick-making families work their kilns as a full-time occupation, but, from the general standard of living of those who do, it is apparent that not a lot of money is to be made in this work. The return for labor is adequate, but no one can work a full year. Damp weather stops the drying operation, and lack of buyers at certain times of the year keeps the family from working. Many of the operators say they make only about four kiln loads a year. It is for this reason that most of them have other occupations.

There are two tanneries and harness-making establishments (*curtiembres*) in Tobatí, an expanding, bustling one owned by an Argentine, which keeps four to six people busy, and another operated more desultorily by one man. The larger one, because of the capital outlay and the number of workers involved, is more of an industry than a professional specialization and is included in the present section for this reason. Tanned cowhide is sold in bulk in Asunción, and saddles are also made up for sale in Asunción and locally.

When the larger tannery was built in 1947, it cost 1,200 guaranis, but in 1949 it was worth at least 2,000 because of the inflation. About 0.80 guarani per kilogram is paid for hides, which may average about 30 kilograms in weight, or 24 guaranis per hide. After processing, the hide will weigh about 12 kilograms and is sold for 3.50 guaranis per kilogram, or 42 guaranis for the same hide. It takes about a month to complete the tanning, and the tanks (at the date of the information) contained forty-five complete and ninety half-hides. This is an average production of three complete hides per day, or 60 guaranis per day gross profit. Tannin, transportation, and other costs subtract about 10 guaranis from this total, which then comes to about 10 guaranis per man-day of labor. Inasmuch as the personnel is familial (one man and his son-in-law and their respective families), this seems to them a handsome profit. These are exceptionally energetic and ambitious people, and it is quite possible that a "man-day" of labor as they represent it is considerably more actual work than is usually understood by the term. We have repeatedly seen the whole family straggling home from the tannery after dusk. They had probably worked a good eleven- or twelve-hour day.

This tannery is obviously a profitable enterprise, and the owners are struggling to expand it. Their *patrón* buyer in Asunción will take all the hides they can send him, and they cannot even fill the local demands. Their tanks will hold 150 complete hides, but lack of capital has kept them at only a little better than half of capacity. Credit in any quantity is difficult to find and expensive, so that expansion must take place largely through accumulation of savings. Curiously, no one else seems particularly interested in establishing another tannery to take advantage of the current demand for leather products. This Argentine owner feels that this is due to "Paraguayan lassitude" and general lack of enterprise—a statement one hears often, even from Paraguayans. Lack of capital and credit facilities, combined with the great difficulties in transportation and marketing, are undoubtedly the important deterrents, however. Lack of information as to the profit possibilities may also be important, as entrepreneurs are very close-mouthed, and many do not keep any written accounts.

Agricultural Industries

Although purely rural, the production of rice, petitgrain, and *yerba mate* is as fittingly called "industrial" as are any of the previously discussed enterprises in the town, which are, except for the *fábrica de coco*, merely medieval-like cottage industries. Especially in the case of rice production, there is more mechanization, more capital invested, and more workers hired than in town. All the important rural industries, however, are owned and managed by commercial interests from the town.

Rice is grown in the modern manner, except that the equipment is ordinarily not up to date. Three of the eight establishments own old threshing machines, and the other rice farmers rent them. Other implements used are plows, disk harrows, and rake harrows. These are all drawn by oxen, except in the case of the Rizzis, who recently purchased a new tractor. Such large enterprises cannot easily be broken down into reliable labor and equipment costs, so we make no attempt to do so here, but some idea of the productivity may be gathered from the following data. The Rizzi *arrozal* of 95 hectares averaged 1,300 kilograms of threshed rice per hectare. This was felt to be below average, 3,000 kilograms being the most usual expectation. Padre Pedro Martínez planted 17 hectares but cropped from only 12 hectares. His yield was 35,350 kilograms, or 2,080 kilograms per hectare. A government agricultural expert informed us that this was poor, as in the Department of Misiones 6,000 kilograms were sometimes realized. (Most of the large mechanized *arrozales* are in Misiones and Pilar, with a few in Encarnación.) Rice sells for 0.40 guarani per kilogram, if transported to Asunción. Transportation by truck costs about 0.025 guarani per kilogram.

Petitgrain, or *essencia*, is an oil extracted in very small amounts from the leaves of the bitter-orange tree and exported to European perfume manufacturers. It is a very old industry in Paraguay, and, although only a few individuals actually participate in bitter-orange production in Tobatí, most peasants in Paraguay are familiar with the work; for this reason we present a description of the process in fuller detail than its local importance warrants.

Seeds are extracted from the oranges and washed and dried, after which they are planted in a small fertilized garden patch. In about one and one-half to two years, when the trees are about a foot high, they are transplanted to a field. Usually three people participate, one digging up the small plants and one carrying them to the field, where the third is digging the holes and transplanting them. The field must be hoed about twice a year, and in about three years the plants are large enough to provide the first harvest of leaves. If well cared for and healthy, the mature trees may be harvested twice a year, but usually a longer interval is necessary. The trees may continue to produce for as long as thirty to forty years. When the tree is too tall for easy harvesting, the trunk is sometimes cut off to allow shoots to grow from the stump. The greatest threats to the trees are prolonged dry spells and ants.

In harvesting, the branches are cut off the trees with a machete and brought to a central location, where they are cut into small pieces. After this, they are carried to the boiler or sold to someone who has one. Sometimes, while the leaves are being cut and carried to the "essence factory," two other men are operating the factory at the same time. The original cutters can work the factory, however, after they get the leaves all cut and transported, as it does not matter if the leaves get a little dry.

The "factory" consists of an apparatus designed to pass steam through the leaves, thereby extracting the oily "essence," after which the vapor of steam and essence is condensed. An oil drum full of water is set over an open brick fireplace, and steam is carried by a pipe from the top of this drum to the bottom of an airtight barrel full of the orange leaves. The pressure of the steam causes it to pass through the leaves and into a copper pipe on top of the barrel. This pipe is then spiraled through a barrel of cold water. The condensed vapor drips out of the pipe at the bottom of the cold water barrel into a can. The "essence" rises to the top of the water in the can, like a light oil film. The can has a pouring spigot near the bottom, so that the water can be poured out from under the essence which is floating on top.

The average factory has a leaf barrel which holds about 250 kilograms of leaves. This is called a "one-kilo factory," as 250 kilograms of leaves will produce about one of essence. Some larger factories produce up to 2 kilograms. Two men can process two loads a day; thus a "one-kilo factory" can produce 2 kilograms of essence per day at capacity. The residue of leaves from the process is not of any use, though some people say cows, sheep, or goats may be taught to eat it. People do not eat the fruit, but the grated skin of the fruit is sometimes used to make a dessert called *dulce de naranja ágria.*

A "one-kilo factory" represents an investment of about 1,500 guaranis. Inasmuch as two men can process two loads a day, one kilogram of *essencia* represents about one man-day of labor. The 250 kilograms of leaves for one load can be purchased for 7.50 guaranis, and fuel costs about 1.50 guaranis. One kilogram of *essencia*, which sold at 11.00 guaranis per kilogram in July, 1949, thus costs about 9.00 guaranis in cash—or a net profit of 2.00 guaranis for one man-day of labor. This is not much of a return, but it is possible that the price was at an exceptionally low point. Informants say that in past years it has risen as high as 21.00 guaranis per kilogram. However, the individual entrepreneur must sell his product promptly; he cannot store either leaves or essence in order to sell when prices are high.

Like *essencia*, the production of *yerba mate* is such a traditional enterprise in Paraguay that we include a few details, even though there are only two *yerba* plantations in the *partido* —both small and planted long ago. The *yerba* is a bushy tree (*Ilex paraguayensis*) native to the region, which produces a leaf from which a tealike infusion is made which has been the traditional beverage in Paraguay, southern Brazil, Uruguay, and Argentina since early colonial times. (For details on preparation of the beverage see Appendix IV.)

The general procedure in planting and harvesting the leaves is similar to that described for bitter orange. The small branches are carried to a central location, where they are individually toasted over a fire, in order to remove the bitterness of taste. The small twigs and leaves are then stripped from the branches and laid like thatch on a drying frame called a *barbaquá*. This is a latticework, dome-shaped frame which varies in size from a couple of meters high to nearly the size of a small house. The leaves are laid thickly on the top of the frame, and the sides are draped with blankets, so that heat from the drying fire will have no escape except through the leaves. The fire is so arranged that it may be fed through a tunnel arrangement from outside the frame. There is also a tunnel designed to draw off smoke from inside the *barbaquá*. The drying process usually takes twenty-four hours, after which the leaves are bagged for sale in Tobatí.[2] Larger *yerbales* ship the leaves to factories in the city, where they are ground and packaged for export or local sale, but the two in Tobatí are not of this size.

2. A description of Paraguay in 1813 by J. P. and W. P. Robertson (*Four Years in Paraguay* . . . [2 vols.; Philadelphia, 1938], II, 91–101) describes this entire process as exactly the same, except that the fire was then built directly under the *barbaquá* instead of conducting the heat through the underground passage.

CHAPTER VII

Standards of Living

THE various advantages available to the upper class and the sharp social distinctions maintained do not seem to represent themselves in important general cultural distinctions and levels of consumption to the extent which one would expect on the basis of experience in urban areas, where differences in income are more easily judged from outward manifestations. This is not to say that the differences do not exist but merely that they are not clear cut and that perhaps the rural Paraguayan does not think so immediately of putting money into his house, furnishings, and various modern comforts. This impression fits with those of many North Americans who have noted the same relative lack of interest in household comfort, convenience, and beauty in other areas of rural Latin America among people who could easily afford more lavish homes.

The same can be said for class symbols, or "badges of pecuniary strength," in general. Tobatí is a small society and a relatively stable one so far as economic mobility is concerned. Everyone knows quite a lot about everyone else, especially where he belongs socially and economically. In the larger, more impersonal, and more mobile urban environment material symbols of economic worth can be much more impressive and convincing than in Tobatí.

The very wealthiest families of Tobatí no longer live in any particular locality in the town. Until recently the central plaza was the site of the homes of the wealthiest families, and the economic and social position of a family was directly related to the distance of its home from the plaza. With the partial overthrow of the plaza tradition, however, there has been no move to concentrate in a suburb or in any other particular region. There is a tendency for the town to expand toward the creek, so that the newest of the modern houses are located in that direction; but some of the older of the homes belonging to equally wealthy and important families are scattered in other localities. Two of the six very richest families still live on the plaza in large but old-fashioned and unpretentious houses, and a few quite poor families also live near the plaza. The other new homes which are scattered about the town may be each entirely surrounded by the ranchos of the very poor.

Three of the six wealthiest families have new modern-style homes. Paraguayans in general do not seem to consider spaciousness of the home as particularly important—either in number of rooms or in size of the rooms. The number of rooms and their size vary upward generally with the long-term economic fortunes of the families, but, although the newest houses are of the "California" style, they are not large.

These new houses are constructed of brick. Cement is used sparingly as mortar, and sometimes only adobe is used. This is the only type of house likely to have window glass. It may also have a tile mosaic floor, though not all of them have either window glass or tile floors. The outbuildings of the homes of the *hacendado* group are also usually constructed of brick. They include the usual kitchen and storage shed, sometimes a stable for a horse or two, and small living quarters for servants. All have as servants at least a cook, and perhaps her children, who help with the work, and sometimes a man who takes care of the horses, the yard, and the garden.

A typical new home of one of this group has four rather small rooms inside the house and a large veranda facing the interior patio. The married couple and three children (aged seven, six, and four) live here. The outbuildings are three small rooms connected in a row; kitchen, *depósito* (for storage), and sleeping quarters for a cook. Both the house and outbuildings are of whitewashed plastered brick with tile roof. There is a stable for three horses and a corral for seven cows. There are also thirty chickens, two ducks, five geese, two pigs, and eight dogs. In front of the house there is a small dance floor of mosaic tile.

Inside the house the floors of the living- and dining-rooms are of tile, without rugs, and the bedroom floors are of brick. The walls are plastered and whitewashed. The living room is small and furnished with wicker chairs of the summer-porch-furniture type. The small table is also of this material and holds a small table-model radio, powered by an automobile battery which sits on the floor.

The dining-room has a long unfinished table and several locally made wooden straight-backed chairs. Shelves hold the thick china plates, cups, glasses, and knives, forks, and spoons. These items are of the restaurant type, but they are not cheap by Paraguayan standards. The distinguishing thing in such a home as this, however, is not so much the quality of the china and utensils as the fact that there are plenty of them. The average family has hardly enough to serve its needs, while this particular family can set a table for several guests if necessary.

The bedroom furniture consists of a metal double bed with a cotton-stuffed mattress. A movable wardrobe, a chest of drawers, a couple of chairs, and a chamber pot complete the furnishings.

Lighting in the wealthy homes is by Coleman lamps, which give much more light than wick-burning lamps but which are more expensive. There is no interior heating arrangement in any Paraguayan home. A simple fireplace would be of great utility, as the people—rich and poor alike—are very uncomfortable on cold winter days.

None of the rooms contain wastebaskets, ashtrays, or other such receptacles; ashes or waste are simply thrown on the floor. There are no rugs, so the tile floor is easily swept clear of debris whenever it accumulates. In poorer homes people may expectorate or throw garbage on the earth floor, but this is not done in the sort of home just described.

Standards in clothing tend to be more noticeably different in quantity than in quality. A Paraguayan peasant family is always short on clothing and may own no shoes at all. The wealthiest families have plenty of clothing for all concerned, but in the rural-town environment formal or business clothing is needed but rarely and, besides, is very expensive. By city standards, the clothing of even the very wealthiest families is of poor-tomoderate quality. Clothing must be washed, as there is no dry cleaning, so one may often judge the age of a person's suit by the way it fits, especially if it is a wool suit. If it is too big, it is new. If it fits fairly well, it has probably been washed once or twice, and if too small it is old. Needless to say, a wool suit will be washed very rarely.

The *hacendado* will usually wear *bombachas* (the full-cut bloomer-like pantaloons), a pair of expensive limp-leather riding boots, and a short waist-length jacket and a neckerchief. Often no shirt is worn underneath. A felt hat, or sometimes a sun helmet, is worn rather than the otherwise universal straw hat. A business suit is worn to church, but it must be remembered that most men attend church only if it is a very special occasion. Except in the coldest part of the year, the business suit is most typically of white linen, with the cut verging more toward the "zoot" style than is customary among middle-class men in North America.

Women's dress clothing is of European style—though often somewhat out of date. A silk dress for a party and often a suit of white linen for church occasions seem to be most usual. Hat and gloves, however, are never seen.

In Tobatí dress is not a particularly important item of social stress, and it seems probable that a much smaller proportion of the incomes of upper-class people is spent on clothing than would be the case among people of a similar income level in North America, despite the fact that clothing is relatively much more expensive in Paraguay.

The food consumed by the wealthier, as distinguished from the lower-income, groups is, like clothing, largely a quantitative rather than a qualitative difference. They eat the same foods that are known to the whole population but probably eat more, waste more, and have a greater variety of dishes. The variety is most noticeable during periods of relative scarcity of some items, which, because of the higher price, are absent from many tables. Esoteric or foreign items are normally not present. Wheat bread and wine (both largely imported) may occasionally be served for some special entertainment, but normal food tastes are roughly the same for all classes. Fiesta dishes which are relatively expensive, like *sopa paraguaya*, *chipa*, and *pasteles*, are served often at social gatherings, the budgetary difference here being chiefly due to the fact that the wealthy entertain more often than poorer people. Liquor is also a bigger expense for the same reason.

A large budgetary item for the wealthiest families consists of the frequent contributions to municipal affairs, especially the fiestas. This usually takes the form of money contributions to some committee. Sometimes an *asado* (barbecue party) is held to welcome a visiting dignitary, and in such a case the wealthiest families donate the biggest food items, such as the steers or sheep.

The *hacendados* of Tobatí spend more money for all the various forms of recreation than do the poorer people. The recreation itself, however, is of the same general nature as that indulged in by other families, the difference being in the fact that the wealthier families, being more important socially and politically than others, usually occupy the leading roles in community recreational affairs and are also invited more often to smaller social affairs.

Much recreation, except for visiting, gambling, and general intrafamilial sociability, is rather formalized and involves large sections of the community who attend the fiestas, *sortijas*,[1] horse racing, and soccer-football games. Two activities which are enjoyed almost exclusively by upper-income families are listening to the radio and taking frequent pleasure trips to Asunción.

Townsmen of Middle Income

Those families which occupy the intermediate position, above the peasants in income and below the wealthiest *hacendados*, are those engaged in business and in the few skilled or professional occupations. This group is basically composed of the numerous store-owners but also includes political office-holders, school-teachers, butchers (who are essentially middlemen as well as skilled workmen), brick and tile producers, two druggists, two leatherworkers, and three tailors. Their incomes vary, of course, but they do form a rather clearly delineated income group when compared to *hacendados* and peasants.

1. A contest of horsemanship in which the rider tries to spear a small suspended ring with a twig while riding at full tilt.

This middle group does not tend to live in any particular locality, although the store-owners usually live in or near their places of business. In a few cases they have built homes on the outskirts of town toward the arroyo. These homes, though new, are not so large nor so elaborate as those of the *hacendados*.

The most usual houses are of the colonial style. They are sometimes of brick but more often of wattle and daub (*estaqueo*), plastered with adobe and with the front, at least, painted with kaolin wash. Roofs are of thatch or, more lately, of tile— sometimes laid over the original thatch. Floors are of brick, both inside the house and on the veranda formed by the front overhang of the roof.

Middle-income people are likely to have real beds in their homes, or at least one for the mother and father. Sheets are of poor quality factory cotton or homespun. The bed will usually have a cotton mattress. Wool blankets are scarce and are used as bedcovers and also as ponchos for men and wraps for women in cold weather. The bedroom may also have a wardrobe and a chair and perhaps a trunk or box for valuables.

Windows are barred but are without glass and without curtains. The house may sometimes have a *baño*, a small room with a drain in the floor, where one may bathe by splashing from a washbasin. More rarely, the house may have a *baño de lluvia*—a suspended bucket perforated to shower water.

Furnishings in the rest of the house are meager, but, inasmuch as the inside of the house is used for social living (whereas the poor man's rancho is not) there are usually several straight-backed, locally made chairs and a table. Kitchen and dining utensils are fewer than in the wealthier homes and often do not consist of much more than the family itself uses, for entertaining at meals is very infrequent. Only a few of these people have a radio (there are twelve in the town), and two or three have Coleman lamps. Interior decorations consist of potted flowers and pictures, usually of religious subjects.

Outbuildings include a brick outdoor toilet and a kitchen— sometimes, but not always, made of brick rather than of wattle and daub. The cooking is done with charcoal in the brick fogón, a raised fire bed with a grate in the bottom. Baking is done in the universally used beehive-shaped oven. Sometimes middle-class families keep a few cows and horses as well as chickens, and in such cases the outbuildings include a corral, a stable, and a shed for the storage of feed and implements.

Full-time servants are not usual among these families, but there is often a schoolgirl from the rural areas who works for her keep while attending school in town. She lives with the family rather than in a separate servants' quarter.

Kitchen equipment in middle-income and even in wealthy homes seems meager. The most omnipresent and necessary utensil is a large iron pot, or olla. Most of the everyday Paraguayan dishes, such as puchero (stew), *locro* (maize soup), boiled and roast beef, and boiled manioc are cooked in the pot over an open fire. There is often, also, a small metal pan for boiling milk, eggs, or beans. A teakettle is an essential, especially to heat water for the *mate*. An earthenware casserole is in common use for baked dishes. Of implements used in food preparation, the wooden mortar is found in homes of all classes. It is used for grinding maize and peppercorns and for pounding meat. With the addition of a large knife and a large spoon to the above items, the kitchen is virtually complete. People save old bottles, tin cans, and jars as containers, but few of these are needed, as people do not customarily lay in supplies of anything; food, including condiments, is bought only in sufficient quantity for each day's use. A kitchen does not include shelves, cupboards, and other food-storage places; a few wire hooks for hanging the day's meat and the baskets which contain the day's manioc, maize, and vegetables are all that are needed.

So far as clothing is concerned, this middle group tends to approximate the pattern of the *hacendados* and to regard this type of clothing as a class symbol distinguishing them from the straw-hatted, barefoot peasant. Thus shoes are worn more and valued more, a European-style felt hat is desirable, and a linen suit is indispensable for public occasions.

Women of the middle-income group are less active socially than upper-class women and have fewer dresses, but their tastes are similar. A few of the younger upper- and middle-income women may be observed at a festive occasion wearing pearls or costume jewelry, and lipstick. Under everyday conditions, ornaments consist nearly exclusively of simple gold earrings and rings. Hair ornaments such as combs, barrettes, and ribbons are rarely used. Both sexes wear wedding rings.

A few women have had permanent waves, which may be obtained in Caacupé and Asunción, but no one has them consistently. The hairdresser from Caacupé comes to Tobatí before the patronal fiesta of December 8, and some women get permanents at that time. In 1948 the hairdresser worked in the hotel patio for two days, in terrible heat, drying hair by fanning it. In this fashion he took care of four customers a day, charging 2 guaranis and up. The upper- and middle-class young women prefer a medium-length bob, while older women and working-class and peasant women wear their hair in long braids or in a bun.

All women wear *rebozos* (shawls), which may be of various types. Wealthy women usually wear black silk ones of excellent quality. For churchgoing the *rebozo* is replaced by a mantilla-like net or lace scarf. Poor women wear white homespun *rebozos*, elaborately hand-embroidered. Except for the *rebozo*, colonial styles have practically disappeared. The most usual dress for women in town is a knee-length rayon print or white cotton.

The type of food consumed by middle-class people is like that of the *hacendados*, except that certain expensive items appear less often. Bread and wine are more rare, and beef fat and pork lard are used more in cooking than vegetable oils or olive oil. Townsmen in general purchase much of their food in stores, so that there are certain foods which are used more often by them than by countrypeople. Coffee, sugar, macaroni, rice, tomatoes, lettuce, and cabbage do not displace the locally produced staples like *mate*, manioc, and maize, but townsmen are more familiar with them than are the more isolated peasants. It seemed to us that townsmen of both the upper- and the middle-income group are well nourished; the food is more than adequate both in quantity and variety, except for the iodine and calcium deficiencies which affect all Paraguayans.[2]

2. Emma Reh's study revealed that small town people in general have a better diet than either urban or purely rural people (*Paraguayan Rural Life* [Washington, D.C.: Institute of Inter-American Affairs, Food Supply Division, 1946], pp. 85–90).

The biggest difference among families of varying incomes in town lies in the proportion of the family budgets which are spent for food. Probably none of the upper-income families spend as much as one-fourth of their incomes on food; middle-income families may spend about half; the town poor spend nearly all of their incomes on food, even though they often have supplementary gardens. As a consequence, the food consumed by a family is not a good index of the family's financial position. The quality of clothing and character of the house and its furnishings are more revealing. Probably the best index of all, but difficult to ascertain, is the amount of money spent on contributions to the church and community functions.[3]

Peasants and Town Working Class

The typical lower-class house of Paraguay, the rancho, is similar in town, hamlet, and country, though there is variability within limits. It is nearly always one small room. In the country it has a long roof extension, or ramada, which provides shade and protection from rain for a small table and a bench or two. Most of the "living" in rural Paraguay actually takes place here, and most of the sleeping in summer and even in winter if the small room is too crowded. In addition to sleeping and eating, sedentary work and social functions all take place here in the shade. The small, dark rancho room should be thought of not as a *home* but as a storage place and as a refuge when the weather is uncommonly cold.

This type of house may vary in its wall construction from simple pole or post sides with unchinked interstices (used by the very poor) to the more common type chinked with adobe. In a few cases the *estaqueo* is fully plastered and smoothed with adobe and may even be painted in front with a locally made kaolin wash. This type is called *pared francés* (French wall). A more common style is an intermediate one in which the exposed sides of the house are *estaqueo* but the front, which is protected by the ramada, is plastered and perhaps whitewashed.

---

3. We collected data on the daily expenditures for a period of one week of five families, representing different income levels. This material and various conversations and impressions form the basis of the above judgments.

The most common difference between the rancho in the country and that of the town is the size of the ramada. Probably so much more varied kinds of work are done in the ramada in the country that it needs to be larger. In town most family activities take place under a shade in the rear of the house, eliminating the need for a ramada in front. The typical town design is called a "one and three-quarters" house. The roof and frame are constructed about half again as long as wide, perhaps 6 × 9 meters. The room is walled in a square shape, and the overhang is usually left as a ramada or porch in front. Thus the room is 6 meters square, and the ramada is 3 × 6 meters in size.

The rancho roof is thatched with a strawlike tall grass which grows profusely in parts of the campo. Double handfuls of straw are bundled together, the butt ends of the bundles are dipped in adobe mud to consolidate them, and the bundles are then laid shingle fashion on the roof. Some people use wire or string to tie the bundles, but this is more expensive. Some roofs slope from one end of the house to the other, and some are gabled. In the latter case, a row of overlapping tiles is laid along the crest to protect and retain the row of adjoining butts of the thatch bundles. Tile is, of course, considered better than thatch because it lasts much longer.

The floors of both the ramada and the house itself are of clay, which is quite serviceable, as it is so hard and smooth that it can be swept clean of debris without sweeping away the floor itself. The door of the house is small, and, though iron hinges are sometimes used, hinges and door fastenings of leather are more common. The one or two small windows are barred, and a wooden panel is used to shut out wind and rain.

Rancho construction proceeds as one might logically expect. Four corner logs are cut to required lengths and set upright into holes. If the house is to be gabled, two longer logs are also set in their proper places at the sides. All these posts have large notches at the top, into which are set the ends of the heavy crossbeams, shaped to fit the notch. Poles and slabs of various sizes are set in the ground along the sides and nailed or tied to the crossbeams at the top. Then long lengths of vine are woven among the upright poles to strengthen them and to help hold the adobe chinking. The doors and window frames are usually made by a professional carpenter. Some of the poorest people have no windows in their huts at all, and the doors are merely openings covered with a blanket.

In the rarer cases when walls are made entirely of adobe bricks, the builder erects the four or six posts and then builds up the walls in the fashion of regular bricklaying. The thick adobe is mixed with a small proportion of fine sand—no other binding material is used—and placed in a wet hand mold over a wet board or table. After the top of the brick is smoothed, the mold is slid off the board and turned quickly sidewise, so that it can be carried without the brick falling out of the mold. The bricks are exposed to the sun for a day or two, depending on the weather, and then turned on edge for an equal amount of time. Finally, they are stored in a place sheltered from rain until they are actually used in construction. In wall-building they are laid face down, long edge exposed, and cemented in place with a thin mixture of the same adobe mud.

Outbuildings are similar in purpose and function for all three income levels, but they differ in construction material, as do the houses themselves, depending on the economic status of the owner. All homes have one separated shed which serves as a kitchen. This custom is very old and firmly established. It is said that it is unhealthy to have a fire in the house and that a kitchen attracts flies. Screening against insects is unknown and economically impossible. The kitchen is a mere lean-to or unchinked shed. Cooking is done over a wood fire on the ground, and the smoke escapes through the many openings in the walls and roof. All baking is done near the kitchen in the dome-shaped brick-and-mud oven, which is commonly about a meter high and a meter in diameter. There is one ground-level square opening in front and a small hole in the rear for draft.

In town the other usual outbuilding is a privy. It is a law of the municipality that all housebuilders must construct a privy and that all homes around the plaza have brick ones. This law is the result of the relatively successful Rockefeller antihookworm mission, which worked in Paraguay in 1929–30. Among the poorer town people, the privy is a hole in the ground surrounded

by a small log stockade, sometimes crudely roofed. In more isolated rural areas, the people go to the woods or bushes a short distance from the house. Sometimes a family may have a storage
shed or an extra ramada for some special use, depending on their
particular needs. Peasants are likely to have such a shed to store
the harvest. If a pig is being fattened, a pen of stakes may be
built, though often the animal is merely tied to a tree by one foot.
Crude chicken-houses are sometimes in evidence in town, but
usually the chickens roost in the trees.

The home furnishings and utensils of a typical town rancho of
a man, his wife, and four children consist of the following items:

1. An *estaqueo* house of one room, a ramada and a kitchen-
depósito, and a privy.

2. Two rawhide beds and two hammocks. The husband and
wife sleep in one bed (which is about a meter wide), the two
oldest children in the hammocks, and the other two children in
the remaining bed.

3. Three or four battered wooden straight-backed chairs, a
long low bench, two or three low stools, one small table, and a
chest or box.

4. Two or three china plates, two glasses (no cups), two or
three gourd *mates*, six tablespoons (no forks), one or two table
knives, one kitchen knife, one large clay pot, one iron pot, one
iron casserole (no frying pan), and one wooden mortar and
pestle.

5. Two dogs, one cat, and a pet bird or so.

The above inventory is also fairly common in the rural *compañías*, except that many families do not own as many beds,
plates, glasses, and utensils as enumerated above. In all cases, tin
cans, glass bottles, and paper sacks are rare and valuable. Any
family will keep these when possible. Because of the limited supply of plates and utensils, grownups usually eat first and the
children later, or two or three children may eat simultaneously
from the same plate. Water is passed around from person to person in one glass.

It seems curious that, in the typical absence of the ability to
purchase enough knives, forks, spoons, and plates to serve a
whole family, some kind of homemade, makeshift utensils are

not used. Spoons, for example, could be easily whittled out of wood, and it would seem that pottery plates could be made cheaply. But we never saw people making or using such things, and even questioning of old people indicated that the people have been accustomed to enamel, chinaware, and metal utensils for generations past and have no thought of using anything else.

It can readily be seen that food-sharing between families cannot be a convenient social form among the poor. *Mate*-sharing is important and goes on at intervals all day with considerable formality, and *caña*-sharing is also important but much less frequent because of the expense. The countrypeople are exceedingly gracious, and hospitality is a great virtue, but it consists of openhandedness toward a stranger or someone in need rather than a planned gathering or dinner among friends or families. The *asados* ("roasts"—outdoor barbecue parties) are more frequent in the upper classes, but even the latter do not entertain friends at dinner. Instead, food is often served incidentally, buffet style, at a dance, or outdoors, picnic style, and the gathering is thought of as having some purpose other than that of sharing food.

The diet of the peasant differs from that of wealthier people chiefly in that he is much more dependent at any given time on what he has available from his *chacra*, while the town upper and middle classes are more able to afford scarce items. A secondary factor is that many peasants are so far away from town that even if they can afford to buy food, they lack the opportunity. This is especially important in regard to beef consumption, for, although beef is cheap and traditionally felt to be the very basis of the Paraguayan diet, many people cannot get it as often as they would like, simply because they are unable to be present at the time the beef is available. There is, of course, no refrigeration storage, so that beef must be sold within a few hours after butchering, especially in summer. There is beef available nearly every day in town because of the concentration of buyers, but, even so, both the supply and the demand are so independently and unpredictably variable that many people cannot count on being able to buy meat on any given day. In the small hamlets, beef is slaughtered only sporadically and rarely. Sun-dried beef (charqui) is sometimes made in small quantities and used in *locro*, a maize soup. Pork is usually made into sausages.

Chickens, eggs, milk, and cheese are highly regarded foods among the peasantry but are not items of everyday fare because of their scarcity, especially in certain seasons of the year. Dried legumes, such as beans and chickpeas, and a kind of porridge made of peanuts are eaten more regularly, especially in areas where beef is difficult to obtain.

The typical peasant's daily fare seems to us exceedingly meager and unvariegated. On arising an hour or so before dawn, the family gathers around the fire in the cooking shed and passes around the hot *mate*, served by the oldest woman. The peasant then works for several hours in the fields, until nine or ten o'clock, when he may come back for a snack of cold manioc or fruit. The dinner is served at noon. It usually consists of some sort of a stew, or roast meat if available, or a soup of *locro* or *porotos*, accompanied by large quantities of manioc. After a long siesta, hot *mate* is taken again, and work is resumed until near twilight. The supper is very light: a leftover from noon or often a dish of mashed peanuts sweetened with honey is all that is served.

There are clearly many inadequacies in the Paraguayan peasant's diet. Rural people eat very few fresh vegetables; onions provide about the only green food for much of the year. There are obvious calcium and iodine deficiencies, as shown by the extremely bad teeth and the extraordinary prevalence of goiter.

The most characteristic items of dress which distinguish the peasant from the wealthier townsman are the broad-brimmed straw hat, the *faja* (large sash), and lack of shoes. The shirt and trousers are not distinctive in style, but, because clothing is quite expensive in Paraguay, the peasant wardrobe is very limited and often extraordinarily tattered and patched. Footgear of any kind is usually absent; even homemade sandals are rarely seen. *Alpargatas* (fiber-soled sandals) may be purchased cheaply in Tobatí, but only a few townsmen use them, chiefly as house slippers. The nature of the soil may have something to do with this; the ground is not hard or rocky and not likely to bruise the bare feet, even in the town streets, but there is so much sand and deep dust that sandals or low shoes constantly need emptying.

Peasant women wear cotton dresses, usually white and sometimes of homespun material. The style is that of a few years back, when dresses were of knee length. Some of the old countrywomen still wear floor-length skirts and long-sleeved blouses, most often in winter as protection from the cold. In cold weather women drape their heads and shoulders in blankets instead of cotton *rebozos*. Men wear ponchos if they have them.

The peasant family's participation in community affairs, whether political, religious, or purely recreational, is necessarily limited by lack of funds, lack of social standing, and often by the distance of the home from community centers. Peasants who do attend town functions are bystanders rather than participants. So far as politics are concerned, the peasant is unrepresented—the vote is meaningless, and he has no organizations which can bring pressure on political bodies. As for religious participation, peasant families often live too far away to attend services in Tobatí, and the functionaries of the church organizations are "respectable" upper-income people. For this reason, local informal saints' cults are more important in the rural areas. Many peasants attend fiestas in town and get drunk and have a good time, but that is about the extent of their participation. Community recreational functions, such as horse races and football games, are organized and run by wealthier townsmen.

CHAPTER VIII

Attitudes toward Economic Advancement

THE economic life of rural Paraguay is most accurately characterized as "peasant," even though we are not as yet accustomed to applying this term to peoples of the Western Hemisphere. We find not only that production and exchange are essentially similar to what has been described as peasant behavior in Europe but that much of the religion, morality, and general attitudes and sentiments of the people are also similar. Raymond Firth's comment on the general nature of peasant life in other parts of the world is applicable to rural Paraguay:

> The principle recognized by the economist, of reward proportioned to total productivity, is not easy to recognize here. Such a principle does exist in this type of system. But its operation is conditioned by other factors—social factors. In such circumstances economic relations can be understood only as part of a scheme of social relations. What I have said about the peasant society studied by the anthropologist is very much what the historian has described in other language for the economic life of the Middle Ages. One can translate this into various propositions. One may say that in such a peasant society ties are personalized—that is, relationships as economic agents depend on the social status and relationships of the people concerned. Put another way, labor is given as a social service, and not simply an economic service. Its reward is therefore apt to be calculated in terms of the total social situation, and not merely the immediate economic situation. Economic means tend to be translated into social ends.[1]

To refer to the Paraguayan agriculturalist as a "peasant," however, should not convey the notion that he is in any sense a dependent serf. Peasant farming in Paraguay is individualized and independent and exists in a society which is dominated by markets, both internal and international. But the peasant is not directly a functional part of this economic society. He partici-

---

1. Raymond Firth, *Elements of Social Organization* (London, 1951), p. 137.

pates in the regional market to a limited degree, but his participation is geared to subsistence requirements and is not normally accompanied by any idea of expanding an investment.

Typical peasant attitudes are those we associate with Europe before the spread of the "Protestant" or "capitalist" ethic. "Individualism" and "competitiveness" have no role as ideals in the peasant community, and, as we have seen in the fuller discussion of peasant land tenure, even ownership of land is not considered particularly desirable. This does not mean that the peasant is not acquisitive, that he does not desire a better living for himself and his family, but the acquisitiveness does not take the economic-ideological form that it does in a middle-class urban milieu. His experience, and that of his ancestors, is that consistent application to his work could be expected to maintain him in the status in which he was born but with no chance of enhancing it. A rich man whose family was not "always wealthy" must have gained his position as a result of luck or influence. We never discovered any sentiment among the peasants that hard work and intelligent management or enterprise could achieve other than a small and ephemeral reward.

The peasants' attitude toward those families who have acquired wealth as entrepreneurs is one of hatred as well as envy. Men like the original Rizzis, who acquired their fortunes through extremely hard work, self-deprivation, and shrewdness, were widely regarded as "cheats." Another view held by the peasants is that hard work had nothing to do with the building of the fortune; the Rizzis had found a barrel of treasure in the forest years ago but would not admit it. In neither interpretation, however, is the Rizzis' economic rise regarded as creditable or normal.

The rural Paraguayans, incidentally, are inveterate treasure-hunters. Presumably there is some basis for the belief in the prevalence of buried treasure, because wealthy families fleeing before the foreign armies in 1869 undoubtedly did sometimes bury and abandon their valuables. We have never met anyone, nevertheless, who actually found any treasure.

The conception that economic improvement can be achieved only through the aid or influence of a *patrón* is also very prevalent, in spite of the fact that for many years there have been no agricultural haciendas. The most usual response from a peasant who is queried about his economic and technological difficulties is not that he needs a steel plow, better seed, or a yoke of oxen but that he needs a good *patrón* who will help him.

Credit usage among the peasantry is normally borrowing for purposes of consumption rather than for investment and is very like the attitude in the Middle Ages in Europe which regarded loans as usury. A peasant tries to borrow money because of some personal or familial crisis such as sickness or crop failure, perhaps to pay for a funeral, or, more rarely, to finance a wedding. These emergencies are most usually taken care of by other relatives, *compadres*, or friends, but, if the sum is too great to be acquired in these traditional ways and the need is dire, the peasant may go to a merchant for an advance against a forthcoming crop or with some prized possession as security. The interest rate may be sometimes as much as 20 per cent monthly, or less if the merchant has confidence in the borrower. Needless to say, peasants are very opposed to such usury and resort to borrowing only in cases of absolute necessity.

The average peasant does not seem to have a very clear idea of simple interest calculation, nor is he very good at predicting future crop prices. Time and again we found instances of peasants who had borrowed money at a time when the prices were unusually high, before the harvest. At harvest time, when prices were lower, the same peasants were surprised to find that their crops did not fetch the expected return necessary to cover the loan.

Private loans at high rates of interest are actually illegal and are not consummated openly, and neither the borrower nor the lender has any legal recourse should the mutual confidence be misplaced. The nationalized Banco del Paraguay has a farm-credit program of supervised loans for agricultural investment and has a Tobatí businessman as a local representative. This bank program, incidentally, is known as the "Banco Norte" because the peasants believe (erroneously) that it is supervised and financed by the United States of America.[2] Because the program

2. At the inception of the program the Banco del Paraguay used advisers from the United States, and since then STICA representatives have collaborated in the extension of the program.

makes loans for investment but not for emergencies, it is only the few wealthier, commercially oriented farmers who understand its purpose. Thus it seems to the peasant that "only the rich can get a loan because they have influence." We have no evidence that "influence" determines who shall get a loan, and all the supervisors of the program that we have interviewed, from the chief in Asunción down to the local representatives, seemed to us to be people of exceptional personal integrity, who were, moreover, extremely conscious of the potential danger of charges of "influence." The local agent in Tobatí showed us all the recent applications made to him for loans, and it was readily apparent that most of the applicants misunderstood the intent of the program. We were told that most of them thought it was merely an easy way to get hold of some cash to use on a "three-day spree."

The behavior of peasants in a wageworking context is instructive. The more overt and idealized attitude is that, in working for someone, you are doing him a personal favor; the wages received in return are presents or tokens of esteem. More covertly, working for wages is seen as a means of raising a little cash for some specific purpose. Labor is not seen as a commodity, impersonally bought and sold, nor is working for an employer viewed as a possible means of making a living. The labor turnover on the few plantations and in the brick factory is rapid, because, usually, as soon as a worker saves the small amount of cash which was his goal, he quits. Foreign employers in Paraguay have decided, in some instances, to pay higher than prevailing wages in order to obtain the highest-quality labor and to have satisfied workers who would be more permanent. The consequence of the higher wage rate was the opposite; the labor turnover was accelerated.[3] It was not understood that those who work for wages do so only occasionally in order to obtain a certain sum of money; the sooner that amount is reached, the sooner they quit. Actually, even the higher rate does not constitute a living wage for a man and his family, so the peasant is undoubtedly perfectly wise in refusing to get caught up in the superficial attractiveness of a weekly cash income.

3. We have heard that this is a familiar story in many of the rural zones of Latin America.

Labor is sometimes exchanged in the rural areas, but rarely does money change hands. The *minga*, as the labor exchange is called, is a neighborly way of helping a person plant or harvest a crop or perhaps build a house. Neighbors, relatives, and friends who help out in this way expect to be helped in return, but the institution is not particularly formalized in a way which insures reciprocity, nor is it formal in terms of accompanying social behavior. Some kind of refreshment is usually served, but the occasion is not particularly festive.

The relation between *patrón* and *peón* in a wageworking context, while in actuality an impersonal pecuniary relationship, tends to take the social form of personal reciprocal obligations. Thus a *patrón* hires a person as though he were asking a personal favor, and the *peón* responds as though he were obliged to grant it. The payment of the wages is played down, almost as an undercover act. Often an employer will hire a *compadre*, or the *patrón* and *peón* may become *compadres*, as a sort of reinforcement to the working relationship. If a *patrón* wishes to fire a worker or if a worker wants to quit, each tries to create a situation which would make the other actually commit the act which destroys the relationship. The community would censure an employer for firing a worker, so he tries to anger the worker in some way so that he will quit instead of being fired. A worker who wants to quit, correspondingly, will do poor work, find excuses for not coming regularly to work, or in other ways try to force the *patrón* to fire him.

In one case involving friends of ours, it was known to us and to other "insiders" that the worker, a truck-driver, had been trying for at least two months to get the truck-owner to fire him. The two men had become *compadres* earlier, so there was an added caution on the part of the two men, as community feeling is strong in such a case. When both men finally blew up over a trivial incident and severed their working arrangement (though not, of course, the *compadre* relationship), the repercussions affected a large part of the town and created antagonisms between people who were, circumstantially at least, far from any involvement.

Even the middle-class people completely committed to buying and selling as a way of life lack many of the attitudes associated with the "capitalist ethic." Each seller has his own personal circle of customers, and it is a grave breach of morality for one store-owner to bid for another's customers. When we first came to settle in the town, it became obvious to us that we were regarded as being very wealthy and therefore as exceptionally desirable customers, but in no case did any of the store-owners indicate in any way that they would like to have us trade with them, except by showing that they were disposed to be friendly. A newcomer is faced with a delicate *social* situation in his initial buying, rather than with an economic situation, for to change from one store to another takes the outward form of a change in personal allegiance. There are often extraordinary differences in the selling price of an item from one store to another because of the absence of competitive wholesale purchasing, and a consequent ill-defined price level. But even in the face of such differences, the people usually stick to a single store, no matter how important a saving they might make by shopping around a little. It seems like exceedingly uneconomic behavior on the face of it, but perhaps it is not, under the circumstances, for the personal social relations themselves always have a very strong economic undercurrent in the sense that friends must always be ready to help each other. In the buying-selling relationship this may mean that a friendly customer who "helps" the store-owner by always buying from him may also expect easy credit terms from the same store in a time of need.

Commercial people are, of course, committed to shrewd dealing and acquisitiveness as a condition of their survival, but this is not overtly admitted. *Naked* acquisitiveness clearly clashes with the ideals of the community at large and must be sublimated or disguised in various ways. Paraguayan social life in its most general aspects has as its basis the face-to-face personal relations of a predominantly agricultural noncompetitive tradition. This does not mean, however, that there is an inflexible "genius" or "pattern" or "theme" of the culture which precludes the possibility of change. The recent increase in wage-earning and buying-selling activities and the limited, but possible, economic mobility in terms of these activities have created the beginnings of an ethic, as yet localized and largely unarticulated, which causes an important conflict in the ideals, if not in the behavior, of a few people. Most strikingly, the primary obligations to the great extended group of relatives, *compadres*, and friends may sometimes take the form of nepotism and favoritism—"unfairness"— under some of the new conditions and may even be ruefully recognized as such. An ambitious young man of the small commercial group in Tobatí may thus get caught up in contradictions. To strike out for one's self and to rise in the economic and social hierarchy involve competition. Successful competition normally involves an evasion of the usual economic responsibilities toward family and friends which hamper one's activities and cut into the working capital, and passing into a higher social status involves at least a partial severing of the normal social ties to the family and to the friends and *compadres* which are supposed to last until death.

So far it is rare that a man actually casts off these ties and becomes as independent as his urban counterpart, even if he moves to another town or to Asunción to promote himself. Such individualism is unusual because the opportunities for advancement are unusual, not because the desire for advancement is not strong. The most normal understanding of the possibility for economic and social mobility actually occurs in the realm of politics, not in business. Mobility via political office-holding or political favoritism has in the past been virtually the only way an ambitious and able man could find a way to financial success, and even today it is seen as more normal than any other way.

The political parties are not compact and disciplined with a pretension to an ideology related to policy; they are, rather, loose aggregations of small bodies or factions of would-be office-holders, professing personal allegiance to their leaders but continually jockeying for greater power by forming new alliances and destroying old ones. The absence of the old aristocracy, the lack of strength of the middle class, and the political inertness of the great body of peasants result in a government without a following, unworried about public opinion, responsible to no large segment of the population, but in constant danger of being overthrown by an ephemeral coalition of other politicians who were formerly friendly. Many of the politicians and office-holders, even occasional presidents, are ambitious men from the rural towns. Office-holders come and go within the government, and the presidents themselves may not complete their terms of office. For these reasons, politicians are often the crudest adventurers, who expect to make their fortunes in one swoop on the public treasury. The ancient prototype of the politician, the backwoods *caudillo*, is still close to reality.

The conception of individual economic advance through politics rather than through business or a profession is in some ways like the prevalence of treasure-hunting among the peasants, especially in the sense that both are born of raw acquisitiveness but take the place of the "capitalist" conception of the means of advance. Interesting in this regard is the contradictory absence of lotteries in the rural scene. Paraguay has a national lottery, and lottery tickets are in some evidence in Asunción, but we noticed only a few townsmen in Tobatí playing the lottery. It would seem that such gambling would be exceptionally congenial to the economic sense of the Paraguayan rural people. We cannot explain its absence; we can only guess that perhaps it is so new in Paraguay that it has not yet become understood in the agricultural areas.

PART III

Society

CHAPTER IX

Status Groups

SOCIAL ranking in Tobatí is somewhat different from the economic groupings previously discussed, although there is an important relationship between the two. The economic groups are rather easily definable in terms of occupation and income (which are largely coincident), resulting in a basic twofold division between subsistence-oriented poor peasants, on the one hand, and commercial-oriented merchants, petty industrialists, and the very few capitalist rancher-farmers, on the other. The top few of the latter may be separated as a subgroup, if desired, for purposes of economic analysis. Each group is distinctive and reflects clearly the important differences which are associated with the basic kinds of occupations.

Social ranking corresponds in general with these extremes; it could be said that there are basically two groups, which might be called "society" and the "people." In practice, however, the gradation of *individuals* from top to bottom is continuous—sharp distinctions between the two groups are not made. In the consciousness of the people, the characteristics which divide the population into social ranks are multiple and often contradictory. Even though, in an ultimate sense, these factors are derived from occupation and income, they create subgroups and individual borderline cases.

Social classification may be regarded in two ways. The society may be seen as composed of certain consistent groupings, distinguishable from one another in terms of actual observed social behavior. The observer may then attempt an analysis or explanation of the composition of these groups in terms of his own evaluation of the correlation between the observed grouping and such attributes of the personnel of each class as seem relevant or determinant. Or the observer may describe the groups and explain them in terms of the people's own conscious evaluations of each other's positions and the criteria that they have in mind when they "choose" their companions. We have no desire to enter into the argument which has been prevalent in sociological circles as to what social class *really* is. It would seem that often the two opposite arguments consist in what is to be considered an adequate *explanation* of the phenomenon of social distinctions: what the people themselves consciously think as they choose their companions or what the observer decides as he analyzes the underlying historical and economic factors. For the present purpose, which is essentially descriptive, it seems desirable to include the natives' own feelings about the nature of their classes, but we feel that this is not in any sense an explanation of the class phenomenon; the reasons given by the participants need explanation as social data just as much as any other observable phenomena, for they are merely the verbal aspect of the behavior which is to be analyzed.

Many aspects of the people's conception of social class are clearly derived from the economic relations of the colonial epoch. Viewed as a national phenomenon, social class became fixed first in the pattern of felt superiority and actual economic dominance of the Spaniards, and later their mestizo sons, over the native Indians in the encomienda system and then in the landholding system of the early period of independence. In those days the two classes were clearly demarcated in the minds of everyone; the coincidence of landownership with wealth and political power was complete, and the various personal attributes, such as education, sophistication, stylish dress, knowledge of Spanish, and family pride, were normal concomitants of this economic demarcation. There was very little economic mobility, so that a person was born into his class and thought of as a permanent member of it.

Many of the same assumptions about class membership are still present today, but a great many things have happened to Paraguay since its independence was achieved, which, however little they may have affected the people's own conscious comprehension of social class, have actually caused significant changes in the nature of the classes. The great War of the Triple Alliance almost wiped out the native *hacendados*, and subsequent events have tended to keep their descendants from re-establishing themselves to any important degree. The few who remain are still accorded a popular status as descendants of "fine old families," but as a group they have not been dominant economically or politically, especially since the revolution of 1947, which ended the rule of the Liberal party. Many of those who were active politically prior to 1947 had to leave the country and are now in residence in Argentina and Brazil; others have remained in Paraguay in political obscurity, sometimes impoverished, although they are still accorded considerable social respect by those who knew them in their previous higher estate.

The socially dominant group in the capital today is a heterogeneous one, made up of eminent politicians and high military authorities, a number of foreigners who have sufficient wealth to wield political power without actually participating overtly in politics, a few members of old families who have "turncoated" but who remain for this reason slightly suspect, and members of foreign diplomatic missions. Lawyers and professional men are highly regarded, as are literary people and artists. Regardless of their family background, they are conceded a relatively high social position.

Below them, in the capital, are the *commerciantes*, or tradesmen, primarily of foreign ancestry—such as Italian, Argentine, Levantine, and German—who form a middle social class. They are rather a small group in the population and do not control enough wealth to be politically influential. They keep rather to themselves socially or mingle with such *déclassé* Paraguayan families as welcome them. This has been an insignificant class both numerically and economically.

The wars, revolutions, emigrations, and the slow but noticeable revival of trade have created in recent years the possibility of economic and social advance for lower-class Paraguayans. As discussed previously, politics offers the quickest way up, but this kind of success may be ephemeral. Business activity of one kind or another is the other possibility. Economic advance is not exactly the same thing as social advance—social advance follows only slowly after it. Nevertheless, it appears that, however slow, an economic rise is the only sure road to a higher social position.

The people of "society," who in Tobatí clearly owe their social superiority to the economic success of their recent ancestors, nevertheless say that money *should* have nothing to do with social position. "Education," interpreted broadly to mean not only formal education but also good manners and modern sophistication, cleanliness, and uprightness in conduct, should be the most important criterion for entrance into society. These attributes come only with a "good family background." Nevertheless, many members of the upper social group admit cynically that financial power in the hands of an upstart can force social recognition. Actual cases of such mobility are still rare in Tobatí but are coming to be such an ever increasing possibility, at least, that members of the present upper social class are aware of it. The feeling about education and background is strong enough, however, so that, even though there is a possibility of a person's rising in the social scale, there is less probability that one would fall rapidly in social esteem because of loss of wealth, presuming that he and his children retained the personal attributes of upper-class behavior associated with the notion of "good breeding." In time, of course, an impoverished family would lose status, but most informants denied this possibility.

Although in the opinions of the people there is a continuous gradation of individuals between the polar upper- and lower-class extremes, there is, in actual behavior, a manifest twofold distinction between *la sociedad* and *la gente*. This is revealed in several ways, but most clearly in the fiestas in which the whole population participates. Most noteworthy are, first, the attendance at the *baile oficial*,[1] as opposed to the *baile popular*, and, second, attendance at barbecues held in conjunction with municipal functions. Upper-class weddings and private dances are revealing, too, for, if these functions are large enough, there never seems to be any doubt as to who is to participate and who is to be merely in the crowd of spectators.

1. We never were able to find out just why the upper-class dance was called the "official dance."

All the towns we visited held to the distinction between *baile oficial* and *baile popular* and seemed to regard it as a most suitable way to make social distinctions crystal-clear. Sometimes the *baile popular* and *baile oficial* were held on different nights as well as in different places during a fiesta, and sometimes they were held at the same time. In Tobatí they are usually held simultaneously at the municipal building. The *baile popular* is held outdoors at the side of the building on the tile dance floor, and the *baile oficial* inside in the main room. Men from the *sociedad* sometimes went out and danced with the *gente*, because the floor was better or perhaps to show off a little, but people from outside never came in, though they always clustered at the doors and windows to watch.

One night at one of these dual functions the authors danced on the floor with the *gente* and were received graciously and, by a few inebriates, exuberantly. Afterward we were advised against this by friends from both groups, because, they said, the people would lose respect for us. It was felt important that we should be accorded extraordinary respect on festive occasions. On many other less formal occasions, however, we were fortunately in an anomalous position, classless, as it were. As foreigners and as friendly observers, we could be invited to both upper- and lower-class functions without particularly disturbing the social order. The *oficial* and *popular* social dichotomy was so clear, however, that it was a valuable guide to us in determining the positions of individuals in the town hierarchy.

Attendance at *oficial* barbecues given to honor some visiting dignitary revealed again the same social lines that were drawn at the dances. The barbecues were, of course, always outdoors, so that it was possible for the *gente* to observe the function from a short distance. The crowd of observers never seemed to be an embarrassment to the *sociedad*, and normally no sign of recognition was ever made that outsiders were watching. Private dances or weddings at the homes of members of the *sociedad* also indicated that the personnel of the group remained unchanged. Sometimes smaller affairs are attended only by more intimate personal friends, but it is said that it is difficult to limit attendance without offending someone, as people are jealous of their membership in the upper social class. We can attest to this because we once held a dance at our home and failed to invite a particular upper-class family which had not been very friendly toward us. This was a bad mistake, we soon discovered, and it affected our relationship with them for the rest of our stay in Tobatí.

No one we spoke to was able to give us a coherent and consistent account of the criteria of class membership, beyond a vague sense that "education" was most important. It is apparent to an observer, however, that there are several attributes which obviously pertain more to the upper-class people than to the lower; therefore, we made an attempt to find out how the people of both classes felt about them. Responses varied, of course, and often no clear-cut feelings could be elicited. We found, in fact, that many of the following attributes associated with class membership are not consciously regarded as criteria at all, however striking the correlation might seem to the observer.

Wealth

All our informants admitted that the amount of wealth a family controls is in some way a determinant of social status, but people of all classes felt that this should not be so, that it would be vulgar as well as unwise to permit "money" to be the determinant. It was clear, however, that they meant *new* wealth; it was essentially business achievement which they deprecated. If wealth is an objective attribute of upper social status in Tobatí, it must be understood as relatively permanent wealth— family wealth. Merely to have possession of a certain amount of money at any given time does not necessarily assure an individual of any particular status; past wealth and, very importantly, the expectation of future wealth must go along with the present wealth.

Whether one is ever likely to be forced to resort to menial labor may possibly be the most important consideration of all. The people do not phrase the importance of wealth in just this way, but it is so obviously revealed in such a great number of circumstances that an observer cannot ignore it; one is accustomed to menial work or one is not, and an upper-class person never has been and never expects to be placed in circumstances where it is necessary.

Any family which can hire labor, as servants or as employees in some enterprise, immediately achieves a considerable amount of deference from the poorer townsmen. The peasantry, also, regard wealth as the real source of personal power and freedom —an attitude which is expressed most clearly in the *patrón-peón* pattern of behavior. In some circumstances the terms *patrón* and *peón* are used with the specific meanings of employer and wage-worker respectively, but they are also among the most common terms of social demarcation. A peasant normally will call any upper-class person *patrón*, and a peasant is referred to as a *peón* (though not in direct address). Usually any person who is poor and is from a poor family is a *peón* whether he has ever worked for wages or not, and any rich man is a *patrón*.

Wealth confers the power to do favors or harm to other individuals, of course, and this is an important reason why status is ascribed to a wealthy person; but it is probably also the reason why there is always a feeling that wealth *alone* should not be a sufficient determinant of high status. A person should somehow merit this power because of exceptional personal qualifications, such as education, intelligence, and good breeding: he should be a superior person. In some cases a purely political office may give some kinds of power over individuals, independently of possession of wealth. This is usually merely a temporary power, however, while family wealth confers power more permanently. People who are important enough politically are often admitted to society but can expect to be dropped as soon as their power wanes.

Symbols or badges of wealth and power are of two kinds: those which suggest or prove more permanent familial wealth and those which are merely signs of strength that may be merely temporary. Formal education and good manners are obviously the external concomitants of wealth of the more permanent kind, as the term "breeding" suggests, whereas such things as expensive clothes, houses, or furniture are not. In Tobatí it is the former which are significant, and symbols of the latter kind are of much less importance than they would be in a more impersonal urban milieu, where temporary economic advance is a much more common phenomenon.

Education

All informants felt that "education" was the most typical characteristic of the *sociedad*. This means formal education and also graciousness, and knowledge of formal etiquette—"fine" rather than "crude" behavior. In actual fact, very few members of the upper class have had more than a few years of primary-school education, and their manners are not always particularly "fine," though they respect both education and manners. In a few individual cases there are people below them in the social scale who have more education and better knowledge of etiquette but who, significantly, are not very powerful economically. Nevertheless, except for these few individuals, the *sociedad* is clearly set off from the mass of the *gente* in this matter. Also worthy of note is the fact that, although some of the most prominent members of the *sociedad* are rather crude, little-educated cattlemen, they are raising their children in a very genteel fashion and plan to send them to Asunción for higher education. They obviously hold their high rank mostly because of their wealth and feel just a little guilty about it.

It might be well to mention that respect for education and good manners does not mean that an effete man is esteemed, for Tobatí is, after all, a rather rough-and-ready country town, and the top of the *sociedad* consists of cattlemen. A man should be *macho* ("masculine") as well as educated. Our male author, being bespectacled and apparently extraordinarily educated (*un doctor*), found himself continually being put to various tests of manliness. A visitor is unobtrusively put in the position of having to demonstrate his qualities, much as a "tenderfoot" was tested in the old West in the United States. He is often given a chance to demonstrate his marksmanship and horsemanship. On most social occasions the men drink a considerable amount of liquor, and a newcomer is often tested for his ability to drink raw *caña*. It is important to be a "good fellow," a little drunk, spirited, and ribald, but one should be always friendly and never discourteous or vulgar in the presence of ladies.[2]

2. Education and social conduct are treated more intensively in chaps. xvi and xiv, respectively.

Town and Country

Town dwellers are, in general, considered a step above countrypeople in status, other characteristics being equal; they do, of course tend to be somewhat more sophisticated, and their children have better opportunities for education, than is the case with countrypeople. This does not mean that living in the country of itself necessarily lowers a person's status, for there is a scattering of farmers who once lived in town and who retain their earlier standing. In the remote agricultural hamlets there is a local group which feels above the rest of the peasants and above the town poor, as well. But usually a *campesino* is regarded as a lower order of humanity than the townsman. People from larger towns regard people from smaller towns as somewhat inferior, and again, in general, it is true that wealth, sophistication, and social grace decrease with the degree of rurality. The sharpest break occurs in the conception which inhabitants of Asunción have of the members of rural communities. Here is found the Latin-American city man's contempt and even fear of the rural people and, with it, mixed and contradictory, the attitude that the peasants are "cute," wonderful, and "pure Guaraní" and that the countryside is *muy tranquilo*.

Ownership of agricultural land is not an important factor in the social relationship of townsmen to peasants. A few upper-class families in town own agricultural land on which a few tenants and more squatters reside. The hacienda system in agriculture, with the attendant social values and the very high social status accorded the landowner, is not a striking feature in Tobatí life. Status distinctions between agriculturalists themselves do not include landownership as an important criterion. (See chap. iii, "Land Tenure.")

The most striking cultural differences between upper- and middle-class townsmen and the peasantry in general have to do with "education" and general modern sophistication. These differences are clearly enough delineated to be considered subcultural, for they are recognized by the people themselves and also are readily apparent to an observer. The peasants' speech, dress, and manners vary from those of the townsmen. The peas-

ants are largely illiterate; they speak Spanish poorly or not at
all; they are uninterested in and do not participate in politics
and are relatively ignorant of national and world affairs. Family
life and respect etiquette are more intense in the country, and
courtesy and hospitality are more important. Religious festivals
and religion include more informal *santo* worship and semi-
secular *juegos* ("games") than formal church worship, and
there is a great deal more supernaturalism in accounting for
natural phenomena and in the treatment of disease. These differences are all so clear that the peasant is socially uneasy in the
presence of townsmen. In fact, each of the above traits taken
individually can be considered a sign of low status, though, of
course, they form a complex.

Marriage

Sexual unions are of several common but distinct types which
carry varying degrees of status. A church marriage is the most
desirable, and a civil marriage is less so. Free unions or consensual
marriages are very common and have more or less status, depending on the degree of stability of the union. Some families of
this sort are very stable; the couples behave as though they had
been married in the church, and they have the expectation of
lifelong association. Some unions last several years and then break
up for one reason or another. Successive short-term monogamous unions are also common. The extreme end of this gamut
is promiscuity, but this is rare and is regarded with contempt.
True prostitution is not found in Tobatí.

The status associated with these different kinds of unions is
from highest to lowest, in the above order, and it should be
noted that this order is from the most permanent or stable forms
of union to the least permanent. Also of importance is the fact
that status pertains to *family* permanency and not to constancy
in sexual behavior, as such. A married man of highest status who
takes care of his family is not censured for extramarital sexual
exploits. Adultery or promiscuity on the part of a woman is
severely criticized because she is the focal point of the family.
Young unattached girls are not censured particularly for sexual
activity—it is assumed that they have appetites which they will

satisfy—but once the opportunity is at hand for a permanent union, they must not threaten it. A full-grown woman who is promiscuous, to the extent that nobody knows "who the fathers of the children are," is the most socially degraded person in town. In a society where *family* is considered so important but where sex morality is not puritanical, it is not surprising to find a double standard of behavior, for male promiscuity does not necessarily have an effect on the stability of the family itself.

Marriage in the church is rare outside the *sociedad*. The social obligations associated with the ceremony are so demanding that the expenses are far beyond the means of most people. Most of the present upper-class people have had church weddings, but several members of the upper class are themselves *naturales*, children of unmarried though respectable parents. Among the elite of the town there is a case which throws some light on the attitudes of the ultrarespectable. Many years ago a woman had married in a civil ceremony a man from whom she separated after bearing him four children. Later she lived in Tobatí in free union with the town's biggest merchant and had several more children. All the children were treated equally and were raised as if they were full brothers and sisters. The couple were greatly respected in the town and were valued members of the *alta sociedad*, but the woman never attended any public functions; the children were always accompanied by their father or by other relatives. She entertained visitors in her home, but she herself went out only informally to small gatherings at the homes of close friends or relatives. After many years, when the children were grown, she arranged a Mexican divorce from her first husband and married her *compañero* in the church, thus legitimatizing all the children. Although she herself had behaved as though her earlier free union was not entirely respectable, we could discover no sentiment among townspeople of any class that was not fully respectful toward her. Her circumspect behavior earned the admiration of the entire community.

The rare peasant who has been married even in only a civil ceremony is the object of considerable awe. It was a common experience for us to be riding through the countryside and have our *campesino* companions point out a house to us: "Fulano lives there—he's married." During our first few weeks of making acquaintances, our friends invariably took us first to the homes of married people and usually announced the fact to us as though it were the most important attribute the family possessed, or at least the one most likely to impress strangers.

Illegitimacy

Illegitimate birth is, like consensual marriage, of several different kinds. An illegitimate child who is *reconocido* ("recognized," i.e., bears his father's family name) and whose family forms a stable consensual union does not suffer any social stigma. Among the majority of the poor but respectable population, most of whom live in fairly stable free unions, the children bear the father's name and suffer no apparent loss of status as a result of illegitimacy. In fact, a recognized child of an upper-class father may himself be considered a member of the upper social class, particularly if he is given the appropriate education and training. Very often a man of good family may have one or more children by a lower-class woman before he is married. If he recognizes the child, financial provision is sometimes made to enable the mother to care for it, or the child may be raised in the household of one of the young man's relatives.

A child born of an adulterous union cannot bear his father's name, and he suffers both socially and financially. He has no legal right to share in his father's estate, as do his half-siblings of the father's marriage. Such persons are usually found on the fringes of society in cases in which the father was socially important and in which the legitimate descendants are currently important. The products of adultery are, in a sense, half in and half out of the upper class and are nearly always at an economic disadvantage. But it seems apparent that it is their lack of expectation in the inheritance which leaves them outside the pale, rather than the moral stigma of adulterous birth.

It is the unrecognized illegitimates, usually the offspring of the single women who form the bulk of the town poor, who suffer most. Here, again, it is difficult to determine how much of their low social status is due to the poverty-stricken economic circumstances of their lives and how much is social stigma attached to this kind of illegitimacy per se. Certainly an un-married mother who is hard-working and not promiscuous is regarded with considerably more respect than a slovenly, lazy, promiscuous woman the father of whose children is literally unknown. But the two factors are closely related in the sense that it is the very poorest women who have the fatherless children.

In the preceding pages we have indicated that the various kinds of upper-class illegitimates suffer losses in social status corresponding closely to their respective losses in the inheritance divisions. This is strikingly illustrated in the individual cases of the descendants of the original Rizzis. There is a large number of Rizzi illegitimates of various kinds, who represent, as well, a full gamut of all degrees of participation in the inheritance division. The correlation of status with property in these cases is virtually complete.[3]

We find a similar status-property correlation occurring with respect to differences between daughters' and sons' inheritances and in the affinal diffusion of status and property. Females of the upper class inherit property equally with males. As they marry and bear children, their own nuclear families tend to have the same status as the families of their brothers, higher than that of recognized illegitimate half-brothers. Status is diffused affinally to their husbands, just as the wives of the brothers may acquire a new status. But status is not passed on to the other in-laws to nearly the same extent. There are six clear cases of socially prominent inheritors (three male, three female) who married "beneath them," and in all cases the spouse was brought un-equivocally into "society," but the close relatives of the spouse were not, though obviously the in-law families gained in pres-tige within their own social circles.

Race

The somewhat apparent physical difference between the classes is very rarely phrased explicitly by the native Paraguayan and would appear to be unrecognized, until the observer has had time to sort out various minor hints that such a distinction is in

3. The subject of illegitimacy will be discussed more fully in chaps. x and xi.

actuality understood. In general, the peasants and the town poor are darker-skinned and look more "Indian" physiognomically than the upper classes; but this is only relative, and there are many exceptions to it. Occasionally one encounters a blond, blue-eyed peasant, and often a high government official or a member of an upper-class family is quite Indian in appearance.

In Paraguay it is most inappropriate to use the term "Indian" (*indio*) for any person of Guaraní heritage. As in Latin America generally, "Indian" refers more to a cultural condition than it does to physical appearance, except that in Paraguay the customary use of the Guaraní language is not in any way a sign of "Indianness." It is only the naked savages of the wilderness, who do not practice Paraguayan culture, who are "Indians." The tribal Guaraní who are considered the racial (and cultural) ancestors of the Paraguayans are not regarded as having been "Indians"; thus Paraguayans often refer to themselves as "Guaranís" without meaning that they have any "Indian" attributes.

Terms which are more completely a recognition of physical differences are *rubio* ("fair"), *blanco* ("white"), *moreno* ("brunet," "swarthy"), or *negro* ("dark"), and *cambá* (Guaraní synonym for Spanish *negro*). The Spanish word *cambujo* ("half-breed Indian"), which may be related to *cambá*, is not used, nor is "mestizo." *Negro* and *cambá* both have the dual usage so common in Latin America; they may be used as insults to a stranger and as terms of affection to a lover or to a member of the family. *Cambá* used abusively is normally modified by an adjective like "old" (*cambá tuyá*), and used affectionately, by a diminutive (*cambá-mi*), as Spanish *negro* usually turns into *negrito* in these contexts. *Indio*, on the other hand, is never used except as an insult, for it would attribute lack of culture, "wildness," to a person. Sometimes an old, ignorant peasant woman known as a *curandera* or as one who can prepare magic love potions may be spoken of as *muy india* ("very Indian").

A dark skin is not considered so beautiful as a light skin. In conversations describing a person, especially a woman or a baby, the term *morena* or *negra* is coupled with the notion of ugliness, while *rubia* or *blanca* is associated with beauty. In the upper class, and among the more sophisticated generally, standards of beauty are like those of Europeans. Blond hair, especially among women, is very highly regarded, and a blond child is greatly admired. We saw a blond boy of six or seven whose hair had never been cut. His locks had been pledged to the church to provide a blond wig for one of the images of the Virgin. He was extravagantly admired for his beauty, and no one, not even his playmates, seemed to regard him as a "sissy." Upper-class women try to stay out of the sun, so that their skins will stay as light as possible. It seems, however, that, while beauty may in some sense be regarded by the upper class as a more usual attribute of their own group, blondness and darkness as such, do not seem to be consciously recognized as class attributes, and certainly blondness is not a *requirement* for upper-class status.

Language

In many parts of Latin America customary use of a local Indian language in place of the national language is an important criterion of "Indian" status, which is usually the lowest social rank. But in Paraguay Guaraní is felt to be the true national language and may be spoken as a household tongue by members of any social group; it is not in any sense regarded as pertaining to any particular ethnic group or class within the nation. All true Paraguayans, of whatever status, may speak Guaraní most of the time.

Spanish is a language more or less artificially grafted onto Paraguayan life, but it is the official language; classes in the national school system are taught in Spanish, radio announcements are in Spanish, and most of the newspapers are in Spanish. Knowledge of Spanish is more rare than knowledge of Guaraní, and, in general, the more educated and sophisticated a person, the more likely he is to know Spanish. The members of the *sociedad*, therefore, speak Spanish more often and more fluently than the *gente*, and townsmen in general more than country-people. The more isolated peasants may know only a few words of Spanish. The ability to speak Spanish thus correlates rather directly with the other attributes of upper social status.

Inability to speak Spanish, however, is not admitted to be a mark of social inferiority. Any Paraguayan would angrily reject any suggestion that it is "better" to speak Spanish than to speak Guaraní; he would probably argue the opposite. Spanish is, of course, much more useful to a townsman, and one cannot be literate without it. Most people appreciate the financial and social advantages of a knowledge of Spanish and try to encourage their children to speak it and at the same time to retain their love for Guaraní. Spanish is slowly but surely on its way toward replacing Guaraní in normal speech, but Paraguayans fight hard to hold back the tide, for the Guaraní language is felt to be *theirs* in an intense, personal, emotional way.

Paraguayans who are fully bilingual say that they feel that Spanish is more formal, "cold," and business-like than Guaraní. Guaraní is a better language to use among friends and relatives; it is the language of love—"you can say sweeter things in Guaraní." There is a tendency (but not a rule), then, to regard Spanish as the language to be used in a formal situation, especially if a person desires to show respect to one above him in status. The use of Guaraní, on the other hand, would seem to suggest an intimacy which might be offensive. We noted this usage most usually in cases in which two passers-by casually greeted each other. Two people of equal status or two friends or relatives conventionally greet each other in Guaraní. But one who wishes to show respect to the other will greet him in Spanish.[4] The reply may be in Spanish if formality is desired or in Guaraní if friendliness is to be indicated.

The difference between Guaraní and Spanish may also enter into familial relations in bilingual families. The father and mother may address their children in Guaraní but require that the children reply in Spanish as evidence of respect.

4. Even those countrymen who cannot speak Spanish know at least the Spanish salutations and use them when etiquette requires.

CHAPTER X

Composition of the Household

IN BOTH town and country and in all classes of the society the individual household tends to be identical with the functional family unit. It is quite rare that persons other than mother, father, and children live under the same roof. In the country and among the poorer townsmen about the only deviation from this generalization occurs when a dependent relative is included. Among the wealthier townsmen, a related child from the country, semiadopted in order that he may attend school in town, may be considered as part of the household but not entirely of the family.

The household also tends to be a social and economic unit, recognizing and valuing the ties of kinship with other related households but having no particular regularized dependence upon them. In the rural areas the households are often scattered, the land is worked individually except for neighborly help in time of emergencies, and many of the families change their location often. In town there is very little interfamilial economic co-operation. The Rizzi co-operative enterprise, which includes affinal as well as blood relatives, is the only outstanding exception.

Sometimes families may acquire a kind of economic advantage through the aid of relatives, but even such "connections" as these seem quite infrequent. The only cases we know of in town are the following: two brothers share in slaughtering and meat-distributing opportunities, while one of their illegitimate relatives retails for them; two families were lent money to start enterprises by a more affluent in-law family; and a tanner took his young son-in-law into the business. It is, of course, very common for individuals to help relatives in sporadic, minor ways, such as patronizing a relative's store or giving work to a poor relative whenever possible. The reason for the infrequency of co-operative familial business enterprises is not that the inclination is not there but merely that there are so few enterprises big enough to involve more than one family.

The strong patriarchal extended family so often ascribed to Latin America is a very rare phenomenon in Paraguay; it really pertained only to the idealized rural gentry of colonial times, with its "big house."[1] The nuclear families in both town and country today mostly go their own economic courses. In town, status and wealth differences, economic competition, and political differences are further divisive factors, so that, even though the propinquity of related families is greater in town than in the country, there is no significantly greater association among them. When it is feasible for adult relatives to have close social and economic ties, these are usually reinforced by the ritual ties of *compadrazgo*, so that such cases can be better discussed in that context.

Types of Households

The complete household is felt to consist of a man and his wife and several children. If they are wealthy, they may have servants, but the servants live separately in an outbuilding or in their own rancho elsewhere in the town. Such an ideal household should, of course, be a stable one; the couple should be married, preferably, although it is understood that many perfectly respected couples live in lifelong harmony in a free union. In the rural areas actual marriage, even if only by a civil ceremony, is much more of a rarity than it is in the town; nevertheless, the unions themselves seem to be generally more stable.

It is regarded as a good thing for respectable town households to take in a child of a poorer country relative for schooling or even to take in informal adoption an illegitimate child of a poor relative. Girls seem to be favored, possibly because they are of more utility as servants in the home. An aged single relative

1. Gilberto Freyre, *Casa grande e senzala* (2 vols.; Rio de Janeiro, 1943).

might also be taken into the family, but it is not considered desirable for two families to live together or even for an adult unmarried girl with children to continue to live with her parents: "Children will fight, and then the mothers will fight"; a girl with children should have a place of her own.

The presence of aged relatives in several households seems to be less a disruptive factor than in North American communities. There is no "retirement age" in Tobatí; the aged keep active for as long as they are able. Thereafter, their children and other relatives take care of them, but there seems to be a tendency for the aged to prefer to live alone and not to make many demands on the young. But, even if the old parents cannot remain independent, they remain highly respected, which may be one of the reasons why there is so little of the querulousness and bitterness so often found among the aged in North America. There is some tendency for old people to feel that things were better in the "old days" and that the young are no longer so serious and hard-working as they should be, but this attitude is not particularly tendentious.

As might be expected, the aged in the agricultural zones are relatively more independent than in town, and potential sources of conflict with their children are fewer. Old men are not able to keep authority over their sons by control of the land, as the sons tend to carve out their own independent *chacras*, so one does not find the sort of extraordinary deference to the "old man" that one finds in southern Ireland, for example.[2] But, if the children are not dependent on the father for a share in the land, neither is the aged father likely to become dependent on the children, for the work involved in making a modest subsistence for himself is not particularly arduous, and any help required would be for only very short intervals.

In spite of the value placed on family life and the high regard held for separate residence and stability, a great many of the unions in town have been only temporary, and less than half the households include both a man and a woman. Of 301 households, only 133 are complete, and, of these, 101 are of couples

2. Conrad Arensberg, *The Irish Countryman* (London, 1937). See esp. chap. vi, "Boys and Men."

who are married or claim to be. One hundred and thirteen households with children are headed by women alone. The rest of the households are of variable, miscellaneous composition.[3] The household consisting of a lone woman with children is such a common feature of Tobatí town life that it must be discussed in as much detail as the complete family.

In the households headed by lone women, the children may or may not be recognized by the father, or some of them may

TABLE 4

COMPOSITION OF FAMILIES

	No. of Families	No. of Children
Complete families (man, woman, children):		
Complete families, man and woman married (church or civil marriage alone)	101	334
Complete families, man and woman unmarried	32	72
Total	133	406
Incomplete families:		
Mother alone with children	113	228
Woman alone	11	
Man alone with children	0	0
Man alone	11	
Married couples without children	18	
Unmarried couples without children	6	
Total	159	228
Single women over eighteen, without children, living with relatives	82	

be, but in any case the father seldom contributes to their support in any substantial way. Ordinarily the women must work outside the home at least part of the time and may also work in the home at cigar-making, ironing, weaving, sewing, and so forth. Since there are so many households of this type, the competition for such work is intense, wages are very low, and steady work is difficult to find. Despite these severe economic handicaps, the families seem remarkably well managed; the children are clean and well cared for and are sent regularly to school. There are, of course, some families who are in very bad straits,

3. See Table 4, "Composition of Families."

barely surviving, and the woman may turn to a series of temporary alliances with any man who will keep her at the moment.

The complete families, those 133 headed by males, include a total of 406 children. Other members of the households include only 17 grandchildren, 7 parents of one spouse or the other, 11 siblings of one of the conjugal pair, and 25 more remote relatives. Significantly, in only two cases did any of the appendages include the spouse of one of the sons or daughters of the family —the starting point, that is, of a true extended family. Other appendages of the complete families were 28 adopted or semi-adopted children, 8 servants, and 2 boarders.

Of the 113 female-headed households, 86 of the women were unmarried and 45 others were (or claimed to be) widowed, divorced, or separated.[4] Three of these women, who say that they are now married, list their "husbands" as members of the household but say that they are themselves the heads of the family. This could mean that the women earn the living and own the house and also that the male companion is more a visitor than a resident of the house. The 113 households (or 110, if the above three problematical ones are excluded) contain 228 children, which is about 1 child less per household than in the case of the complete households (2.07 children to 3.05). They also include 44 grandchildren (about two and one-half times the frequency of grandchildren found in the complete families), 2 siblings of the household head, 2 parents, 21 more remote relatives, and 9 lovers or spouses of a grown son or daughter (see Table 5). There are only 12 "adopted" children and 4 servants, but there are 6 boarders. This relatively small number of adopted children and servants and the greater number of boarders could be explained by the generally lower economic status of the incomplete households. The large number of grandchildren (44) is probably also to be explained by the fact that most incomplete households are of the lower economic class. Thus an illegitimate daughter of a lone woman is more likely

4. The discrepancy between this figure for formerly married females and the twelve males who so claim might be due to several factors: more women might *claim* to have had an earlier marriage because it has more status value to them; women outlive their husbands, especially because men are usually much older than their wives; more men emigrate than women.

to find herself dependent on her mother for help in housing her own illegitimate children.

It is not common for men or women to live completely alone; there are only twenty-two instances, eleven for each sex. Such individuals often actually have a sexual partner who is in a sort of visiting status rather than in a residence status. One such lone woman, on being asked if she had a *compañero*, laughingly replied: "De noche no mas" ("Only at night").

TABLE 5

COMPOSITION OF HOUSEHOLDS

	No. of Households	No. of Persons
Children under fifteen years of age........	230	647
Own children, nieces, nephews, grand-children.........................	212	587
Criados, boarders, or adopted children...	46	60
Other relatives in household...............	....	79
Aged parent:		
Household with male head...........	....	7
Household with female head........	....	2
Sister or brother:		
Household with male head...........	....	11
Household with female head........	....	2
Spouse (or lover) of a son or daughter:		
Household with male head...........	....	2
Household with female head........	....	9
More remote relatives:		
Household with male head...........	....	25
Household with female head........	....	21

In a complete family, the father is recognized as head of the household, at least nominally, but in practice it is the woman who is the most important in maintaining family stability, in encouraging close ties with relatives, and in managing the household. Women usually control the household finances and even bring in additional income. Men, on the other hand, are treated respectfully, sometimes almost like guests, but they seem to play a less important role in the internal life of the family. This is not true in all cases, of course; occasionally a strong family orientation will be found in a particular father, but the more usual case in town is the contrary. Men customarily spend a great deal of their leisure time outside the home in the company of other men and often may, in fact, provide very little or none of the family income. Men generally have little to do with the rearing of children, especially in the early years.[5] In external or public affairs, the father is the family representative. He makes all arrangements for important events, such as baptisms, weddings, or funerals, and negotiates major financial transactions, such as purchase of a house, although usually in accordance with his wife's plans or wishes.

When a woman is deserted by a man with whom she has been living in a free union, she ordinarily retains possession of the house and sometimes may be paid a small sum by the man to help raise the children. Most of the homes in town owned by single persons are owned by women who have children but who have never married or who have been deserted or widowed. Single men, on the other hand, generally do not try to maintain households, preferring to live with a woman companion or with a relative's family. Illegitimate children recognized by the father are sometimes adopted or taken in by relatives, but more commonly by a relative of the mother than by one of the father. The father's recognition of the children does not necessarily involve further obligations on his part. There is some class difference on this score; a man from a family of some financial means is more likely to provide benefits for his recognized illegitimate children (see Table 6).

Household types other than the kinds already discussed are rare. Only twenty-four couples live alone without children, and in the majority of these cases the couples are old and the children are living elsewhere. There are various other expedient household combinations, most of them temporary. There are a few cases of a brother and sister and her illegitimate children living together; a mother, two daughters, and their children; two sisters and their children; or two women friends and their children. This latter combination is more shifting and unstable than the others, inasmuch as relationship ties between the two adults are not present. In the extreme poverty in which they live, each is constantly looking for a better situation, and friction is inevitable.

5. Intrafamilial social relations are treated more fully in chap. xiv, "Some Aspects of Daily Life."

Adoption

Adoption is almost never legalized, and it is usually impossible for an observer to know whether the living arrangement is temporary or permanent. Many people are eager to place their children with a family which can give the children advantages. We hardly dared admire a child, even if it belonged to people we barely knew, because it might be offered to us forthwith. The arrangement is normally made by verbal agreement only and

TABLE 6

ILLEGITIMATE CHILDREN

	No. of Children
Acknowledged illegitimates:	
Recognized by father	198
Unrecognized	124
Information on recognition lacking	47
Total	369
Residence:	
Living with mother	249
Living with mother and own father	51
Living with father's family (i.e., with stepmother)	12
Living with grandparents	32
Living with older sibling, aunt, or uncle	15
Living with other than above relatives	10
Total	369

is subject to termination at the whim of the child, the parents, or the foster-parents.

The most common conditions for such adoption are for children of rural people to be taken in by town families and for illegitimate children of a young mother to be taken by a related family. In the former case the children do light household work and run errands and are commonly called *criados* for that reason. The latter case, which more typically involves illegitimates, is closer to true adoption and is a more permanent kind of arrangement. In cases in which a man of some means has illegitimate children by a lower-class woman, he may take one or more of the children into his own household after he marries.

The legal aspects of the rights of illegitimates and the questions involved in adoption are complex and seem not to be fully understood by the parents. The adjustment seems to be one of avoidance of legality. Of one hundred and thirty-nine children "adopted," only one was adopted legally. This informality and the impression of possible lack of permanence in the relations of the child to the household, however, do not seem to result in any apparent social disadvantage to the child under most conditions, even including cases where they must live with legitimate offspring of the foster-parents.

Illegitimate children recognized by the father often have certain advantages over the unrecognized ones, largely because this recognition is a sign that the father has agreed to help financially in some way within his means, and, if he is wealthy, the children may receive a small share in the inheritance. Unrecognized children are usually a product of youthful, rather promiscuous sex relations. Even if the father was known, he may have been so young and his relationship to the mother so ephemeral that he does not want the responsibility of fatherhood. The same woman may later set up a permanent household with another man and have children recognized by him, but her older children do not seem to suffer any social stigma in comparison with the others, nor do they apparently suffer in intrafamilial relations.

While an unrecognized child does not inherit from the father, even when the father is known, neither does the father himself have any rights over the child. If the child is the product of an adulterous union (i.e., if the father was already married to someone else), the man cannot recognize the child or claim him in any way, even if he wants to. Usually, of course, this is more disadvantageous to the mother and the child than to the man; consequently, adulterous unions would be quite rare unless the father were willing to make some informal financial provision for the mother and child. Most informants stated that the wealthier men have many more illegitimate and adulterous children than poor men and that the reason is that they are able to provide financial security for the woman and children. It is often claimed that certain of the older wealthy townsmen have as many as thirty unrecognized offspring. The son of one of these men recalled that his father had fifteen such children, which would indicate that there is at least some basis for the rumors. Fortunately, children are highly desired; hence the care of the numerous illegitimates is not so serious a problem as it may sound. Some relative of the mother or of the father, or even an unrelated person, is almost always pleased to "adopt" and give loving care to any child for whom financial provision is lacking.

Marriage

Marriage unions are of the three usual Latin-American types: consensual marriages, or "free unions," civil marriages, and church marriages. The free unions are by far the most common type. Church weddings are the most rare and also the most desirable and must be preceded by a civil ceremony. Some people in town are united by civil ceremony alone. It is said that civil marriages are increasing to some extent in the town because women are more aware nowadays of the advantages of legal protection, but the civil ceremony alone does not guarantee added social status.

People claim that church weddings are infrequent because of the expense, especially that incurred in the fiesta. This is regarded as an obligatory celebration and is always as large and pretentious as the two families can possibly afford. Civil and consensual marriages do not require a fiesta, but some small festivity for the family occasionally takes place. The cost of a civil ceremony is 20 guaranis, plus 5 guaranis for the health certificate which is apparently automatically issued on payment of the fee. If a church wedding is also planned, the priest is consulted about a date. A wedding at night usually costs 12 guaranis and a marriage in the morning as little as 5 guaranis. It is considered "more decent" to get married at night, and most marriages take place as late in the day as is feasible financially. Every few years the bishop visits the country areas on his *gira pastoral* and performs marriages and baptisms free of charge. After such mass weddings no fiesta is considered necessary, but these weddings normally legalize free unions of couples who already have children.[6]

6. In 1938, between March 6 and 13, there were forty-six of these marriages, and thirty-four of them legitimatized 117 children. The average number of children per couple was 3.4.

It is difficult to evaluate the data on the ages at marriage. The youngest people often live in free unions, the beginnings of which are not marked by any formality, and many civil marriages are of couples who have been living together for several years. In 1948, of 36 civil marriages, the average age of the females was slightly under 25 years and that of males 31.5 years. Ten females were under 20 years of age, while only one male was under 20. Fourteen men but only nine women were over 30.[7] Even allowing for some falsification of age by the women,

TABLE 7

AGE DIFFERENCES BETWEEN COUPLES
(In Free Unions and Marriages)

Age Difference (Years)	Man Older (No. of Cases)	Woman Older (No. of Cases)	Age Difference (Years)	Man Older (No. of Cases)	Woman Older (No. of Cases)
0	9	9	13	2	
1	8	5	14	1	1
2	9	5	15	1	
3	13	4	16	2	
4	6	2	17	1	
5	9	1	18	2	
6	7	1	19	3	
7	6		20	1	
8	7		21	3	
9	6		22	2	
10	10		23	1	
11	7		Over 25	5	
12	7	1			

their age at marriage was substantially lower than that of men; on the average, the male was 6.8 years older than his marriage partner. In only five cases was the woman older than the man she married. The figures are altered somewhat when consensual unions are included (see Table 7). Of census data that we gathered on 148 cases of unions of all kinds, women were older than men in 20 cases, and, of the 128 cases where the men were older than the women, the average discrepancy was 8.3 years. In general, it can be said that, although some women do

7. Five women were between 30 and 40, two were 40, one was 45, and one was 50. Of the males, nine were between 30 and 40, two were between 40 and 50, one was 54, one was 65, and one was 84.

marry after the age of twenty-five, the chances of marriage after that age have so diminished that she is usually regarded as a spinster. But there seems to be no limit to the time when a man can marry, and many men express a preference for marrying after thirty. A boy under twenty-five is not considered capable of supporting a family unless his parents can help him for a few years.

It is a stated value in the case of legal or church marriages that the bride be a virgin at marriage, but informants could think of no example of a man leaving the bride, or even of complaining, because his new wife was not a virgin. After marriage both partners are supposed to be faithful, but actually infidelity is common among men. It is believed that a man is very likely to desert his wife and that the woman must tolerate any behavior on his part in order to preserve the marriage; but there is evidence, too, that women are not always as submissive as the ideal.

In free unions the virginity of either partner is not a matter of concern and is not expected. A common type of alliance, which may endure for many years, is one in which the man goes to the woman's house to sleep and spends the rest of his time at his own place or with his relatives. In these cases the man is more free than the woman. She must be faithful to him or risk the criticism of the community for her loose morals, but she is also quite capable of casting the man aside if he is not reasonably faithful to her.

It seems clear that the ceremony of either church or legal marriage does not necessarily contribute to the stability of the union. Legal problems may arise in case of separations or divorces, but the marriage is not held together by the formal bonds. The great value placed on the home is the main influence toward marital stability, and this applies in cases of consensual as well as legal or church unions, so that the actual ceremony is only a form. Only in the upper classes do legal and social considerations prevent separations; in such cases, if the man wishes, he may maintain separate establishments for other women. It was the opinion of the priest that the family was no less stable now than ever. Wars, revolutions, and economic instability have always contributed somewhat to insecurity of the home; the Chaco war and the recent political unrest were no more disruptive, in his opinion, than previous disturbances had been.

Separations are frequent but take place mainly among those who live in free unions. Legal divorces, on the other hand, are rare; most separations, even of married people, are by common consent, and, since there is little or no censure of subsequent free unions, legal relationships are relatively unimportant unless inheritance problems are involved. When divorces do occur, they do not seem to carry any particular stigma, in spite of the fact that the population is entirely Catholic.

A legal divorce may be secured by either husband or wife, after either a civil marriage or a church marriage. A second marriage of a divorced person whose previous marriage had been civil may be performed in the church. A second marriage of one whose first marriage was a church ceremony, however, may be a civil ceremony only, and it must be performed outside of Paraguay. Most individuals who want such a ceremony go to Argentina. Divorces involve legal advice and court costs, and the expense is prohibitive to all except the well-to-do.

CHAPTER XI

The Extension of Kinship

THE nucleation and separation of related households and geo-graphic mobility tend to reduce the importance of extended kin ties to a quite unexpected degree. Kinship ties are felt to be of great importance; in terms of ideal behavior kinship obliga-tions are to be regarded as next to sacred, but in actual practice they are frequently less functional than those of *compadrazgo*.

Recognition of genetic relationship is extended horizontally more than vertically, which is to say that sociological factors are actually the important consideration rather than genetic descent itself. In spite of the considerable confusion in genea-logical lines resulting from the numerous cases of successive consensual unions, adulterous children, or illegitimate children born prior to marriage, a study of the genealogies collected re-veals that wide recognition of relatives is extended only one generation above and below the individual. This is generally true even in cases where only one side of the family (usually the maternal side) is known, and the only exception is in those cases where vertical descent lines assume importance in connection with inheritable wealth. Even in the latter case, descent lines are traced back only so far as necessary to show relationship in a direct line to the wealthy ancestor. Thus, in eleven genealogies collected, four of the informants could name no grandparents, three could name the maternal grandmother, and one could name both the maternal grandparents but not the paternal grand-parents. Three were able to name all four grandparents, but only one of these could name a great-grandparent, this one on the paternal side. In two of the cases where all the grandparents were known, an inheritance was involved. Only six of the eleven

PLATE I

The Church Plaza in Tobatí

PLATE II

A Typical Rancho

A Typical Main Street in Paraguay

PLATE III

The Town's Wells

Typical Colonial Architecture of Paraguay

PLATE IV

A Cemetery

PLATE V

A Homemade "Santo"

PLATE VI

The "Toro Candil"

Procession of "Santos"

PLATE VII

Plantation Laborers

Potters

PLATE VIII

Carpenter

A Respected "Mayordomo" of the Church

PLATE IX

Laundresses

Manioc-grinder

PLATE X

Sawyers

Preparation for Maize-planting

PLATE XI

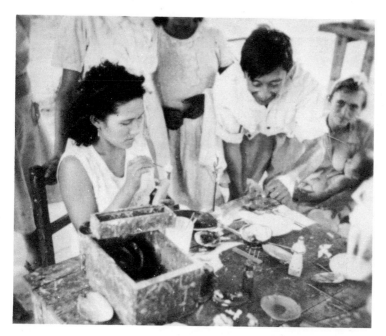

A Family of Professional "Santo" Manufacturers

Baking "Chipa"

PLATE XII

Hauling Timber

informants could name a great-aunt or a great-uncle. Six of the informants knew relatives of both their father and their mother. The other five did not know any relatives on the paternal side—two because the father was unknown or foreign, two because the father had no siblings or cousins, and the fifth because the father was a single man who had many children, none of them recognized, to whom he paid practically no attention.

Informants could readily name their aunts and uncles; sometimes their parents' first cousins; their own first cousins; often their own second cousins; and, of course, their own siblings and usually their half-siblings. Children of full siblings, half-siblings, and first and second cousins are called "nieces" and "nephews." When naming nieces and nephews, particularly if they were small children, there was little assurance about the name, or even the sex, of the child. In fact, in speaking of a relative's children, an informant will often say, "He has four or five, all small." Children are dearly loved and cared for, but the general feeling about them seems to be that they have no significance—that they are mere *criaturas*—until they are near puberty.

There are three major factors which influence the nature of the social relations of kindred: inheritance of property, marriage customs, and social propinquity. It has already been mentioned that a potential inheritance tends to increase the importance of the vertical descent line. For example, the parents of Guillermo Rizzi were first cousins, children of Italian brothers who took Paraguayan women into concubinage. The only recognized offspring of the brothers, one son and two daughters, inherited their estates, which were largely in land. The legitimate descendants of these three heirs have retained the bulk of the family fortune in their hands, although a number of illegitimate and adulterous descendants in the direct line have received small settlements from the estate or informal gifts from the legitimate heirs. Although any of the recognized illegitimate heirs are able to trace their relationship to the original sources of the fortune, the legitimate heirs tend to exclude them from genealogical consideration in a way which is not done where an inheritance and social standing are not involved. Thus a closed system, including only legitimate direct descendants, is in the process of formation.

Those who are not a part of the inheritance line are not denied a place as relatives through shame of their illegitimacy. On the contrary, they are freely recognized as kin, and kinship obligations to them are observed by the legitimate heirs. Two of the brothers have taken into their households adulterous children of their father. One brother has in his home his own illegitimate unrecognized daughter; she is being raised as a *criada*. An illegitimate son of Guillermo is being raised by Guillermo's aunt. Even though these children may be well treated, they can never anticipate a share in the family fortune, and their children will be further separated from the members of the inheritance line and perhaps not even recognized as relatives by them.

The second important function of genealogical reckoning is related to marriage customs. Recognition on a horizontal level is most significant for exogamy and must include in the system even socially distant half-siblings and their descendants, except in cases, like the above, where the status position of the wealthy acts automatically as a bar to marriage with illegitimate relatives. The family of Felipe Saenz demonstrates the difficulties in horizontal recognition which may result from successive free unions of both parents. Felipe is a young single man, though he is the father of four children by two consensual unions, and he must recognize exogamous relationships to a large group of agemates, including five half-siblings by five successive unions of his father and three half-siblings by two unions of his mother. He can name both parents of his half-siblings, even if the latter were not recognized by their fathers. His own siblings and the half-siblings who were raised with him in his mother's house are the most important socially; his full cousins and other full kin are more important than his half-siblings by his father, all of whom were raised by their mothers. Only in cases in which the father is literally unknown, as in the instances of true promiscuity, or in cases in which the father is from a distant location or is a foreigner is the father's side of the family completely lost. José Melgarejo, whose father was a foreigner, named two uncles and two aunts on his mother's side, thirteen first cousins, one sibling, fourteen children of his own (five of them natural), thirty-five grandchildren, nine nieces and nephews, and nineteen grandnieces and grandnephews. He also knew of fifty children of his first cousins (called "nieces" and "nephews"), though he could not name them all. Moisés Prado, son of an unknown man from another part of Paraguay, counted as relatives, all on his mother's side, three uncles, four aunts, four half-siblings and seventeen of their children, and two grandchildren of one half-sibling. His own eight children, nineteen grandchildren, ten first cousins, and sixty-two children of cousins (of whom he could actually name all but twenty-one), and many small children of theirs, make a total of more than one hundred and twenty-nine relatives, an impressive number in a family one-half of which is completely lost.

Marriages of first cousins are more frequent in the upper class than in the lower, possibly because the choice of mates of equal social position is more restricted and also sometimes in order to keep estates from being dispersed. Among the peasants first cousins occasionally marry, but there is a feeling that it is somehow wrong to do so. Such people are said to be *como lagartos* ("like lizards"—which supposedly eat their own tails). Several peasants told us that the marriage of first cousins was not possible; on further questioning, they finally admitted that it was possible with the permission of the priest but that it was not right. Actually, marriage within any degree of known relationship is supposed to require a dispensation from the church, and a special fee is paid which is greater the closer the relationship.

A type of marriage between "relatives" often mentioned by informants is that between a widower and a sister of his deceased wife (the sororate). It is regarded as eminently proper and is believed to be common though not obligatory. We could discover only four cases of its actual occurrence, however, in the combined knowledge of the informants. Feelings about the corresponding levirate—a widow's marrying her dead husband's brother—were not clear cut, although such a marriage would not be censured. We have no statistics on either of these types of marriage; however, the impression gained from questioning is that both levirate and sororate marriages occasionally happen but that the latter is more clearly sanctioned.

The third important factor which affects the relations of kin is social circumstances. This is well illustrated by the family of Elena Hernández, whose knowledge of and association with relatives on her mother's side completely overshadow her father's side. She can name her half-siblings, the children of her father, but she has no interest in them or in their children. She was raised by her mother, in close association with her mother's relatives, and it is they who constitute her family in a functional sense. Her own sisters and brothers and their children, her aunt on her mother's side and her first cousins by that aunt, are close to her. Members of her father's family are acknowledged as relatives but are verbally rejected as of no consequence. If they did not live near by in the same town, they would in time be forgotten. In another case, that of Epifanio Gamarra, seven siblings and nine half-siblings on his father's side by four different mothers were all recognized and raised in close association. His father took an interest in all of them, and Epifanio can count his relatives on both sides as equally close.

The social relationship of relatives to one another always varies greatly with circumstances of location and living arrangements. The successive families of the father of Felipe Saenz (described above) are completely separated households. In the Rizzi family all but four of the household groups are associated in a large enterprise. In the case of Elena Hernández a line of almost pure matriarchal type, composed of single women and their offspring, has maintained its members in close association, although in separate households, for three generations. The ideal pattern is seldom carried out. This would involve the obligation of parents to provide food, clothing, and schooling for their children; in turn, children should respect their parents and help them in later years. Aunts, uncles, and cousins should help in crises and extend shelter and hospitality at all times. Brothers and sisters should be especially close and should help each other throughout their lifetimes. In reality, this pattern is modified by circumstances of proximity, by desertion of the family by the male parent, and by "adoption" of children. Half-brothers and

-sisters may be very close if they have been raised in the same household but may be nearly strangers if they have not. In-law relatives may be very close or not important at all, depending on economic circumstances and political or social class differences. Illegitimate kin are recognized without shame in all classes and may be as close as legitimate kin if they are raised together and if an inheritance is not involved.

In general, the terminology and respect attitudes of kinship, like the real need for mutual assistance, are more important among the poor; but the actual tracing of descent may be more important economically and socially in the upper classes. Members of the upper social group can usually trace their genealogies much more completely than can other people because of the greater frequency of stable marriages, the less frequent moving of families, and the much greater amount of property to be inherited in family lines. The ability to trace more relatives genealogically, however, does not mean that the social ties between those related individuals are commensurately stronger. There are certain disruptive factors which pertain more to the upper class than to the lower. The individual nuclear families, being stronger economically, need not depend so much on one another for aid. There are cases of closely related upper-class families who do not associate because of jealousies over inheritance divisions. Sometimes related families may even be in business competition with each other. Added to all this, of course, is the fact that in a town upper class, and even more so in an urban milieu, individuals are not so dependent on family and close relatives for general social life as they are in more isolated rural areas.

Relations between families whose children have married are so variable that it is impossible to generalize. They are supposed to be close; in the ideal situation the two families would actually have planned the match with a view to cementing a working alliance between them. The modern trend to extreme neolocalism and nucleation of individual conjugal pairs, however, has made this a relatively unlikely result of marriage. Economic factors are more of a determinant of marriage in town than they are in the country and, naturally, are more significant among the wealthy than among the poor. A rural couple would feel that they should be aided by either family and should aid them in return and that their two parental families should be friendly because of the marriage; but, in the words of one of our peasant friends, "people move around too much. Out in the *compañías* the people do not live close enough to each other, and they move and you lose track of your relatives. You don't know if they are sick or hungry or what, and they have to depend on whoever their neighbors are instead of their children or relatives."

In-law kinship terms are not used between two families unless at least a civil ceremony unites the couple. Since the majority of couples live in free unions, the degree of social relations between "in-laws" is limited. A free union does not carry the expectation of permanency, so that in-law relatives may be, in effect, "here today and gone tomorrow." The great numbers of unrecognized illegitimates are naturally limited to a recognition of only half the possible number of kindred, those on the mother's side only. Even a recognized illegitimate may be restricted in association to only his maternal kin.

Kinship Terms

Kinship terms in use by people who normally speak Guaraní instead of Spanish actually conform to general Spanish categories. For some relationships there was no original Guaraní term, or the term has been lost, and the Spanish term is used even by persons who cannot converse in Spanish. The words for aunt, uncle, cousin, nephew and niece, grandson and granddaughter, relatives, father-in-law and mother-in-law, are always Spanish and in common use by otherwise non-Spanish speakers. Most people now use Spanish terms for all categories most of the time.

The following list includes Guaraní terms in parentheses (*she* means "my" in Guaraní and is commonly prefixed to the kin term in address):

FATHER: *Padre, papá* (*she-ru, taitá*). *Papá* and *taitá* are affectionate and are commonly used in direct address.
MOTHER: *Madre, mamá, mamita* (*she-sý*).

UNCLE, AUNT: *Tío, tía* (*she-tió, tiá;* note that the final letter is accented). In usage no distinction is made between cross- and parallel aunts and uncles, and the father's and mother's side are equivalent. Sometimes a cousin of the father or mother is addressed by these terms if the cousin is socially close.

GRANDFATHER, GRANDMOTHER: *Abuelo, abuela* (*taitá guazú, she-sý guazú—* "my big father, my big mother"). Great-grandparents normally are addressed the same as grandparents in both languages. Brothers and sisters of grandparents are called *tío* and *tía* ("uncle," "aunt") in address.

BROTHER, SISTER: *Hermano, hermana* (*she-ryk'ý*, "older brother"; *she-ryvý*, "younger brother"; *she-ryké*, "older sister"; *she-kypy'ý*, "younger sister").

SON, DAUGHTER: *Hijo, hija* (*she-ra'y, she-ray'ý*).

GRANDSON, GRANDDAUGHTER: *Nieto, nieta* (absent in Guaraní).

FIRST COUSIN: *Primo hermano* (male); *prima hermana* (female) (*she-primo;* sex distinction absent). This term is used for *first* cousins only.

SECOND AND THIRD COUSINS, ETC.: *Primo, prima* (in Guaraní usage, simply "relatives": *pariente* or *she-gente*. If one of these relatives is socially as close as a first cousin, he may be called *primo* in address; if less close but recognized as relatives, such cousins would be referred to as "my relatives" or "my folks").

NEPHEW, NIECE: *Sobrino, sobrina* (*she-sobrino;* sex distinction absent). A nephew's child is called *sobrino* by ego, and ego is called *tío* in return. A child of a first cousin also is called *sobrino* and ego called *tío.*

BROTHER-IN-LAW, SISTER-IN-LAW: *Cuñado, cuñada* (*tobayá;* sex distinction absent). *Tobayá* can be used only in direct address, but *cuñado* is a term of reference as well. In-law terms are not used unless the couple have been formally married, at least in a civil ceremony.

FATHER-IN-LAW, MOTHER-IN-LAW: *Suegro, suegra* (*she-suegro;* sex distinction absent).

SON-IN-LAW, DAUGHTER-IN-LAW: *Yerno, yerna* (*she-yerno;* sex distinction absent).

RELATIVE: *Pariente* (*pariente* or *she-gente*). This term is used only in reference and applies to any person recognized as a relative when the degree of relationship is unknown, uncertain, or distant.

Family Names

The inheritance of surnames follows Spanish custom, but with this important difference of degree: whereas, in Spanish formal usage, a person's name includes his baptismal name and both his father's and mother's patrilineal family names in that order, in Tobatí the mother's family name is almost never used, even on civil documents. The only exception is that of unrecognized illegitimates, who use the mother's family name. Our door-to-door census, for example, reveals that only eleven persons gave us dual family names, out of the 1,368 persons listed. Often an older married woman signs documents with only her husband's surname, leaving out her own, as "María de Núñez" instead of "María Pérez Rodríguez de Núñez" or even "María Pérez de Núñez."

In normal social usage, the people are (it seems to us) surprisingly unconscious of surnames, especially among the *gente* as distinguished from the *sociedad*. This was very noticeable from the beginning of our residence in Tobatí. Someone would attempt to give us directions by saying "next to Panchita's house." But which Panchita? There are several in town. The answer usually was, "Panchita the laundress" or "the fat one." If we asked for Panchita's family name, the informant was usually nonplused. In gathering census data, we found that people often could not remember the family names of their immediate neighbors. And in the upper social levels, where recognition of surnames is more common, we found that people rarely knew the family names of their servants. Most surprising of all, perhaps, was the difficulty people had in recalling surnames even of their *compadres*, who are, of course, supposed to be very close and valued friends. We encountered this especially when we were gathering data on ritual kinship; an informant might consult with several other people to recall the surnames of even half of perhaps ten or twelve *compadres*.

There are two obvious factors in Tobatí life which account for this, at least in part. First of all, Tobatí is a small rural town where face-to-face relations dominate social life. As in European peasant villages (and probably in all of medieval Europe), Christian names are in use nearly all the time, and, if respect is to be shown, a title is added: "Sir Harry"; "Don Juán." The use of surnames was originally imposed in Europe by civil and religious authority as the keeping of records on tax collections, marriages, and inheritance divisions became important for the purposes of the state. Personal identification in an impersonal context pertained more then, as today, to urban than to rural life. In Tobatí people call one another by Christian names (often with a diminutive), or by nicknames if they are well acquainted; if respect is to be shown, the title is *don* or *ña* (*doña*, the full form, is almost never used). *Patrón*, *señor*, and *señora* are used in address but not often in conjunction with a surname.

Another reason for the ignorance of surnames is the lack of family stability. Many people are unrecognized illegitimates, bearing only the mother's family name. Many families include an unmarried father and mother with children of their own, and other children of the mother, some of whom may be recognized by their father and others not. Such a case would mean that three family names would be found among the children. There are several examples, in fact, of four surnames represented among a group of children occupying a common residence. This means that there are fewer of the usual short cuts by which a person may know another person's surname; knowing his brother's name or his mother's or father's, or what house he lives in, is often no help at all. This proliferation of surnames also has the effect of subdividing and dispersing a family line, and it becomes difficult to trace relatives for this reason. Because of these genealogical complexities, surnames do not function alone as a sign, or even as a suggestion, of actual relationship.

A proliferation of some family lines and a dying-out of others is a continual process in any community. Therefore, a stable ingrown community will have, through time, fewer and fewer family names, each representing a greater number of households. The town of Tobatí, on the other hand, has a surprising number of family names for the size of the town. Excluding the few foreign-born residents, we find that there are 98 family names for 290 households, which represent 1,350 people. This is a striking number of family names compared with what might be expected for an old rural town. Moche, a much larger town in Peru, had only 44 family names for a "true Mochero" population of 3,273.[1] In Tobatí the most frequent name ("Núñez") occurs in seventeen households, but only four other names occur in ten or more. Forty-three names each pertain distinctively to only a single household (see Appendix II).

Only one surname, "Arepocó," is possibly of Guaraní origin. There is no apparent way of distinguishing the "more Guaraní" families from the upper social group by means of their surnames or by their choice of Christian names.

1. John Gillin, *Moche: A Peruvian Coastal Community* ("Publications of the Smithsonian Institution, Institute of Social Anthropology," No. 3 [Washington, D.C., 1945]), pp. 5, 102–3.

CHAPTER XII

Ritual Kinship

As IN other parts of Latin America, bonds of ritual kinship arising from *padrinazgo*, the godparent relationship, are important means of extending the range of social kinship and of intensifying bonds between relatives; in short, they provide a sort of kin-oriented social security for both children and adults. The parents select a godfather and a godmother (*padrino* and *madrina*) for a child's ritual ceremony, such as baptism, and these *padrinos* are thereafter obligated to care for the child as substitute parents in time of need. The ties between the godparents and the real parents also become highly formalized. In fact, the coparenthood (*compadrazgo*) aspect of the relationship is probably more important than the ties between the child (the *ahijado*) and the *padrinos*, for *compadres* must ever after aid each other in all things and treat each other very respectfully. They are so "close" that they may not marry or have sexual relations with each other; such relations would be incestuous. Should one of the *compadres* insult or fail the other, he would be severely condemned by the community.

In Paraguay confirmation and marriage are the only other occasions besides baptism which involve the selection of godparents.[1] The *padrinos* of confirmation, however, are of little importance. They are called *padrinos* by the child and *compadres* by the child's parents but are not regarded as of the same closeness as *compadres* of baptism. For a marriage ceremony

1. Sometimes rich people may be honored for their contribution to a project, such as the building of a chapel, by being named *padrinos* of the project at a dedication ceremony. Despite the use of the term *padrino*, however, a relationship between individuals is not created.

the bride or the bride's parents choose a *madrina*, and the groom or groom's parents choose a *padrino*. Their function at the ceremony is similar to that of maid of honor and best man. Afterward, they are supposed to act as mediators in case of quarrels between the married couple, but such intervention is not common, and usually they have no formal obligations beyond their duties in connection with the marriage ceremony itself.[2]

The choice of *padrinos* of confirmation is a matter of importance only in that it honors the person so selected or permits him to honor the parents who select him, if they are of lower status. It does bring another individual into the relationship of friendship and respect, but not very closely and often temporarily. We found that many people did not recall the names of children for whom they had acted as sponsors for confirmation; some parents did not recall who had served as sponsors for their children; most often the *padrino* or *madrina* of confirmation was remembered only by the child itself.

In choosing *padrinos* of marriage, the bride and groom often select personal friends with whom they welcome a closer, more formalized bond. Sometimes these may be individuals who will later serve as *padrinos* of their children. In other cases, good friends of the parents of the bride or groom may be selected, thus providing an older, more established set of godparents to the young married couple. The direct obligation of the godparents, as witnesses to the marriage and as providers of a wedding gift (which, in any event, they would have given as friends of the young couple or their families), is not so important as the fact that they are brought into a system of warm, confidential and generally helpful relationships, so that the young couple may turn to them for advice given without self-interest. But the truly enduring and important ties are those between *padrino* and *ahijado* of baptism and between *compadres* so contracted. The greatest care is given to selection of these godparents, and many considerations are involved.

2. The *compadre* system in Paraguay is not nearly so extensive as in Moche, Peru, where fourteen kinds of ritual occasions involving selection of *padrinos* are listed in a single community. (See John Gillin, *Moche: A Peruvian Coastal Community* ["Publications of the Smithsonian Institution, Institute of Social Anthropology," No. 3 (Washington, D.C., 1945)], p. 103).

There is considerable variation in the function of the *compadre* system between rural and urban areas and between class groups.[3] In the cities and among the upper classes, the relationship is primarily an observation of Catholic ritual. The *padrino* and *madrina* of baptism assume responsibility for the cost of the baptismal ceremony and give gifts to the godchildren at the time of baptism and on occasions such as birthdays and confirmation. They assume a nominal obligation to care for the child should the parents die, but ordinarily in families of some means the necessity does not arise. Even if the godparents took the child to raise, the financial means would be provided by inheritance. The *padrinos* of confirmation among upper-class groups have no duty beyond attendance at the ceremony. City children are instructed in the catechism in classes, and an exceptionally interested godparent of confirmation might assist the child in his studies before confirmation and would give him a gift at the time of the ceremony; but the relationship is ordinarily transitory and of little significance. Among urban, upper-class groups, the relationship of the *padrinos* of marriage is entirely a social one.

Among rural and lower-class groups, on the other hand, godparenthood is much more functional economically. The *padrinos* of baptism are expected literally to assume responsibility for the child in case of the death of the parents, and, if they cannot themselves raise and educate the child, they must try to find someone who can. They are expected to give gifts to the child on special occasions and, if they are able, to give some assistance in providing clothing, pencils, notebooks, and so forth, when the child reaches school age. Their obligation to the parents of the child, their *compadres*, is one of mutual aid and respect. They must provide assistance at times of illness and death, lend help at times when fiestas are given, and give favors any time they are requested.

Many families do not feel able to assume the financial burden involved in being *padrinos*. They have large families of their

3. For an excellent discussion of the differing functions of *compadrazgo* as it adapts to varying economic circumstances see Sidney W. Mintz and Eric R. Wolf, "An Analysis of Ritual Co-parenthood (Compadrazgo)," *Southwestern Journal of Anthropology*, VI, No. 4 (1950), 341–68.

own and cannot provide even the small gifts required, nor can they contemplate the possibility of adding orphaned offspring of their *compadres* to their own families. Therefore, it is fairly common for a *padrino* to be chosen from within one's own family, a sibling or a close cousin often being asked to fill this role. The same godparents may be asked to serve for successive children. Such choices intensify family relationships or strengthen the ties between already established ritual kin. Another alternative, among the poorer groups, is to request a man of some means, perhaps a *patrón*, to be a *padrino*. Thus, while the pattern of ritual relationship may be used to strengthen already existing blood or ritual kin ties, it is also used to cut across class lines, and in both cases for reasons of poverty.

Less frequently, a distant relative or a *patrón* from a city, who is considered to have money or power which would be advantageous to the child or to the parents, is chosen. Even less often are *compadres* sought among visitors or foreigners, because the obligations could not be maintained properly by a nonresident. When a foreigner does act as a baptismal sponsor, he is expected to provide a high baptismal mass, which gives prestige to the *ahijado*. In addition, he may be expected to make a handsome gift to the parents. But most rural Paraguayans do not have contact with such individuals; hence, this is not a relationship of great importance.

We were once honored by a request to serve as baptismal godparents, but, as we did not know the child's parents very well, we consulted the priest. After some consideration, he decided that we should not accept, on the grounds that we were not members of the Catholic church. We discovered later that he had used the technicality to keep us from being exploited by persons who had hoped to get large gifts of money from us. It would have been difficult for us, in truth, had he not made this decision, for we very likely would not have had the courage to refuse an invitation which is normally considered the greatest honor one person can offer another.

In daily life in the small towns and in the rural areas the ties of ritual kinship are of constant social as well as economic significance. A child visits his godparents as frequently as possible. At Easter the child takes a token gift to the godparent, and the *padrino* is expected to reciprocate on a larger scale. Sometimes the godparent provides a fiesta meal for the child and for his family. A child calls his godparents *padrino* and *madrina* and addresses them with respect. When he greets them, he should always first ask their blessing and wait respectfully until it is given. Since there is no formal grammar of address in Guaraní, the Spanish-speaking residents in the backward areas customarily use the *tu* form among themselves; hence there is no overt linguistic evidence of the respect relationship as there is in other countries where the *usted* form must be used. Well-brought-up children in the urban upper and middle classes address their godparents with the *usted* form, though their godparents speak to them in the familiar form or in Guaraní. In the latter case the child should respond in formal Spanish, as a sign of respect.

Between the parents of the child and the godparents, the *compadres*, the term of address is *compadre* (*comadre*), which connotes great respect and confidence. The bond is not broken by the death of the child or even by a quarrel between the *compadres*. In general, the godparent of one's children is expected to help out in any possible way in any family crisis or at any great fiesta, such as a wedding. The parents of the child may approach the *compadre* with a request for help whenever necessary. Theoretically, the reverse is also true, but in actual practice the parents of the child have less obligation to their *compadre* than the godparent of their child has to them. The relationship of mutual respect obtains between them, but the practical obligations are somewhat lopsided, and in cases where a man asks a superior to act as his child's *padrino* they are completely one-sided. Except in so far as the parents of the child owe a rather loosely defined "loyalty" to the *compadres*, their immediate practical obligation seems to be nonexistent. Only in cases in which blood kin are additionally bound by *compadre* ties or in which the ties of *compadrazgo* are multiple, and thus stronger and closer, does the obligation seem to approach reciprocity.

In some instances the terms *compadre* and *comadre* are extended beyond the actual coparents. Most commonly, a child's godparents call the child's grandparents as well as the parents by these terms. It is not usual, however, for the child's real parents to extend the terms to the parents of their child's godparents, although we have been told that both usages existed in the past. It is also customary to extend the term to the spouse of a *compadre*. For example, two *compadres* would address each others' wives as *comadre*, even though the marriages took place some time after the *compadrazgo* bond between the two men was established. This extension does not apply in free unions or in civil marriages. *Compadre* terms do not extend to siblings, and it should be noted that the godchild itself is *ahijado* only to the actual godparent and addresses no one else as *padrino* or *madrina;* but the terms *pa'ino* (*ma'ina*) *guazú* may be addressed by the child to the father or mother of the godparent. These terms mean "big godfather (mother)" in Guaraní. We never heard a similar extension in Spanish.

People are very serious about the correct use of godparental terms in address. For example, we once heard the uncle of a small child severely reprimand the child for calling his aunt *ma'ina:* "You must never, *never*, call her *ma'ina*—she's your *tía*." The aunt intervened, saying, "Don't be so hard on him; he's only a baby. He hears his sister call me *ma'ina*, and he doesn't understand that I'm her *madrina* but not his. It will make him jealous." The uncle was adamant, however: "He's *got* to learn. He mustn't say this."

When ties of ritual kinship exist between a *patrón* and a *peón* or between any persons of unequal status, the individual of lower status may go more freely to his *compadre's* house and may expect to be received with somewhat more friendliness and hospitality than another of his class. The *patrón*, on the other hand, expects to be treated with great respect; complete intimacy does not enter into the relationship when it crosses class lines. The *patrón* expects extraordinary loyalty from his *compadre*, but less in the way of gifts and favors. Between equals, however, ritual kin ties imply mutual respect, admiration, trust, and confidence and also go together with greater intimacy and familiarity, even to the point of privileged "disrespectful" joking. For exam-

ple, José Melgarejo stood in the simultaneous relationship of
padrino, relative, and *compadre* to the local priest. Such a relationship is so close that great familiarity is understood; José was
able to chide the priest, jokingly, about such matters as illegitimate children and sexual power.

There are no set rules or procedures for selecting godparents.
Sometimes the same *padrinos* serve for all of a couple's children;
often each child has different *padrinos;* in some cases nonrela-
tives are the sponsors, and in others only relatives. It is said to
be preferable to select a female sponsor for a girl and a male for
a boy. This may be because, in 1919, the priest taught the people that the godparent of confirmation should be of the same
sex as the child and this later became extended to baptism. Nevertheless, it is not a rule, and anyone who is selected by the parents may be a sponsor for a baptism.

It is permissible for a child to have only one godparent instead of two, and certainly the selection always seems to be based
on one individual. If the sponsor is married, the spouse is automatically included. Thus a woman might speak of "María" as
"my *madrina*." Asked if María's husband is not therefore a
padrino, she will say, "Yes, of course," but the relationship to
María is clearly more significant.

Figures taken from baptismal records show the actual practice
of godparent selection to be roughly in correspondence with our
informants' opinions; but there is one interesting variation
through the years. In 1919, the earliest year of recorded baptisms available, there were one hundred and thirteen baptisms.
Of these, fifty-two boys each had only one godparent, a male,
and forty-eight girls had only one, a female. Only seven girls
had a male godparent alone, and five boys had a female godparent alone. Seven children were sponsored by married couples,
and there were two cases of unmarried cosponsors who were
related to each other. This is strong evidence that parents believed that boys should have male sponsors and girls female
sponsors, if there was only a single godparent.

In 1948, there were one hundred and eighty-eight baptisms
recorded. Again, only seven children had married couples as
sponsors. In the cases of single sponsors, however, there is an

interesting shift. Thirty-one boys had a male sponsor alone, while forty-three boys had a female alone. Sixty-two girls had a female sponsor alone, while only thirteen had a male sponsor. For the boys, at least, the selection has almost reversed itself toward female rather than male sponsorship. It is apparent that, when informants express what they think is the customary preference in choosing godparents, they reflect the earlier situation, which does not completely accord with present behavior.[4]

From the point of view of the security of the child who is to be baptized, married couples are favored as *padrinos*, since they represent the ultimate of stability and are thus more likely to be able to provide a home for the child should it be necessary. There are not enough married couples to act as *padrinos* for many children, of course, so that widows and, less frequently, widowers may serve. Young single women who are respected in the community often are asked to serve as godparents; single young men, less often. It is important that the person chosen be respectable, stable, and well established in the community—a person worthy of trust and aware of responsibility.

When a poor man is choosing a godparent for his children, he hopes to get someone better off than himself and may often ask a man of considerable wealth—in particular, his employer or a landowner who hires him for occasional work. In such cases the parents of the child may often expect direct benefits through the *compadre* relationship, such as financial assistance or seasonal work. Respectable wealthy men are so often chosen for this reason that they may find it difficult to keep up with their obligations. José Melgarejo, for example, is a very respected old man, now a widower. He has twenty children and many *compadres* through them. He is also *padrino* to the children of many other families. In all, he has over forty godchildren and well over a hundred *compadres;* there are so many he "can't take care of them very well." He now tries to avoid additional responsibilities, but it is difficult for him to refuse.

María Venturo is highly respected, is married, and is of the

4. Church records of confirmations reveal the behavior to be in accordance with the rule; there was only one sponsor per child, and always of the same sex as the child.

sociedad. She has no children, so that she has acquired *compadres* only through her sponsorship of their children. She has eleven *compadres* through baptismal ceremony and one through confirmation. She calls numerous other people *compadre* by extension of the term through marriage or kinship ties. María takes these relationships seriously, even though they are all one-sided; she bears all the usual responsibilities to the *compadres* and their children but needs no aid in return.

Jacinto, the pharmacist, has only one godchild by baptism, and his *compañera* cannot be a *madrina,* because they are living in adultery. His own two children have *madrinas* of baptism; one is his own single sister, the other his stepmother. Jacinto could not remember who the *compadres* were and had to ask his *compañera;* he was somewhat embarrassed about this carelessness and confessed that he had been out of town at the time of the baptism of both his children. He obviously does not take *compadrazgo* very seriously.

Patricio Pérez and his wife Julia are both well aware of their *compadrazgo* relationships. Patricio is an enterprising, striving lower-class man of Argentine birth, and Julia is a local girl. Patricio and Julia have six children, and each of the children has a separate set of godparents of baptism. They count as *compadres* Guillermo Rizzi and his wife (perhaps the most powerful family in town) because the latter are godparents to Patricio's small granddaughter. Both Patricio and his son-in-law have worked for Guillermo, as has the nephew of Julia. They also have as *compadres* an upper-class couple who were godparents of a child now deceased. In addition, another Rizzi married couple served as wedding *padrinos* for their oldest daughter. In all, there are fifteen of these *compadres,* most of them in a higher social status than that of Patricio and Julia. It is clear that they have sought to acquire as many different *padrinos* for their children as possible; there are none of the more usual duplications, nor are any of the godparents relatives of Patricio or Julia. On the other hand, Julia has sponsored only one godchild, now deceased, and Patricio has sponsored none. They say that it is a very serious obligation, and they cannot afford to undertake it. This is a good example of how godparenthood can be used for ultimate personal advantage; *compadres* are acquired without taking on any of the godparental obligations in return. We never heard any criticism of Patricio and Julia for this behavior, however.

Luís Gómez, a married man with eight children, has only three *compadres* and *comadres* who are godparents of his own children, having asked the same individuals to serve for more than one child. On the other hand, he is *padrino* of baptism to five children of different families. He is also *padrino* of matrimony to two young couples. He is very serious about all these relationships, and, although poor, he is highly regarded as a *padrino* because he is married and respectable.

Elena Contreras, a single woman about thirty years old, has an aunt as her own *madrina* and her aunt's husband as *padrino;* they served for both her baptism and her confirmation. Her illegitimate son, Domingo, has a married couple living in Asunción as *padrinos.* They are not related to Elena. Her illegitimate daughter has a single woman, a relative of the child's father, as godmother. She has no godfather. The same woman will also act as godmother of confirmation, according to Elena, but other informants said that the godparent of confirmation must be different from the godparent of baptism, and the priest agreed. Elena has no godchildren and says that she will not accept the obligation. She thus has only one *comadre* in Tobatí and no *compadre*, and apparently she does not desire more. Although she is very poor, working at home as a cigar-maker, she is respected as intelligent, honest, hard-working, and not promiscuous (her two children are recognized by the father); her failure to participate more fully in the godparental and coparental network is not due to her being in any sense a social outcast. She apparently has restricted her participation purposely. In spite of her poverty, she has a strong feeling of independence.

Nicasio Alvárez, the former *compañero* of Elena, now living with another woman, has two *compadres* and two *comadres*. Two of them, one *padrino* and one *madrina*, who live in Asunción, are the godparents of Elena's two children. The others are a couple who were godparents at the baptism of his child by his present *compañera.* He has no godchildren. He said that single men such as he are not often asked.

Juán de Dios Núñez reported that his two married sisters chose their own mothers and mothers-in-law as godmothers for their children; thus the child of one sister had her maternal grandmother as *madrina*, the child of the other her paternal grandmother. The parents of the children thus stood in the relationship of *compadres* (*comadres*) to their own mothers and to their mothers-in-law. Elena once told us that she thought of asking her mother to act as *madrina* to her daughter and said that many single women do this. She herself, however, thought it was better to ask a younger person.

To generalize about the factor of selection, it seems that the wealthiest people may choose either relatives or friends as co-parents; friendship and respect for the person chosen are the only considerations. In the town middle class, horizontal ties within that class are usual; relatives are frequently chosen, and *compadrazgo* is not generally viewed as of great importance. Among peasants and the town poor the alternatives may be more strictly limited to either a *patrón* or a close relative. Friendship becomes less important and real economic advantage more significant. In a *patrón-peón* situation the bonds of *compadrazgo* may serve to bind the *patrón* to assist his *compadre* in raising his children and to favor him in economic matters. Conversely, the *peón* is bound to his *patrón* by loyalty and gratitude; he becomes more dependable as a laborer.

Among town wageworkers, a *patrón-peón* relationship is likely to be more unstable, and ritual kin ties between worker and employer are therefore subject to much strain. For example, Patricio Pérez had as *compadres* his two employers, Guillermo Rizzi and Mario Ventura. They helped him with the expenses involved in the illness and death of a child, and they provided medical care when he himself was ill. When his employment with them as driver of the combined bus-truck became irksome and financially less rewarding than his own small leatherworking business, he was unable to give notice and quit, because of his obligation to be loyal to his *compadres*. In the end a serious quarrel resulted when his request for higher wages was ignored. One day, under difficult circumstances when the truck broke down, he spoke "disrespectfully" to Mario; tempers flared on both sides, and Patricio returned home to town on foot, leaving his *compadre* with the broken-down bus. Then he was "fired" and concentrated his energies on his own work, as he had wished for a long time. But he had to be *fired;* he could not quit the job.

In spite of the considerable variability in the pattern of *compadrazgo* in Tobatí, the system clearly is important to most of the people, not only in the times of crisis but also in normal daily life. In rural Paraguay the family is seen as the primary source of all emotional and material security. The institution of *compadrazgo* can extend kinship obligations more widely, or it can intensify the pre-existing bonds. It is in its nature extremely viable. The circumstances within which it functions may be widely divergent, and the motives of the participants may be opposite in intent. Thus a poor man may look outside his family and class for economic advantage and more security for his children; a *hacendado* can make his tenants more personally loyal. It is only in the context of buying-and-selling relationships and those of pure wageworker and employer that the system tends to lose some of its effectiveness.

CHAPTER XIII

The Church as a Social Institution

THE church in Paraguayan towns serves as an important focus of social activity, chiefly through the religious societies and the fiestas which the societies sponsor.[1] It provides the only social functions in which all classes participate. Rich and poor associate on the closest basis of social equality which they ever achieve, and often the time of a fiesta is the only occasion when families from the remote hamlets participate in town functions.

In terms of this integrative effect the fiestas of local patron saints assume the greatest importance, in the sense that the fiesta of the patron of any one *compañía* may attract visitors from the neighboring *compañías* or even from the nearest market town. In the same way, adjacent market towns may participate in each other's patronal festivals. The celebrations in some of the larger towns may even attract national attention. One of the most noteworthy examples occurs annually at the town of Caacupé in celebration of the day of the Virgin of the Immaculate Conception. This particular image of the Virgin is believed to have miraculous powers and is ordinarily referred to as "The Virgin of Caacupé" or "The Miraculous Blue Virgin." Thousands of people from all over Paraguay make an annual pilgrimage to this shrine. Elaborate secular arrangements are made, including bands, dancing, and sales concessions, so that the fiesta resembles a small-town carnival in the United States of America. Although many people are attracted primarily by the carnival activities, the feeling of awe and reverence is pervasive to a greater degree than in any other religious fiestas that we observed, with the exception of the ceremonies connected with Holy Week. Most other local

1. See Appendix III for ceremonial calendar.

184

patronal celebrations seem to inspire little religious feeling, and many are almost entirely profane.

Certain festivals, such as Christmas, Three Kings' Day, and the Easter observances, are celebrated everywhere at the same time, so that the interregional integrative function is absent. The participants are all residents of a particular locality, and the effect is that of uniting classes within a regional unit.

The various saints' fiestas are the responsibility of societies of laymen. In Asunción and in some of the larger towns there are many religious societies, including brotherhoods which are dedicated to various kinds of activities such as support of orphans, education and medical care of poor children, and general charitable work. Usually in small towns the societies are loosely organized and function only at the time of preparation and celebration of the fiesta for which they are responsible. The head of a society and a few associates assume the full responsibility for arrangements of the celebration. Other individuals are drawn in only as needed for some minor assigned duty. During the rest of the year the society is inactive.

Probably the largest society is that of the Three Kings. We do not know the actual membership, but there are 50 images of the Three Kings which appear in processions in the town and about 70 in Colonia 21 de Julio. The head of the society, who is appointed by the priest, is responsible for the collection of funds to pay the church for the religious celebration and for expending them as necessary for the profane fiesta. Most of the members live in Colonia 21 de Julio, and it is they who plan the profane entertainment of games and masked clowns and provide their own local band. The Comisión Profana de María Auxiliadora is also one of the larger societies, with 65 images. María Auxiliadora is also patroness of a barrio of the pueblo, although some of the members of the society live outside the barrio. The society has an elected president, a *mayordoma*, and a treasurer. The Society of San Antonio also represents a barrio of the pueblo and has an organization of elected president, *mayordoma*, and treasurer. There are 112 images of San Antonio, but many of them are from outside the barrio. All owners of the images help provide funds for a Mass and procession; all profane celebration is in private homes and is optional. The Cofradía del Carmen is a different type of religious society, which can be entered only by men and women who are living a life of practicing Catholicism. They must be married in the church, confess at least once annually, live a good, serious life, and serve the church when called upon. It is not a very large society. Other societies are those of San Pedro and the Liga Rosarina. Such religious societies also exist in the *compañías* which have patron-saint images.

In Asunción some years ago it was considered scandalous that the people of the rural areas brought the images of their household saints home from the church after the Mass and procession in which they were blessed and immediately held profane celebrations. For this reason it was prohibited to bring private images to the Mass. From the point of view of the local priest, however, the activities of the societies and the celebrations in honor of the household saints were good for community *esprit*, and he had this rule revoked for Tobatí. He has actually encouraged the profane celebrations, although he has ruled that such celebrations may not take place in the presence of the image. The people are very fond of the fiestas and games, but the religious aspects of the festivals seem to have little meaning for them. There is practically no training in the fundamentals of the Catholic tradition, and there is a great deal of confusion about the saints and many strange beliefs and superstitions. The local church seems to be not particularly concerned with religious education but more interested in maintaining harmony and co-operation among the people through encouragement of community-wide participation in traditional games and festivals.

The church does provide for lay participation in purely religious functions, however, chiefly by distributing various offices having to do with the maintenance of the church property. There is one office—the *mayordomo de la iglesia*—which has the responsibility of caring for the saints' images and opening the church for visitors. There is a sacristan, who must see that the church is kept clean, that the bells are rung at the proper times, and that candles and incense are available. The *mayordomo de los altares* takes care of the four altars in the church, and there are four families who act as *mayordomos* of four images used in Holy

Week processions. They keep the images in their own homes during the year and clean and dress them and bring them to the church the day before their particular ceremony. Other lay officers are the cantors. One is chosen by the priest each year to lead the prayers in the Via Crucis ("Way of the Cross") and the Pasión y Muerte in Holy Week. Cantors may also be called upon to lead the prayers in family novenas, for which services they are given gifts by the families of the deceased.

These various officials, aided by volunteers, usually from among the young girls of the town, organize the festivals and pageants connected with Christmas, All Saints' Day, and the Day of the Dead and, most important, those of Lent and Holy Week. The *sociedades* have no concern with these activities, which are felt to pertain solely to the church, whereas the primary purpose of the fiestas sponsored by the *sociedades* is entertainment.

The Patronal Fiesta

Perhaps the largest and most important festival in Tobatí is the celebration of the day of the Virgin of the Immaculate Conception on December 8. This is celebrated in many other Paraguayan towns as well, for she is a popular patroness. In Tobatí the fiesta is of local importance only, except that it also represents a time of homecoming for the natives who are living elsewhere.

About a month preceding the date of the fiesta, the society sets about raising money. A group of women make collections for the church, and a commission of men raises money for the profane festivities. Two or three days before the fiesta, vendors come in from other towns and start building their booths for the sale of food and toys and for gambling games. The afternoon of the day before the fiesta, horse races and various other competitive games are held, and in the evening a large public dance is given (*baile popular*). About four o'clock in the afternoon the image of the Virgin is carried in procession around the church plaza, and a vesper service is sung.[2] On the morning of December 8 a Mass is held, followed by Communion and another procession. If enough money has been obtained, a visiting priest or two

2. These events were related by informants, as we were attending the more famous festival at Caacupé.

may participate, and there will be a High Mass with music and a longer procession. In the afternoon games continue as on the previous day, and the fiesta is culminated at night by a dance given for important people of the town (*baile oficial*).

María Auxiliadora

During the period of our residence the fiesta of María Auxiliadora was the largest held in Tobatí. The fiesta of this saint, who is patroness of the army as well as of one of the major *sociedades* of Tobatí, is celebrated on May 24. In 1949 a battalion of army engineers was stationed in Tobatí to build a road to Caacupé, and, also in that year, a large new image of the saint was presented to the church. These special events may account for the elaborate fiesta which was held, although this society is said to "know how to make a fiesta."

Preparations began two weeks in advance of the fiesta with a benefit dance, the music contributed by the band of the engineer battalion. Collections were taken up in the barrio of the *sociedad*. All members were expected to contribute according to their means, and outsiders also were canvassed. Another benefit dance was held the following Saturday night. The fiesta fell on Monday and Tuesday, May 23 and 24, but festivities began the preceding Saturday afternoon with horse races between the army and civilians. Large side bets were made, and a steer and a cartful of manioc were donated as prizes. The man who won was the president of the society, and he used the prizes to give a barbecue and dance at his house on Sunday, after which there was another horse race. There was also a soccer-football game between the Tobatí team and the engineer battalion on Sunday afternoon in the church plaza.

A novena was celebrated before the fiesta, and at noon on each of the nine days the men fired their guns into the air. On the first day of the actual festival, an army band of twenty-three musicians arrived from the large town of Piribebuý. The band played first at the house of the president of the society, then at the municipal building, and finally marched through the entire barrio. During the morning previously prepared decorations had been raised. Poles trimmed with green foliage and strings of red, white, and blue papers were arranged as arches across the streets of the barrio. The streets had been raked clean and the weeds chopped down. In the afternoon there was a soccer-football game between Tobatí and the neighboring town of Atyrá. At four o'clock the procession of the saints into the church took place, proceeding through the barrio from the coco factory to the church. Fifty-three images were carried. About fourteen of them were merely photographs, but the rest were carved wood, ranging in size from four inches to a foot in height. Vesper services were held and the images left in the church overnight. Later that night there was a *baile popular*. There was music by the visiting band, a speech by the commander of the Paraguayan army engineers, much noise, and considerable drunkenness.

Tuesday morning at five o'clock there was a flag raising, accompanied by much shooting of pistols and army machine guns. After Mass the images were taken from the church for a long procession through the entire barrio and back to the church, after which they were taken home individually. This concluded the religious part of the festival. The townspeople and many country-people who had come in for the fiesta played games and held informal horse races. There was much animation, and many private parties took place, during the remainder of the day and night. We attended a barbecue at the home of the priest, given in honor of the visiting commander of engineers. There was *caña* and beer to drink and much food, including barbecued lamb and beef, manioc, and *sopa paraguaya*, followed by dancing, drinking, and general hilarity. At nightfall the flag was lowered, and the fiesta was officially concluded.

Contributions for this fiesta were clearly quite substantial. It is understood that all should give according to their means; yet all share alike in the fiesta, and those who can give less in money may make contributions in products or in labor. A great deal of actual cash was given to pay for prizes and decorations, 300 guaranis for the visiting band (as well as their food and lodging), and 15 guaranis for the local band. There were substantial contributions to the church for the performance of the Mass and procession and for candles, incense, and decorations. Such cooperative efforts involve a great deal of visiting and merriment during the preparations. Facilities for cooking and food preparation are combined, and there is a genuine pride in the results.

The Three Kings

The fiesta of the Three Kings is primarily a secular one, organized for amusement, particularly for the children, although it is celebrated with a Mass and procession of the saints' images on the morning of January 6. Ordinarily, *santos* are brought into the church on the evening of January 5 and are left there overnight and then carried back to the homes the next day after the Mass and procession. The games are traditional ones: climbing a greased pole, blindfold games, bow-and-arrow shooting contests, and the usual horse races and games played on horseback. Prizes may consist of *chipa* bread, money, chickens, or fruit. The Society of the Three Kings is a very old and strong one, both in town and in the *compañías*. At times the celebrations and games have been sponsored by society members in the town of Tobatí, but in recent years the games have been held in the *compañías*.

In 1949, when we witnessed the fiesta, the first small groups of families from the country began to come into Tobatí early in the morning, carrying the images of the kings, Baltasar, Gaspar, and Melchior. After a number of families had arrived, they formed a procession with men on horseback carrying the flag of Paraguay in advance and the women and children following on foot, carrying the images. They were escorted by a small band of drums, flutes, and cymbals, and the masked clowns, the *cambá ra'angá*,[3] cavorted on all sides.

The *cambá* seem to be especially associated with this fiesta. Their masks are made occasionally of leather but more often of the carved root of the *sammuú*, a large tree with a light, corklike root. They should be made by the individuals who wear them, since no one should know who is wearing the mask. Actually, they are often made by specialists. The masks are usually sold after the games are over and not used again, unless in another vicinity. The whole head of the clown is covered, and even gloves and shoes are worn so as to prevent any possibility of recognition. The masks themselves are clever representations of grotesque personalities; some are tremendously ugly, some merely comical, and some part animal and part human. Only men may be clowns, but the representations are often of females.

3. Called *negritos* in Spanish.

The clowns dance, play flutes and drums, sing and talk in falsetto voices, and tell obscene jokes. They are not permitted to follow the procession into the church plaza, because they are considered exceptionally profane.

San Juán and San Pedro

Two other large festivals are those of San Juán and San Pedro, which fall on June 24 and June 29. The religious part of the celebrations involves the usual Masses and, in the case of San Pedro, a procession, but the games played on these two days are special because of the association of San Juán with the fire miracle. In former times one of the features of the profane fiesta was walking barefoot over live coals, but this has been discontinued in recent years. Children do build a great many bonfires and run about with burning torches as a preliminary to the regular games held in the street before the home of the *mayordomo*.

The more traditional, almost ritual games include most typically the *cambá* in a simulated bullfight with the *toro candil*. The bull is made of a light frame covered with hide with a bull's skull fixed in front; the horns are covered with rags which are soaked in kerosene and lighted (Pl. VI). When the man in the *toro candil* dashes around in the night chasing the crowds, the flaming horns make a fearsome sight. Some of the *cambá* taunt the bull, while others stand around playing their flutes and drums. On this occasion, the *cambá* are called "San Juán."

Two other apparitions usually appear at these games, a *ñandú guazú* (rhea) and a man representing a Guaycurú Indian. The *ñandú* consists of a small cage of wood covered with leaves to represent feathers and surmounted by a long stick for a neck. Another small piece of wood simulates the small head and beak of the bird. A child inside the cage walks around inside the circle of spectators and bobs the neck and head down to peck at the *toro* from behind, harassing him while he chases the San Juáns. The Guaycurú, in outlandish rag costume and blackened face, meanwhile dashes around, pretending to kidnap women. Some of the *cambá* chase women with blazing torches; the total effect is one of great activity in the huge crowd, and there is much screaming and laughter.

These games have become part of the celebrations of both San

Juán and San Pedro, but they are supposed to be more appropriate to San Juán. San Pedro is the patron of Tobatí and supposedly has attributes different from those of San Juán. Neither the Society of San Juán nor that of San Pedro is particularly strong or active, so that there is little formal ceremony. The fiesta of San Juán is celebrated by a vesper service in the evening before the games, and a Mass is held on the morning of the saint's day. There is no procession, as the image is supposed to be removed from the church only during Holy Week.

The church celebration for San Pedro is more formal. By long-standing local custom the procession of the Corpus Christi (which should be on June 16) is held on the morning of the day of San Pedro. Each of the four corners of the church plaza is decorated with leaves of palm, laurel, and flowers. The procession stops for prayers at each of these four *sitiales*, after which the people take the leaves home for medicines and the flowers as offerings to their household saints. In some towns the *sitiales* are made of manioc, banana, and sugar-cane plants, and tables are heaped with garden products; it is believed that the blessings will insure good crops in the coming year. In the afternoon the procession of San Pedro is held. There is only one image, that belonging to the church. In 1949 the procession was poorly attended because of bad weather. The man who played the bassoon was very drunk and seemed always to have in mind a different tune from that of his fellow-musicians.

Miscellaneous Fiestas

Other saints' fiestas, such as those of San Antonio, the Virgin of Carmen, the Virgin of Asunción, San Roque, San Miguel, and Santa Librada, are observed by only a Mass and a procession, with individuals bringing their household images (except in the case of the Virgin of Carmen, whose single image belongs to the church). All secular activity is in the form of private celebrations for individual household saints. One society, that of the Corazón Sagrado de Jesús, celebrates a Mass and a procession in which the participants carry their pictures of the Sacred Heart. This is a completely religious society and is small (twenty-four members) because, as one informant stated, "This saint is too serious. It is for old ladies only."

Patronal fiestas which are celebrated in the *compañías* include those of Santa Rosa and Santa Rosalía; the priest goes to the local oratorios to perform the religious ceremonies. The Virgin of Mercedes is patroness of Compañía Typychatý (Villa Mercedes), and there a large celebration is sponsored by one of the Rizzis, who is *padrino* of the *oratorio*. Games, races, and dances are held after the Mass and procession. Colonia Mompox plans to adopt San Fernando as its patron as soon as an image can be made.

Lent

Several religious celebrations are not organized by societies. Of these, the most important occur during Lent and Holy Week. *Carnaval* celebrations, which occur on the Sunday, Monday, and Tuesday before Ash Wednesday, are not so elaborate as in some other parts of Latin America, but there is a considerable amount of clowning and unorganized festivity. In 1949 the celebrations were canceled, owing to the death of the archbishop of Paraguay.

The first religious observance of Lent is that of Ash Wednesday ("Miércoles de Ceniza"), which is marked by a meat fast and by a Mass. Fasting is observed during Lent by abstaining from meat on Fridays, and a few persons make some further voluntary sacrifice. Many individuals also observe the fasting rule at Wednesday morning and evening meals during Lent, but the custom of fasting is not highly developed in Paraguay and is not commonly observed on other Fridays through the year. There are no dances or festivities during the Lenten period, and private parties and drinking are frowned upon. It is a quiet period in the annual round of frequent festivals.

The second formal observance during Lent is a Mass on Día de Dolores, the Friday before Good Friday. It is considered a day of great danger for undertaking any new enterprise or for traveling. Most people avoid doing anything beyond the most routine tasks. From now until the Saturday before Easter, the saints' images in the church are covered with purple cloths.

In 1949, on the afternoon following Día de Dolores, the *encargado* of the image of "El Señor de Ramos" brought the image to the church, preceded by a band consisting of a cornet, a bassoon, a snare drum, and a heavy bass drum. The image is a figure of Christ, mounted on a burro carved of wood and wearing a large gilded crown, dark blue garments, and a cape bordered with gold. The platform on which the image was carried was covered with fine white cloth edged with lace and embroidered in gold, and there were flowers on either side in polished brass vases (Pl. V). The image was left in the church all night, and before the Mass on Palm Sunday ("Domingo de Ramos") the band and a procession of people carrying palm leaves circled the church with the *santo* (Pl. VI). After the Mass the *santo* was escorted in procession back to the home of the shoemaker who was *mayordomo* of this image.

Holy Week ("La Semana Santa")

On the Monday before Easter ("Lunes Santo") there was a heavy rain from 2:00 A.M. on, letting up a little at daybreak, and the Mass was poorly attended. The first performance of the Via Crucis procession was scheduled for that evening, but the weather was cold and windy and there was a light rain, so prayers were conducted in the church under the leadership of Prudencio Molinas, a cantor.

On Tuesday ("Martes Santo") there was an early Mass, again poorly attended, and the word went around the pueblo that the priest was very angry because the young girls had not voluntarily gone around town to take up collections for the Easter festivities and because the people were not sufficiently interested even to attend the Masses. In the evening there was a Via Crucis procession, in which the image of "Nuestro Señor de la Columna" was brought from the house of the *mayordoma*. This image is a nearly life-size representation of the Christ with hands fastened by ropes to a column of wood. The figure is naked except for a lace-trimmed loincloth. Two images of the Virgin were also carried in this procession. About sixty people made the fourteen Stations of the Cross, progressing from one unmarked location to another in the church plaza, making a complete circle around the church. The praying was led by a cantor.

On Wednesday ("Miércoles Santo") there were two Masses. After the second Mass the "Señor de la Columna" was carried back to the house of the *mayordoma*, and in the afternoon the image of "Jesús Nazarene" was brought to the church. This large figure, bent under the weight of a huge wooden cross, was dressed in a long maroon robe. In the evening, the Via Crucis procession was again performed, with the "Jesús Nazarene" and the images of the Virgin of Dolores and Veronica. Over one hundred people attended this ceremony.

On Maundy Thursday ("Jueves Santo") there was a High Mass. Following the Mass, the Host was carried from the main altar to a side altar under a purple and red canopy supported by six prominent residents of Tobatí. The Host itself was carried by a visiting curate; the local priest chanted the prayers. The procession was guarded by two armed sergeants of the engineer battalion. These observances, celebrating the anniversary of the Eucharist, are followed by a feast meal at midday. After the noon meal there is supposed to be no cooking and no work done until after Mass on Saturday. No money is supposed to change hands, and stores are therefore closed until Saturday at noon.

On Thursday evening the last procession of the Via Crucis was held. The procession, as before, circled the church, and at each of the fourteen stations prayers were repeated. The cantor read each station number and related the events which occurred there. Probably somewhat over three hundred people attended on this evening, the majority being young girls. There were a few middle-aged and older women and many children, but very few men were present.

On Good Friday ("Viernes Santo") there was a Mass at six in the morning, called by the *matraca*, a hollow square of wood with metal clappers, which is used in place of the bells until the Saturday Mass. In the afternoon at three the people were again called by the *matraca*, and a pageant of the Crucifixion was performed. An altar had been built behind the church, with a wood frame covered with plants of *caña de Castilla*, *manioc*, banana, lemon and lime, laurel, and sugar cane. In front of this was a black curtain and a Cross with Christ impaled. The figures of the Virgin stood on both sides, and offerings of tangerines and candles were on the altar. Six lay officials participated in this ceremony, wearing white scarves edged with lace. These particular officials were not prominent men of the town but poor peasants. Prayers were repeated by a cantor, followed by a sermon by the visiting priest. After the candles were extinguished by the cantor, the crown of thorns was removed from the image of Christ by the lay officials, who used the white scarves so as not to touch the image directly. The three nails, one from each hand and one from the feet, were removed one by one and placed in the coffin, and then four men together removed the Christ from the Cross. All the men knelt, holding the image in front of the figures of the Virgin, and then placed the image in the coffin, while the church bells tolled the *doble*. A procession of small boys, carrying silver candelabra, a silver cross, and a silver ball of incense, came from the church, and an armed guard of eight soldiers assembled. A funeral procession moved slowly to five prepared altars on the edges of the church plaza, back to the original altar, and into the church itself as the seventh station.

Well over a thousand people must have been present at this ceremony, including many countrypeople. Throughout the ceremony parents explained the events to the children. In general, older women seemed to show the most devotion. Some of the young girls were much more aware of what a charming picture they presented in their best clothes and white mantillas than of what went on in the ceremony. As the funeral procession moved, there was considerable disturbance caused by the children stripping the altars of leaves, which are believed to serve as a remedy for any infirmity.

The Saturday before Easter ("Sábado de Gloria") there was a High Mass (the Misa de Gloria). Before the Mass the holy water for the coming year was blessed and the congregation sprinkled with it. Then, while the candles were being lighted behind the black altar curtain, prayers were repeated. The black curtain was dropped, revealing the lighted candles; the music started, the bells rang furiously, and the Misa de Gloria began. The ceremony was dramatic, and many women wept quietly.

Just after nightfall on Easter eve it is customary to burn a life-sized effigy of Judas made of old clothes and stuffed with rags, dried weeds, and paper. The effigy is usually paraded on a burro through the streets and is later burned at the edge of the church plaza. Toads, cats, and other small animals which have been imprisoned in the stuffing, come scrambling out during the burning.

At dawn of Easter Sunday there was a Mass, followed by Communion, but we were unable to enter the church because of the crowd. Afterward, a procession was held enacting the reunion of the Virgin and her Son following the Resurrection. At least fifteen hundred people were present, and they seemed to take a childlike delight at this happy meeting of the Virgin with her Son. It is a completely happy occasion and is followed by drinking, feasts, celebrations, and dancing. Informants stated that before the revolution of 1947 the town was crowded with people celebrating all night Saturday and all day Sunday, and the jail was full of prisoners who had caused some trouble by drunkenness, fighting, or disturbing the peace.

Although the Lenten observances are by far the largest and most dramatic of the religious ceremonies which are not arranged by societies, there are also other strictly religious observances. All Saints' Day, All Souls' Day, Christmas, and New Year's Day are the most important. November 1, All Saints' Day (Día de Todos los Santos"), is considered to be a day for remembrance of the *angelitos*, or dead children. There is a Mass, and it is customary to go to the cemetery afterward and place flowers and candles on the graves. On November 2, All Souls' Day ("Día de los Difuntos"), a Mass is said for the souls of the adult dead, and, if the priest is paid in advance, he will come to the cemetery at the time of the procession and say prayers for the individual dead. It is customary during the year to visit the graves of children on Saturdays and to visit the graves of adult dead on Mondays. Candles for the dead should be cut in short pieces to be burned simultaneously, it is believed, because, if large candles are burned, the dead will be kept on their knees too long and will tire.

For Christmas a crèche is prepared in the church before the midnight Mass. It is made of several cartloads of branches, decorated with paper stars, balloons, fruit, corn, and watermelon. Statues of animals are grouped facing the reclining figure of the infant Jesus. After midnight Mass on Christmas Eve, a feast is eaten by the participants from a large table which has been set up at the side of the church. Many families make small crèches in their homes or yards. Christmas is generally considered an occasion for family reunions and visiting. On Christmas Day feasting and dancing are permissible, but public celebrations are common only in the capital.

New Year's Day is spent in much the same way as Christmas. It is said that a family should celebrate this holiday as a group in order to insure being together all through the year. Crèches are also used for the New Year observances. An entirely new one may be made, or the reclining Child may be removed and replaced by a standing or sitting representation with the world in his hand. All the toys now face away from the figure of the Child, which is called "Niño del Año Nuevo" instead of "Niño de la Navidad."

In addition to the saints' fiestas and the purely religious observances, which tend to bring people together in co-operative activities regardless of class lines, there also are certain other church functions which have social consequences. All individuals are dependent on the church for the offices of baptism and burial and, at least theoretically, for confirmation and marriage. The very important ties of ritual kinship are dependent on the church, inasmuch as they are sanctified by religion and originate in church ritual.

In contrast to the situation in some other Latin countries, the church in Paraguay has very little wealth, owns no productive land, and has been separated from the civil functions of the government and from public education for many years. This means that, aside from church buildings and such properties as altar equipment and images, the church has no wealth. It is supported by fees and donations and by missions sent from foreign countries, mainly Spain. The priest in Tobatí farms two small plots of land in the name of the church and calls upon the people for donations of bricks, sand, stone, and labor for repairing and rebuilding the church and for contributions of money to maintain the church and to pay his salary. Individuals pay for private ceremonies, such as baptisms, marriages, and funerals; but there is no charge for confirmation, since this ceremony is performed when the bishop comes to the country on his *gira pastoral* every year or two. Contributions are made at weekly Masses. Many people pay off obligations to the church by working for the priest, thus earning special consideration and lower rates when his services are needed. Other sources of church income are first-fruits gifts or the first products of a new home industry. The tithe is not practiced.

The clergy as such does not enjoy a position of great power in Paraguay, although individual priests may achieve such power

TABLE 8

SOME CEREMONIAL FEES*

	Fee (Guaranis)
Marriages:	
Just before or after Mass	3
Other times:	
Daytime	5
Night	12
Funerals:	
Ordinary Mass, at time fixed by priest ("Misa Manual")	3
Ordinary Mass, not at ordinary time ("Misa Rezada")	5
Sung Mass ("Misa Cantada"), at time fixed by priest	10
Sung Mass, not at ordinary time	15
Procession, halfway around church	6
Procession, all the way around church (including cost of bell-tolling—*doble*)	12

* Baptisms and confirmations are usually performed during the bishop's visits (*gira pastoral*) and are free on these occasions.

locally, or even nationally, through political means. The actual influence of the church as a whole is weak, and priests and population alike are poorly educated in religious matters. Men, as a rule, are not much concerned about church activities or religion, while women are more likely to be both devout and concerned with the need for the church blessing on important individual life-events. From the point of view of an individual, contributions and payments to the church, directly for particular ceremonies or indirectly through the religious societies, may cost so much as to constitute a serious problem—so serious in some cases that marriage or a baptism may be considered impossible, and even a funeral service may have to be postponed (see Table 8).

There is great local variation in Paraguay in degree of economic support of the church, in individual participation in religious rites, and in the importance of secular festivals connected with church holidays. In the capital and in the larger towns, there is greater emphasis on religious education and on purely religious observances. In smaller towns, the orientation depends a great deal on the individual priest. Some priests emphasize purely religious aspects; others are more interested in community co-operation and social cohesion, and stress the secular fiestas. In many towns, even in some as large as Tobatí, there is no resident priest. In such localities the residents are dependent on occasional visits by the priest of a near-by town for religious services. They may themselves organize local profane fiestas for particular saints, or they may travel to the neighboring communities to join in their festivals.

CHAPTER XIV

Some Aspects of Everyday Social Life

THE conduct of daily social relations is of several kinds or levels of etiquette, depending on the degree of familiarity or respect which must be shown. It is perhaps easiest to think of these differences in terms of ever wider circles of association, proceeding from the intimate relations within the nuclear families, through extended kin, *compadres*, and friends, and, finally, to strangers. Within these categories are special sorts of conduct related to individual differences in age, sex, and socioeconomic status which also deserve separate consideration. Insasmuch as status groups, family organization, and *compadrazgo* have already been discussed in separate chapters, our emphasis here is concerned with etiquette of the more formal sort which applies in the wider area of relations with fellow-townsmen and strangers.

Correct behavior, meaning rectitude in conduct as well as observance of formal etiquette, is esteemed at all times. Probably the greatest insults are to refer to a person as *sin verguenza* ("shameless") and *malcriado* ("badly brought up"). Nevertheless, formality is not always of the sort which might be called "distant," for the Paraguayans are proud of their reputation as an open, friendly, and hospitable people. Peasants are generally less open than townsmen, but there seems to be a general regard for a "hail fellow," or even a boisterous person, to a greater degree than is generally found in rural Mexico, for example. This heartiness is somewhat formalized as an aspect of etiquette, however, and should not be assumed to mean necessarily a genuine intimacy.

Paraguayans seem to manifest their quality of overt friendliness quite spontaneously; not only are they quick to boast of this, but it may be observed in characteristic behavioral situations. Greetings between friends or even between mere acquaintances seem rather effusive; handshaking and embracing are extended to a wide circle of acquaintances. People do not pass each other on the streets without a spoken greeting, and usually a short exchange of words will follow. Commonly one person invites the other to engage in some joint activity, and the other accepts. Neither takes the other seriously, for this is merely a formula greeting and farewell, slightly more familiar than "Buenos días."

There is some difference of degree in the formality of greetings in town as opposed to the country, chiefly in that the countrypeople more often use older, more complex formal address. In calling at a house, the visitor stands some distance away and claps his hands to attract attention; one should never go to the house itself to knock on the door. After thus alerting the inhabitants, the visitor should call out "Ave María." The response should be "Por siempre" or "Como siempre" ("As always") or, in older usage, "Sin pecado. Adelante" ("Without sin. Come in"). The talk does not turn to informal chatting or to the purpose of the visit until after the host and guest have exchanged formal inquiries about the welfare of the members of the two families.

Visiting hours are restricted to late afternoon and early evening, except for very informal chats between close friends or relatives. It is not common to invite people other than intimates inside the house; hence the more formal visiting takes place in the front yard or ramada. In bad weather and in winter, for this reason, the afternoon calls are very rare. During the seven or eight warm months of the year a great many families go to the arroyo in late afternoon to bathe and perhaps change to clean clothes. Afterward, they may make several brief stops at the homes of friends, usually staying at each one only long enough to take some refreshment. Young girls sometimes walk around together in small groups, but usually they accompany their families. The streets in a summer evening are full of strolling families, and other families are sitting in front of their houses awaiting visitors. Boys and girls do not circle the plaza in the formalized *paseo*, which is so common in some Latin-American countries.

There is a very clear recognition of the difference between informal and formal visits. Informal visits are very common; a friend passing by is asked to stop, or someone calls ostensibly to borrow something or to deliver a message or on some such pretext. An informal visit of this sort may last an hour or so. If a specific invitation is made in advance, however, the occasion is recognized as formal. The visitors dress very carefully in their best clothes and conduct themselves with extraordinary decorum. The hosts prepare special refreshments, and the labor and expense may be considerable. Formal invitations are quite rare for this reason; the people generally prefer the more casual visit.

Some refreshment should always be served at an early stage of any visit. *Mate* is most customary, but, if the host can afford it, a drink of *caña* is most desired by the men. The serving of *caña* is an immediate signal that conviviality is in order, that breaches of formal courtesy may be countenanced, and, therefore, that the host is disposed to accept the guests intimately. In this regard, it is felt that drinking *caña* together from the same glass is the proper thing to do as a sign of friendship. This may have started as a custom because of the shortage of glasses in most families or perhaps as a carry-over from the *mate* drinking customs. The *mate* gourds are cheap, and each person may have several of his own, but courtesy dictates that friends must pass one gourd from hand to hand, drinking in turn. *Caña*-drinking is done similarly, even in a wealthy home where several glasses may be provided. A large glass is filled to the brim and passed around, each person taking a swallow or two. At a large party there are often plenty of glasses provided, but men tend to gather in small groups, a single glass being passed around within the group. When we first arrived in Asunción, some of our friends apologized for this custom, knowing that it was not ours, but defended it on the grounds that it was the "Paraguayan way to drink." Women do not participate in such drinking, and many never touch *caña* at all under any circumstances.

When guests are present for meals, a clean tablecloth is always used, even among families so poor that all they have is a ragged homespun towel. There is always someone, a daughter or the neighbor's girl, if not a servant, who sets the table and then stands by to serve the courses. Boiled manioc is set in a basket to be eaten with all courses. Separate plates are used for each course, and, if there are no extra plates, the used plate is washed and dried and returned for the next course. Nothing is drunk during the meal; wine is used very rarely, and *mate* is strictly a between-meals or breakfast drink. Immediately after a meal, water is served; each person in turn rinses out his mouth and spits on the floor (except in the more decorous *sociedad*). Toothpicks are then used discreetly, the mouth hidden by the palm of the unoccupied hand.[1]

Only a small proportion of men smoke cigarettes; women almost never do. Perhaps more men smoke or chew cigars, but it is the use of cigars by women which has attracted the attention of foreigners most forcibly. It is now said that cigar-smoking among women is dying out somewhat. In the city upper and middle classes it is regarded as a rural or lower-class habit, and most women of the *sociedad* in Tobatí do not smoke, at least in public. Most cigar-smoking women feel that it is discourteous to smoke in the presence of a respected person, although older women, feeling exempted by age, smoke whenever they feel like it. We often noted, in traveling around the rural areas, that when we stopped at a house, the air would often be full of cigar smoke but that the woman had put the cigar away before greeting us. Our cook never smoked when we were at home, even though we told her that it was not offensive to us. She told us she only smoked when alone or at home, never on the street or in any public place, as this was a sign of *mala educación*. It is, nevertheless, a common sight to see barefoot, *rebozo*-clad women at the market or on the streets with the black cigar clamped in the side of the mouth. There is, of course, great variability in this habit; some women smoke all day long, others only after meals, and some not at all. Girls in their early teens often experiment secretly and get sick, for all the world like young boys in other countries. But smoking is not regarded as

1. For details on food and its preparation see Appendix IV.

a vice which is bad for the health. Most members of the *gente* feel merely that it is somewhat unseemly for too young a girl to be seen smoking. It appears that smoking suggests casualness and informality, and a young girl smoking a cigar, therefore, looks immodest as well as disrespectful of convention. The upper social group also regards it as an attribute of *mala educación*, pertaining to the lower class.

Women as well as men of all classes use profanities derived from religion, but there are a few differences between the sexes and classes in regard to the seemliness of certain expletives. Such usages as "Por Dios" or "Jesús María" are the most common. The only likely difference here is that perhaps upper-class women use them less often because they are not likely to express themselves so forcefully as men or as lower-class women. Another difference in the use of expletives is the modification of "A la puta" as used by males to "A la pucha" or "A la pinta" when used by females. "A la puta" is by far the most common expletive in use in Paraguay but seems to be unknown in other countries, so far as we can ascertain. It may be a Paraguayan version of the widespread "[Vete] a la puta [or "chingada"] madre que te parió." Its usage is most equivalent in force to the English "Go to hell," shortened to "Hell" and modified to "Heck."

The etiquette of gift exchange is fairly elaborate in Tobatí. It is especially important to recognize the appropriate occasions for giving certain presents. Friends, *compadres*, and relatives usually observe each other's birthdays by giving small gifts, and New Year's gifts are exchanged within the immediate family. Children are given presents on Three Kings' Day (January 6). Gifts of food are the most common on all these occasions, and a bottle of *caña* or vermouth is a usual gift to a man or as a contribution to a wedding fiesta. The gifts are always wrapped very carefully, and flowers are often sent along with them. Such presents are rarely expensive, but the thought given to the choice of gift and the care given to the decorating is considered important. Presents given outside the immediate family are always delivered by a child or servant, never in person. Inexpensive gifts of food are always appropriate, but sometimes wealthy people exchange things of greater value, such as lace or jewelry or, between men, a horse or a dog. Live poultry, kittens, lambs, parrots, or monkeys are often given to children. Money may be given only under exceptional circumstances and usually indirectly; an older person (such as a *padrino*) might contribute money for a wedding fiesta, or a *patrón* might give money to a *peón* for some special reason, but money is never exchanged between equals. The giving of money implies an attitude too much like patronage.

When a gift or favor is given unexpectedly, it is assumed by the recipient that the giver is asking, in effect, for a favor in return. For example, the giver may indicate at a later time that he wishes some special consideration in a political or commercial matter. This is regarded as correct conduct even in the most impersonal bureaucratic contexts. The principle of reciprocity is strongly adhered to, and such an exchange is not thought of as bribery or as calculating or shrewd behavior.

There is some feeling that in the past generation there have been slight modifications in old social customs and the beginnings of some new ones. Occasionally, for example, a daring young upper-class woman might wear slacks or *bombachas* for a horseback trip. But slacks are never worn on any other occasion, and nearly all women still ride sidesaddle in skirts. Lipstick is used fairly frequently by young women on dressup occasions, but permanent waves are still new and infrequent. It is said that girls go to dances and appear at public social functions at an earlier age than they used to. It is also said that young people are less reticent about showing affection for each other in public than before. In general, the differences between town and country and between younger and older people suggest that the trend in etiquette is slowly toward less and less formality.

Gossip

The conduct of individuals, especially as it concerns rectitude in personal dealings and the propriety of women's behavior, is most effectively held under control by the fear of gossip. People very quickly take sides in case two persons or two families quarrel. The stories of the affair have only the pretense of accuracy; the people have taken sides on the basis of previously established alliances or preferences and embellish the story as a rationale of their favorite's behavior. Gossip about women is continual, and frightful untruths are told, especially by other women.

The envious, maliciously destructive gossip about women, by women, is, of course, an old story to inhabitants of small towns the world over, but it is probable that there are differences in degree from society to society, depending on, among other things, the very position of women in the society itself. Busy commercial women, *almaceneras* and *revendedoras*, and the more educated women whose minds are otherwise occupied seem, in Tobatí, at least, to have less inclination toward maliciousness. Those who are more housebound and uneducated seem to find little of interest except gossip. Older women gossip much more than girls, and the subject matter is different. Young girls take an active, eager interest in the social life of fiestas, dances, and parties and gossip about each other and their sweethearts with little malice, but the older women sit together, apart from the others, gossiping invidiously about other people rather than participating in the festivity.

Commonly, it is only unmarried girls who dance; a young married woman may dance occasionally, but there is always the danger of unfavorable gossip if she dances too often with men other than her husband. A woman must be exceptionally circumspect at all times. She should always avoid the appearance of having a private conversation with a man even on the street in broad daylight. A woman seen alone on the street at night is always suspected of going to a rendezvous with a lover. It is true that there is a great deal of sexual activity outside marriage, as attested by the great proportion of illegitimate children.

The gossip about women's indiscretions sounds extraordinarily vicious, yet the victim of the gossip is not socially persecuted in any way commensurate with the vigor of the gossip. Couples living in free unions are not bothered; a woman having an adulterous affair with a married man is not censured to her face, at least; and illegitimates do not suffer social ostracism. Even a very young girl who becomes pregnant and cannot name her violator is quickly forgiven by the family and the society at large. It would appear, therefore, that, while malicious gossip is just about the only social mechanism which brakes the individual's urge to self-indulgence, it is far from effective. The people are not puritanical about sex, drinking, or any other indulgences, and thus guilt does not seem to be an aspect of the control mechanism. The concern is, rather, with the purely practical consequences of indulgence—it is felt that the pregnant girl did a very *foolish* thing and that her parents made a *mistake* in failing to guard her rather than that she was immoral or lacking in character. Likewise, a woman entering an adulterous or consensual union may be considered unwise or lacking in foresight rather than wicked or immoral.

In the daytime the women of neighboring households call out to each other a choice bit of gossip or news. It is like "back-fence" gossip, except that it is often carried on by shouting from a distance. In fact, an otherwise quiet morning in the home is characteristically punctuated by the sound of women calling to each other, shouting admonitions to children, laughing over some joke that is being passed around town in this way, or calling out to some passer-by. This spontaneity and general noisiness of the women remains one of our most vivid recollections of everyday life in Tobatí.

Practical jokes are very common, and often the humor seemed to us to be rather cruel, concerned typically with someone's misfortunes. But laughing *at* someone is not always a sign of ill-will or malice, and, if the person whose dignity has been punctured takes it in good part, he may find he has established himself as a friendly person. In our bus and truck travels around Paraguay, we quickly learned to capitalize on this. The other passengers on the bus would be curious but quite shy of us at first, but we would try to speak to them in Guaraní, which immediately sent them into gales of laughter because of our mistakes. This served to break the ice and put everyone in an affable mood.

Foreigners are treated very courteously and hospitably, but Paraguayans take delight in clandestinely making them the butts of jokes, especially if, as is so common, the foreigner takes a superior attitude toward Paraguay. Stories concerned with *jodiendo a los gringos* ("fooling the foreigners"), as it is called, circulate widely and excite much more merriment than the merits of the joke would otherwise warrant. The most extreme practical joke we heard of resulted in the breaking-up of an Italian couple's marriage. This couple had an unmarried Paraguayan cook who became pregnant and circulated the rumor that the Italian was the father. The Italian was never able to convince his wife that this was not so, and, although it was common knowledge that a certain Paraguayan was actually the father, no one came to the Italian's defense. Our Paraguayan friends laughed heartily at this story.

Recreation and Games

Social dancing is the most frequent recreational activity. Most of the social occasions which involve both sexes are planned as dances. Other kinds of functions—weddings, *asados*, "picnics," parties of all kinds—quickly turn into dances, for there is nearly always a guitar or two available even at a very small, unplanned gathering. Many families have outdoor dance floors; the wealthier people have them made of brick or tile, and poorer people have fashioned a smooth area topped with clay.

The interest in dancing transcends all classes. The only difference is the greater frequency of large dances with better music among the wealthier people. Traveling in the countryside almost any day, one sooner or later hears the sound of guitars, shouts, and laughter from a rancho, where friends and relatives have gathered to celebrate some occasion with a dance. Nearly any evening in the town similar revelry is heard, perhaps punctuated by pistol shots fired by someone who wants the occasion to be more widely appreciated.

The musical style and usual dance style is the polka, which is thought of as Paraguayan or "Guaraní." The Argentine tango and waltzes are known by the sophisticates but are not often played. The guitar is the most common instrument, and drums, an accordion, and perhaps a violin are used when an orchestra has been hired for a large function. We once saw a small old-fashioned horizontal harp, but this is a rare instrument nowadays. Horns, especially the bassoon and cornet, are used only for band music in church processions and military parades, and flutes are used apparently only by the masked *negritos*.

Most of the dancing is done by couples, the man inviting the girl, and at large affairs "cutting-in" is sometimes practiced. At smaller parties dancing games are sometimes played, especially the *solito* and the *pericón*. The hostess of the party begins the *solito* by dancing alone a few turns around the room, then stopping as the music stops and bowing to the nearest man. He then dances with her, each occasionally doing a few solo turns around the other; then she sits down, and he dances alone until the music stops him in front of his next partner. The *pericón* is a game involving several couples who dance circling the room in the normal way. The music stops suddenly, and the man who is caught in front of the orchestra has to say a little rhyme to his partner. This game is especially interesting to onlookers, for the men dance abstractedly, concentrating on making up a poem or trying to remember one. Complicated maneuvers take place because some men try to get caught when they have thought of something funny, and others are intent on avoiding it until they have made up their poem.[2] The "Santa Fé" is a more traditional dance, involving three couples in a series of sedate, highly formalized, involved phases, apparently derived from the ancient minuet. Most townspeople do not remember how to do it, and we never saw it properly performed.

All people, townsmen and countrymen alike, enjoy daytime barbecue dances in the countryside. They are usually all-day affairs which involve much planning and co-operative effort. Food is donated in abundance, tables and kitchenware are borrowed, and contributions are collected for liquor and to pay musicians. Almost any occasion can be turned into an *asado* outing. A visiting dignitary is typically honored in this way; a wealthy man may give an *asado* in honor of a friend's birthday, or, more typically, a group of friends may spontaneously decide to celebrate some occasion together.

In all cases, prodigality is the chief characteristic of the *asado;* the participants seem eager to exhaust their pocketbooks, their stomachs, and their energy. Vermouth and *caña* start flowing

2. The *pericón* of colonial Argentina was a much more intricate affair, but the essential element of rhyme-making is still present.

early in the day, and the dancing continues all day long. The food is always plentiful, usually including several kinds of barbecued meat, boiled manioc, *sopa paraguaya,* and desserts. Even the otherwise rarely used bread and wine may be served. The food is served at long tables under a tree or ramada, and during the meal a great many humorous speeches, poems, and off-color stories elicit great general hilarity. Everyone eats and drinks too much and sings and dances too long, and by nightfall all are in a state of complete exhaustion.

Any fiesta in the town occasions a considerable number of spectator sports, although there are no athletic clubs or permanent teams. Soccer-football is as common as it is anywhere in Latin America, and the people all understand it and are attracted to the games. Horse races are held nearly every Sunday and always the day before a fiesta. All Paraguayan towns, and even most of the *compañías,* have a race track consisting of two parallel paths about two meters apart, running in a straight line for about four or five hundred meters over level ground. The paths are made by cutting a shallow ditch through the turf, about twenty centimeters in depth and half a meter wide. The paired horses run from a standing start to a finish line, where a judge stands. A great deal of betting goes on; odds are sometimes given but usually not, as a horse is picked to run against its presumed equal.

The horseback games most traditional for fiestas are the *sortija* and a contest something like the colonial "chicken pull" still practiced in parts of Mexico and Argentina. The *sortija,* or "riding at the ring," is derived from an early Spanish sport. Two upright posts are sunk in the ground, four meters apart and about four meters high, with a crossbar at the top; from this a small ring is suspended by a string, so that it is at about eye level to a rider. The horseman rides at full speed between the posts, attempting to spear the ring with the point of a small Y-shaped twig. (The Spaniards used a sword or a dagger instead of the twig.) It is a difficult feat, and only about one rider in ten is successful. Whenever a rider carries off the ring, the band strikes up, and the rider gives the ring back to the officials, who present him with a red silk handkerchief which he ties to his horse's bridle. When the tournament is concluded, the winner is the man with the most trophies. The game so reminiscent of the chicken pull consists of burying a bottle of *caña* or a kerchief in the sand with only a small portion showing. Riders take turns trying to snatch it out of the sand as they lean over at a full gallop. When one succeeds in this, the other riders try to pull it away from him as they swirl around the area in a great cloud of dust.

Bullfights are common at the patronal fiestas at such towns as Luque, San Lorenzo, and Capiatá, but the last one held at Tobatí took place in 1943 or 1944. The bull is not killed, but merely tormented by three or four masked *negritos*, who clown around until the bull is tired. As many as ten bulls may be used in one day, and many clowns thus get into the act. Sometimes money is tied to the bull's horns, and the clowns try to get it off, while others twist the tail or flourish a red cape in imitation of a matador.

Cockfights are technically against the law but sometimes are held semisecretly during a fiesta. The inclosure is formed by several men in a circle, holding ponchos together. Each cock is fitted with the usual single razor-sharp spur. Odds are not usually given in the betting, as the assumption is that the cocks are evenly matched.

Gambling is a very frequent male indulgence and one of some economic consequence, as the men typically gamble for higher stakes than they can afford. The usual gambling games are known in Tobatí. One game called *bofo* is claimed to be purely Guaraní, but it turned out to be very much like draw poker played with Spanish cards. Other common card games, *truco*, *monte*, and *escoba de quince*, are played according to the usual Spanish rules. Dice-throwing and coin-pitching are well known, and so are bingo and raffles. The latter are the only gambling games in which women participate. *Taba* is a game of old Spanish provenience, still common in Paraguay and Argentina, which consists of betting on the toss of an astragalus bone of a cow or sheep. It is like a single die, but the faces of the bone have names instead of numbers. There seems to be no peculiarly Paraguayan (or "Guaraní") game, in spite of frequent claims to the contrary.[3]

3. See chap. xv for a description of children's games.

The Temporal Sequence of Daily Life

Time is calculated by the position of the sun and in town is told by the church bells, which apprise the people of important municipal functions. Very few people own watches or clocks and the only one in a public place is an old alarm clock in one of the two hotels, but it is often as much as a full hour off. The church bells toll daily, approximately at noon (twelve short strokes) and at about four or five o'clock in the afternoon for vespers. On weekdays the school bell calls the children at 7:00 A.M. and 2:00 P.M. To announce a Mass, the church bells ring rapidly at three fifteen-minute intervals, and the people who live in the town start for the church after the final ringing. A funeral procession for an adult is accompanied by the slow tolling of the *doble*, two strokes with the large bell and then both bells together for the third. A child's funeral is accompanied by the less doleful *repique*, the two bells rung rapidly in unison. The *repique* is used because the occasion is supposed to be joyful rather than sad, for a small child is without sin and thus goes straight to heaven to become an *angelito*. On the day before a holiday a *repique* is rung at noon and at vespers, again to foretell a merry occasion. The response to the calls is dilatory, and any large function usually begins an hour or two behind schedule.

The time for retiring and rising varies from summer to winter, but in any season most families are asleep shortly after dark and up before dawn. Trucks leave town as early as 2:00 or 3:00 A.M. in summer and about 4:00 or 5:00 A.M. in winter. Agricultural work is always well under way before dawn. People say they know when to arise in the dark by familiarity with the crowing habits of their roosters.

In summer most of the people are up about two hours before dawn. The family gathers for the leisurely *mate*-drinking and in about an hour are about their tasks. The men and boys go to the fields or other employment, and the women go first to the meat market and then to the milk-sellers and *almacenes* for other things needed for the late breakfast or noon dinner. The sun is barely up before most of the women have completed these errands and have begun whatever is the major task of the day.

Between nine and ten o'clock in the morning many people stop work for a snack and a drink of milk or *mate*. Dinner is at noon, after which nearly all activity ceases until three or four o'clock in the afternoon. Because of the afternoon heat, all doors and windows are tightly closed, and the people may undress completely and go to bed. Activity begins slowly again in the late afternoon with the taking of *mate*. By about five o'clock many families have started for the arroyo to bathe and visit. Many people do not work at all in the afternoon in summer, but they may have worked nearly eight hours in the morning. A light supper of leftovers is eaten in the twilight, and shortly after dark the houses are again quiet.

In winter work begins after the sun is up, because it is not necessary to avoid the heat. Work stops during the siesta, but people are not so likely to go to sleep because of the longer sleeping hours at night. People still go to bed shortly after dark at seven or eight o'clock. There is little visiting in winter unless the weather is warm. In bad weather people stay home, shivering in the dark, closed house, often going to bed to keep warm.

PART IV

Ideology

CHAPTER XV

Informal Education

IN THE care and training of children a clear distinction is drawn between the status of babyhood and that of childhood. In general, babies seem to be completely indulged; they are fed when they indicate the desire and are held and fondled a great deal. They are the center of much attention, and considerable time and effort is spent to keep them amused and comfortable. When a baby begins to crawl and finally to walk, some restriction in its activities is made, but only enough to protect it from harm. Someone, often an older sister, is always present to remove dangerous objects or to distract the child from any potential difficulty. Older siblings display remarkable affection and patience in their association with the younger children. At the ages of two and three years there is a certain amount of admonition and indirect guidance, but it seems to be directed toward some immediate end rather than toward training. At four or five years the gradual transition from an indulged babyhood to a more responsible childhood has been achieved. A few rules of behavior have been made, and a considerable degree of obedience is enforced.

Women usually have their babies with them. A very tiny baby is carried in the arms, wrapped in a towel or a *rebozo*. After the baby becomes stronger, it is carried astride the mother's hip. When the mother is seated, she holds her baby lying in her lap or with its back against her chest, so that it can look around. When the baby is put into its hammock for a nap, the mother rocks the hammock gently and croons.

Toilet training is accomplished without apparent difficulty. There is little scolding or shaming, especially among the countrypeople, whose circumstances of life create fewer problems of waste disposal. The diapers are squares of soft old cloths, doubled and passed between the baby's legs and fastened at the waist. As soon as the child begins to walk, the diapers are discarded, and the child goes around unclothed below the waist. It is not until this time that any attempt at toilet training is begun. The child is patiently taught to go outside the house to urinate and defecate, and eventually the mother begins to carry him directly to the outside toilet or corral or whatever is used by the family. In case of an accident the child is not scolded; the mother merely cleans it up, taking such things as expected. Although the people are pleased when a child learns quickly, the whole attitude toward toilet training is a relaxed one.

It is desirable that a child should learn to walk early, and parents spend considerable time encouraging and helping the child to take its first steps. A baby should be sitting up at three or four months and should begin to creep shortly thereafter. One informant asserted that her child walked at between eight and nine months and that this was possible because foam from cooking *locro* was collected and rubbed on the child's legs. A more common leg-strengthening application is a paste made of ashes of *tacuarilla* leaves. Early talking is likewise desirable, and leaves of a plant called, appropriately, *charlatana* are put in the child's mouth. One informant said that her child talked at ten months, owing to repeated use of this plant.

At about the age of two or two and a half, parents begin guiding the child by admonition but not by force. They seem to expect that the child will not pay attention, but endless repetition is apparently felt to be of some value. The earliest tantrums that we observed in which the parent was firm and demanding occurred at about four years. A few times we saw children of about five slapped on the face or on the buttocks, or dragged into the house crying, but verbal commands are much more usual. A very common method of discipline is to frighten the child by threats. He may be told that the *pora* or *pombero* (spirits) or the *Yasyyateré* (a witch who kidnaps children) will do him harm if he does not obey. Or an impromptu threat may grow out of immediate circumstances. Our cook told her little daughter of four and a half years that our garment bag was to put bad little girls into, which of course destroyed the child's confidence in us and made her afraid to go into the room where the bag hung. Once she told the child that the bag was full of dead little girls who had starved to death in it. Virtually any horrible fate may be threatened if it seems to result in the proper fear reaction. The process of disciplining a child of this age is called "taming"; a good child of five or six should be quiet, obedient, respectful to elders, and willing to help around the house and run errands. At the age of seven children start to school, both in the country and in town, and school discipline is added to the home training, though it cannot be said to supersede it.

Girls are supposed to be particularly well behaved; boys, even at six or seven, are indulged more and allowed to play with other children more. In the homes of the well-to-do, children seem to be given more leeway and to be a little more arrogant and "spoiled," but this may be due more to the influence of higher social position in the society at large than to their home training. But especially in the homes of the rich, boys as well as girls are taught good manners at an early age and are required to assume a deferential attitude toward guests, including the stereotyped behavior of greeting and talking with them, seating them comfortably, and serving them with drinks or food. Children seem to enjoy dispensing familial hospitality in the manner of grownups, and it gives them a feeling of participation. They have an air of social sophistication which always intrigues North Americans.

Training in formal etiquette begins in early childhood. Many of the rules of conduct taught children refer equally to any adult, whether guest or relative. All older persons must be treated respectfully. A child is taught never to interrupt a conversation or to pass in front of grownups. He must always respond politely when spoken to. By the age of three or four, children are taught to address, when in public, all women—their own mothers and grandmothers and even unmarried adult women—as "Señora." Since children are included in all social functions, public and private, they have considerable opportunity to observe and, to a limited extent, to practice adult social behavior.

Much home training of children, at any social level in the community, is concerned with the etiquette of serving. Small boys may be asked to pass a beverage or a plate of cookies, but the training of girls is much more extensive. Girls must learn to serve complete meals at a very early age and in any circumstance will be asked to serve more often than boys. When boys reach the age of ten or eleven, they are no longer asked to help. Even if no young girl is present to assume this duty, a mother will herself take the responsibility rather than ask her son to assist.

Small children are remarkably deft at the complicated, even dangerous, art of serving hot *mate*. The infusions of hot water used in the *mate* gourd are very small, and a child may be kept running back and forth between the kitchen and the tea-drinkers with the kettle of boiling water as much as twenty times in an hour. The *mate* gourd is always handed to the child, who pours about two tablespoons of water from the heavy kettle into the gourd. At first we were always apprehensive that the child might burn itself, but we eventually learned to relax, as we never saw one spill any of the water.

Children are taught always to serve any beverage other than *mate* on a plate or tray, even if it is only a single glass of water. In serving a group, the guest or most honored person is served first and the hostess last. It is emphasized that a person should be served with the right hand, never with the left. There was some feeling among a few of the upper-class informants that left-handed serving, which is considered disrespectful, might be proper among adults who were close relatives or good friends as a sign of intimacy, but children should never be permitted to serve with the left hand.

Girls are taught at an early age to set the table and to help in the preparation of food as well as in serving. In all classes great attention is given to arranging food attractively on the serving dishes or individual plates, particularly when guests are present or when the plate is being prepared as a gift. Lettuce or leaves of other plants may be used to garnish the salad, roast fowl, or slices of boiled or broiled meat. Pimientos, olives, slices of lemon or lime, radishes and onions, sprigs of parsley or other herbs, and even flowers may be used as trimming. Desserts such as puddings may be decorated with meringue, small candies, caramelized sugar, lime leaves, or sprigs of small flowers. Much time and effort is devoted to achieving an artistic effect, and girls are encouraged to attempt elaborate food and floral arrangements when they are very small.

From about the age of six or seven, boys and girls play less and less together, and a division takes place in the kind of household tasks they are expected to perform. There is great affection between brothers and sisters, however, which continues into later life—perhaps because this very sex distinction reduces friction and rivalry. The differences in treatment of boys and girls are in the common Latin-American tradition, though perhaps the indulgence of boys is somewhat greater in Paraguay. Paraguayans believe that more girls than boys are born, and they have an exaggerated idea of the preponderance of women in the population. Some informants suggested that boys are regarded as more important than girls for this reason. Others said that the indulgence of boys is the Guaraní tradition. At any rate, girls are trained to work dependably around the house from six or seven years of age, and considerably less concern is shown for their welfare or happiness than in the case of boys. This difference in the parents' attitude grows greater as the children get older. By the time boys are adolescent, they are almost obliged to act *macho*—to drink, gamble, engage in sexual exploits, and be generally undisciplined. If a boy is too "tame," he is regarded with a certain contempt, and this undoubtedly is the reason that he is treated indulgently at an early age.

Child Play

All small children imitate their elders in their play. From the age of four or five on, boys lose interest in the activities of their mothers and sisters and confine their play to imitations of their older brothers and their fathers. Small girls imitate their older brothers, attempting to play marbles and tops, but girls never become expert at boys' games. Boys' play after five or six is not closely supervised by adults. The boys play about the streets and vacant lots and near the arroyo, in groups of six or seven. Girls, on the other hand, more often play at home or at the home of a relative, where they are more constantly watched.

There is little difference in child play in different classes of society, perhaps because children in upper-class families are cared for to a large extent by the servants, whom they imitate in the same way that other children imitate their parents. An upper-class child will never learn to carry burdens or water, but outside of this their play will be much the same as that of a peasant child. Real dolls and expensive toys do not supersede the child's interest in the adult life around him.

Between the ages of two and a half and four, children play at planting flowers or vegetables, making home remedies, taking care of animals, and playing house. Little girls may play with homemade rag dolls, but doll play is less common than one would expect and lasts a short time, for often there is a real baby to play with and care for. From the time they are able to walk about, girls copy their mothers and older sisters at household tasks. They are given small brooms and learn to sweep; they play at making a fire and pretend to prepare and serve meals, using tin cans and broken dishes as utensils. When the mother washes clothes, the children are taken along to the arroyo, where they are allowed to wash a few small pieces. They play at ironing, grinding corn, sewing, and mending. They model small pottery vessels out of mud, make artificial flowers of paper, and pretend to play cards. When in a group, they carry on a conversation as if they were adults, discussing foods, medicines, and child care in an affected manner and with great seriousness. Often at about the age of four girls are given a small carrying basket and a little water jar or pail, and they accompany their mothers or older sisters on errands and help to bring home the food and water. At five or six they can already balance a small jar full of water on their heads.

Small children playing together often fight over their playthings or quarrel about who shall act a certain part in their make-believe play. Perhaps because they are so indulged by their parents and older siblings, they do not get along well with children of their own ages. Mothers frequently observe that when there are more than two or three small children playing together, there is frequent quarreling. This jealousy and failure to adjust to each other may be made more acute by the shortage of toys. Older children play and work together with less dissension. Only infrequently will a child of seven or eight strike another or use harsh words. Should this occur, the injured one usually leaves the group, sometimes in tears. "Fighting back" is very rare.

Formal Games

Since most manufactured toys are very expensive, there is a good deal of ingenuity in making toys and games from available materials. Balls may be made by stuffing rags, raw wool, or cotton into an old sock. Marbles are made of the same clay as that used for making pottery and are dried in the sun. These are used also for jacks and for shooting from a slingshot. Marbles are most commonly used for a game called *figura en el corral*. A circle is drawn on level ground and a small depression made in the center. Cut-out matchbox covers serve as prizes. Marbles are tossed toward the hole in the center, and the one whose marble lands closest gets one prize. The object is to get as many match covers as possible. Older boys play the same game for money. Other homemade toys include tops, kites, cup-and-ball games, and slingshots. Boys also make bull-roarers and stick-and-hoop games. Small *boleadoras*, like the Argentine bolas, may be made of string and coconuts, small round fruits, or other round objects.

Kañú kañú, or *escondite*, is hide-and-seek, played much as it is in North America. Tag is another popular game. The children count out to see who shall be "it" and then play the game with the familiar variations, tag with safe areas, running tag, or squat tag. *Descanso*, or hopscotch, is particularly liked by girls, but younger boys may join them in the game. All the above games may be played by both sexes, separately or together. Other games which may be played in mixed groups include fox and geese, drop the handkerchief, and various guessing games.

After about the age of five or six, the contacts with the opposite sex tend to be with siblings, except in school, which is coeducational. The brief half-hour of play in the evening, under the watchful eye of a parent or an older sibling, is the only other time when children of both sexes run and play together. By the time the children are ten or eleven years of age, they cease to play games in mixed groups.

Sex Education

Informants of all social classes agreed that parents do not purposely teach their children anything about sex and, in fact, consciously avoid discussion of any such topic in front of children. Informants also agreed, however, that all children "know everything" by the time they are twelve or thirteen and that some may even have had sex relations by that time. It is said that children learn about sex by "figuring it out," by observation of animals, and from older children. Sometimes an older sibling will inform a younger one of the same sex, and it also seems most probable that, especially among the poorer families, children would be aware of their parents' sexual relations, because of the very restricted living quarters.

The people usually say that they have "shame" about speaking of sexual topics to their children, and even siblings are shy in talking to each other, though less than in talking to their parents, who must be shown respect. The daughter of one of our friends was very frightened when she first began to menstruate but dared not tell her mother; finally, in desperation, she went to her older, married sister, who explained it to her. One of our female informants, whose sixteen-year-old daughter was about to be married, told us that the daughter knew nothing about sex. Another informant, a friend of the first, explained that the mother had never told her daughter anything and felt shame that the daughter might actually have learned some things. The daughter pretends ignorance of sex out of respect for her mother.

Children are of course aware of sex differences at an early age, for they run about naked until the age of four or five, and thereafter until near adolescence there are ample opportunities for boys and girls to observe each other bathing or dressing. There is little modesty about nakedness. The excretory functions are not particularly hidden, even among adults; men, especially, are often seen urinating, and, although women are more modest, they are not particularly concerned if discovered in the act.

Menstruation, however, is concealed carefully, and menstrual clothing is washed secretly because of the danger of supernatural contamination (*payé*). Pregnant women feel no shame or embarrassment and make no attempt at concealment of their condition. Children are nursed openly, and the only attempts at privacy are occasioned when there is fear that some onlooker might have an "evil eye."[1]

Despite the concealment of certain aspects of sex from children, there is little reticence about discussing sexual intercourse impersonally among adults. The attitude seems to be that sex relations are very enjoyable and natural. A man is supposed to have more pleasure than a woman and to find sex more irresistible, but a woman, too, may be expected to succumb sometimes to the "demands of nature." It is assumed, however, that a woman can live without a man but that a man must have a woman regularly. Male promiscuity is to be expected, therefore, and even in a sense to be valued, especially in young men. An unmarried woman is granted less license but no great censure is meted out if she has illegitimate children.

There are differences between the upper and lower classes in the degree of sex education a child may acquire. In the upper social class of Tobatí children are much more restricted in their activities, have fewer other children to play with, and are able to observe much less of the life around them than the poorer children. Upper-class people of both sexes are much more modest than the peasants. The houses have more than one room, and boys are more strictly separated from girls in dressing and sleeping; children are fully dressed at an earlier age, as well. Upper-class girls are much more closely guarded after puberty, and the shame and social ostracism resulting from premarital pregnancies are very much greater.

Among most of the population, exclusive of the upper and middle classes in the towns, sex relations soon after puberty are not uncommon. Elders try to protect a young girl from premarital relations, but it is assumed by all (including the girl) that she wants to escape and will inevitably do so and that, if she does get away, sex relations and possibly pregnancy will follow. If

1. The conceptions of *payé* and "evil eye" are discussed in chap. xvii.

this happens, the girl may be scolded and the family may be regretful or even somewhat ashamed, but they assume the blame as their own. The boy is considered the initiator, but he is not censured, as it is "natural" for him to act in this way. If the boy's interest in the girl continues, and he is acceptable to the family, a consensual marriage may take place; but more often the girl's parents will try to break up the alliance, feeling that the couple are too young to set up a household.

Organized prostitution does not exist in Tobatí, although there are a few women who are known to be promiscuous. True prostitutes would probably be driven out of town, as they are considered to be disease-carriers. It was reported that some years ago, when more outsiders came to the big patronal fiesta, a few prostitutes used to come, but the municipal officers did not permit them to stay.

Masturbation is said to be practiced by girls as well as boys. It is referred to by a Guaraní word, *oyupó ipoiba*, which means, literally, "to make thin." When the small, naked children touch their genitals, they may be distracted by the grownups, but they are not scolded for it. Older boys may be punished by their fathers if discovered, as it is believed that the practice actually is harmful. Except in case of discovery, however, usually nothing is said to the boys about masturbation, because of embarrassment. People believe that masturbation causes insanity, pimples, and weakness, and even the story about the growth of hair in the palm of the hand is known and used by older boys to tease younger ones, as in North America.

Sex aberrations are apparently quite rare in Tobatí. The most common stories have to do with boys' experimentations with farm animals. Such acts are considered to be the result of a natural curiosity, rather than as abnormal. Homosexuality is said to be present in Asunción, but we never heard of even an accusation of it in the town of Tobatí, and there was only an insubstantial rumor of it in the countryside.

CHAPTER XVI

Formal Education

THE formal education of the public schools in Paraguay is of particular interest to the anthropologist, for the curriculum is not only designed to give the fundamentals of reading, writing, and arithmetic but also is important in promulgating a universal Paraguayan conception of the national character. The nation's folk history, and kinds of knowledge which can only be described as mythology, are taught in the interest of the extremely nationalistic, almost revivalistic, cultural chauvinism.

During the colonial period education was primarily religious and largely limited to the upper class. Most wealthy families hired tutors or in a few cases sent their children out of the country to study. Following the wars of independence, under Francia's dictatorship, a few private schools existed in Asunción, but they were not encouraged by the government, and the *seminario*, the only secondary school, was suppressed in 1822.[1] Apparently the next dictator, Carlos Antonio López, encouraged education somewhat, but specific evidence is lacking on this point. At any rate, the great war of 1865–70 ruined whatever progress had been made in education. The *Statistical Yearbook* of 1886 reports that 14 per cent of the population could read and write. By about 1890 there were apparently some attempts to begin normal schools, and the Universidad Nacional was giving some courses in law.[2] By 1929 considerable progress had been made. There were seven schools devoted to teacher-training on several levels,

1. Harris G. Warren, *Paraguay: An Informal History* (Norman, Okla., 1949), pp. 175–76.

2. E. de Bourgade la Dardye, *Paraguay: The Land and People, Natural Wealth and Commercial Capabilities* (London, 1892), p. 79.

three *colegios nacionales* (high schools), and a few small technical schools, and the Universidad Nacional had expanded its
curriculum to include several sciences and medicine.[3]

The *Colegio Internacional,* founded in 1920 by the United
Christian Missionary Society, is considered the best of the private
schools in Paraguay. It has expanded considerably since its founding, and today Paraguayan as well as foreign teachers serve on
its faculty. Many of the well-to-do residents of Asunción send
their children there.

A number of well-taken criticisms of the Paraguayan educational system have been made by Teodosio González.[4] He stated
that the primary and secondary schools do not take account of
the practical needs of the backward, illiterate rural people, while
the purely cultural education of the upper classes fits them only
for politics. Schoolteachers are underpaid and undertrained. Of
late there have been some attempts by foreign missions, notably
from the United States, to encourage the teaching of public
health, nursing, and agricultural methods, and there has been an
increasing number of Paraguayan scholarship students who go
outside their country for training. These trained Paraguayans
complain, however, that their skills are not used when they get
home.

The public schools of Paraguay are organized under a central
ministry of education, with an administrative, advisory, and in-
spection staff. All these are political appointive offices which
change with the frequent overturns of the government. This has
resulted in uncertainty and disruption because of the constant
revisions in the curriculums to accord with the particular biases
of the ministers of education. The teachers themselves are civil
servants and are not so directly affected themselves by politics,
but they have no control over the curriculum. But the Catholic
church does not oppose the public school system in Paraguay,
nor did we notice any public criticism stemming from Catholic
ideology. In general, Paraguay stands in strong contrast to many
countries in Latin America because of the political weakness of
the church throughout its history.

3. J. Natalicio González and Pablo Max Ynsfran, *El Paraguay contemporáneo*
(Asunción, 1929), p. 65.

4. *Infortunios del Paraguay* (Asunción, 1931), pp. 427–57.

All financial support of the public school system derives from the government bureau of education in Asunción. Individual towns may allot a playground or a garden to the school, or volunteers may help repair the building; but the towns are otherwise of no influence. A plan of studies is revised and circulated from Asunción to the school directors all over the country, and regional school inspectors periodically check the schools for the orthodoxy of their teaching methods and use of the study plan.

In 1949 the program of study for the first six grades, as published by the ministry of education, was as follows:

GRADE I

Arithmetic: Familiarity with numbers and, by the end of the year, simple addition of sums up to 100
Drawing: Spontaneous interpretation of daily scenes
Manual work: Modeling useful objects with clay, cutting and pasting round and geometric figures, making book covers, and crayoning; all in connection with drawing class
Physical education: Exercises in formations, marching, games, and mimicking natural phenomena and animals and household activities
Artistic education: Songs
History: In language classes, knowledge of national holidays
Reading: Vocabulary-building, around activities of home and school; writing single words and short phrases; conversation on simple, common themes and short recitations; copying exercises and writing from dictation

GRADE II

Arithmetic: Familiarity with numbers to 1,000,000; addition and subtraction, including problems of purchasing, etc.; methods of proving a problem
Drawing: As in Grade I
Manual work: As in Grade I
Physical education: As in Grade I
Artistic education: Singing; addition of new songs
History: As in Grade I
Reading: Continued vocabulary-building, reading simple legends, continued exercises in conversation, copying and recitations, and very simple composition

GRADE III

Arithmetic: Mental arithmetic, multiplication, primary concept of fractions, and division
Drawing: As for Grades I and II
Manual work: As for Grades I and II
Physical education: As for Grades I and II, with addition of instruction in hygiene and emphasis on co-operative and rhythmic exercises and dances

Artistic education: Singing
History: National symbols and biographical information on heroes of Paraguay
Reading and Spanish: Conversation, with emphasis on trades, useful plants, health, agriculture, and animal care; copying, recitations, use of dictionary, rudiments of grammar, and more emphasis on composition

GRADE IV

Arithmetic: Decimals, measurements of length, and time
Drawing: Drawing direct from nature, copying, composition of designs fitting legends, etc.
Natural science: Anatomy, physiology, and hygiene; minerals, plants, and animals
Manual work: Sewing and embroidering (for girls only); agricultural work (for boys, use of plow and other tools, care of trees, etc.; for girls, care of school garden); industries (manufacture of flour from manioc, grinding corn, preparation of *locro*, breadmaking, preservation of meat, milk, and manufacture of cheese)
Geography: Form of earth; concentration on American continents, particularly South America and Paraguay; main emphasis on locations and political divisions
Physical education: As in Grade III
Artistic education: Singing, description of various types of music, and fundamental music theory
History: Discovery of America; discovery and early history of Paraguay, through time of López
Reading and Spanish: Conversation, recitations, conjugations, composition, and grammar

GRADE V

Arithmetic: Fractions
Drawing: Emphasis on form, proportions, and perspective; copying from natural models; geometric and decorative drawing
Natural sciences: Domestic economy, care and embellishment of the house, preparation of food, care of clothing, budgeting, and care of infants
Manual work: Sewing, embroidering, lacemaking, and weaving (for girls)
Industries: Agricultural techniques (for boys); preparation of desserts and candies (for girls); cutting of leather (for girls); manufacture of such items as ropes, brooms, hammocks, soap, ink and dyes, peanut and coconut oil, charcoal, paper, sugar, lime, and pottery
Geography: Intensive study of map of Paraguay and of each department in terms of localities, products, etc.
Physical education: As before, with further emphasis on co-operative and group games
Artistic education: Singing; further study of musical tempo and fundamental theory
Civic and moral knowledge: Duties to family, society, municipality; nationality, citizenship, naturalization, and various forms of government

History: A review from Grade III on; further discussion of *comunero* revolutions, national congresses, government of Francia, and "state of grandeur" of Paraguay at the death of Carlos Antonio López

Geometry: Measurement of lines; angles, polygons, squares, and rectangles; circumference of circles, etc.

Spanish: Oral exercises in conversation, recitations, conjugations, grammar, subjunctive use; written exercises, copying and composition, spelling and grammar

GRADE VI

Arithmetic: Complete review, with emphasis on problems of application

Drawing: Perspective, light, shade, compositional illustrations of stories of historical events, and use of paints

Natural sciences: Minerals, plants, and animals; physics and chemistry

Manual work: Further exercises in tailoring and sewing, crocheting, lace-making, embroidering, and weaving (for girls), agricultural techniques continued (for boys)

Geography: South America, North America, Central America, Europe (particularly Spain), Africa and Oceania

Physical education: As in Grade V

Artistic education: As in Grade V

Civics and moral knowledge: Political principles of the May revolution; study of various constitutions, good citizenship, duty of a citizen to his country, organization of the national government, the law, civil and political rights, and suffrage

History: From the independence of Paraguay through the war with Bolivia; some discussion of "the economic and social evolution of Paraguay"

Geometry: Prisms, pyramids, rounded bodies, cones, and spheres, with emphasis on problems of application

Language: Conversations, with aim of improving mode of expression, conjugations, poetic language, written exercises, spelling, and grammar

The reading and Spanish classes and also the history classes are the primary means by which the teacher indoctrinates the children in the folklore of Paraguay's history, politics, virtues, habits, customs, and mythology. This has a rather unexpected effect, for many items which a stranger regards as folklore or myth and superstition and expects to find only among uneducated rural "folk" are actually propounded in textbooks and are accepted by professors in Asunción as well as by isolated peasants. The intense interest in the posited "Guaraní heritage" has resulted in a reversal of the educational flow, which is usually from city to country. Here the beliefs of the folk are extolled as a sort of Guaraní version of the truth, put into books, taught to teachers, and reinculcated into the folk in a form which changes the original folk beliefs only to the extent that, in becoming part of national history, local variations are homogenized into one single version.

This is not to be taken as an absolute, complete, characterization, of course, for there are many aspects of lore which are peculiar to the peasants and are disdained by the sophisticated and other matters which are understood only by the educated urbanites. We shall make some attempt in the following chapters to separate "nationalized" lore from the superstitions peculiar to the uneducated peasants. Much of the lore taught in the schools has to do with the history of Paraguay and the nature of the Guaraní "race" and its culture. The themes are intensely patriotic, as are the geographic descriptions of Paraguay. Such subjects as the great beauty and healthfulness of the country, the color of the skies, the magnificence of the forests, and the purity and curative qualities of the lovely arroyos are continually extolled in recitations and poems which are memorized by the students.

Much of the history, as might be expected, emphasizes Paraguay's wars, the great bravery of her soldiers and citizens, and the biographies of her great statesmen and generals. Surprisingly, a considerable amount of attention is also given to what is perhaps best called "folk anthropology." However erroneous the teachings actually may be from a modern scientific point of view, there is an extraordinary interest in what are believed to be Guaraní institutions, customs, and traditions and in the characteristics of the Guaraní language. Race, language, and culture are thoroughly confused, but it seems that considerably more emotional interest is focused on the language, even though much emphasis is placed on the practical necessity of learning Spanish.

Many Paraguayan intellectuals have devoted themselves to linguistic studies, undertaken for the purpose of showing that Guaraní has not only the same grammatical categories as Latin (which, of course, it does not) but also some different categories (which it does) and that it is therefore superior to European languages. In other words, it is argued that a Guaraní-speaker can say (and think) all the same things as Europeans and also say (think) certain other things *better* than Europeans. It is felt that language is a direct reflection of racial intelligence; hence it follows that the Guaraní are a superior people. Linguistic evidence in the form of vocabulary parallels is used to argue that the Guaraní at one time had conquered all of South America, including the Caribbean Islands. It is quite a surprise for a North American ethnologist to find himself listening to a barefoot peasant listing some of the similarities between Tupían and Cariban vocabularies which are supposed to prove this point.

Somewhat less emphasis is placed on purely biological traits, but almost any ten-year-old school child can describe how the aboriginal Guaraní were not *Indios* but were light-skinned, taller, braver, with higher brows and more light in their eyes, and so on, than the other aborigines. In the cultural realm the Guaraní are represented (falsely) as having had a highly developed music and art and a complex political organization. They are said to have believed in "God" (*Tupá*), and, unlike the other aborigines around them, they abhorred cannibalism. Many of the surviving colonial traits, such as the polka dance and music, folklore, plant remedies, and cooking recipes, are described as Guaraní. Once we were told that the old-fashioned horizontal harp was a Guaraní instrument.

The Paraguayan personality or national character is supposedly distinguished by certain clear-cut traits which are extolled in the schools as unique racial attributes. Above all, the Paraguayan is fierce in battle and absolutely fearless, and the women are not only beautiful but also extraordinarily valiant. The men are supposed to be exceptionally amorous and generally *macho*, a concept which lumps sex desire and potency with aggressiveness, bravery, pride, and physical vigor into one single characteristic.

The various patriotic themes mentioned above are also drummed into the literate parts of the populace through the newspapers, radio, and literature. Newspapers are censored by the government, and only themes which are desirably patriotic may be presented. The radio is owned by the government and is very propagandistic. Paraguay's literature underwent a considerable ferment and efflorescence after about 1900, when the country was beginning to rise out of the ashes of the War of the Triple Alliance. As might be expected, all the writings were extremely patriotic, and the majority of the popular works were histories of Paraguay by such writers as Manuel Domínguez, Cecilio Báez, Manuel Gondra, Fulgencio Moreno, Blas Garay, and others. Most of these men became national heroes because of their writings, and some successfully entered politics. Some more modern writers, such as Natalicio González, have made great reputations as poetic glorifiers of Guaraní folkways and legends. Paraguay's most famous scientist, Dr. Moisés S. Bertoni, also became a national hero on the basis of his science, which was essentially patriotic. One of his most famous works, on Paraguayan botany, argues that the Guaraní had a native botanical nomenclature more accurate than the Latin one begun by Linnaeus and improved by European botanists and that it is preferable for most uses.[5] These writers are not read by the average Paraguayan, of course, but their works have formed the basis for a great deal of the material taught in the schools.

The teachers are seemingly among the most intellectually able members of the population. Their social status and prestige are high, but the pay is very poor. The wage categories are set up purely on the basis of amount of training, experience or seniority being of no consequence. Salaries for the various categories are as shown in the accompanying tabulation. In addition, a director

	Salary (Guaranis Monthly)
First category	103.40
Second category	89.30
Third category	84.60
Fourth category	75.20
Fifth category	65.80
Sixth category	61.10
Seventh category	42.30

gets 15 guaranis extra in a *superior* school (six grades), 10 extra in a *media* school (four grades), and 5 extra in an *inferior* school (two grades). In the Tobatí town school, a *superior* school, there are ten teachers, one gymnasium director, and one director of the school. Three teachers are in the sixth category, five in the seventh category, one in the fourth category, and one in the third category. The director is in the second category and has been

5. *Diccionario botánico* (Asunción, 1940). See esp. pp. 142–56.

teaching for many years. In the primary schools in the *compañías* of Tobatí, there are eight teachers in the seventh category, three in the sixth category, and one in the fifth category, in ten schools. Eight of the ten schools have only one teacher, who is also director, and two have one assistant each. Nearly all teachers, both in the pueblo and in the country, teach both morning and afternoon, which is considered double duty.

The schools of most towns are fairly comparable in their faculties, but there may be some variations. The nearby pueblo of Altos is practically identical with Tobatí; Arroyos y Esteros has no teacher above the fifth category; the pueblo of Santa Elena has more teachers in the second and third categories. There is a shortage of teachers all over the country, and there are too many students in all schools.

Towns vary considerably in the available facilities, such as buildings, garden plots, and playgrounds, depending on the amount of political pressure they are able to exert to secure funds. In the case of Tobatí a number of students come to the school from neighboring pueblos which have schools inferior in facilities and teachers, and Tobatí has also begun to grow in population, owing to the projected road to Caacupé. It had, even during the revolution of 1947–48, maintained considerable stability, owing to the power of the priest in political affairs and to his control over the local situation, so that it was regarded as a desirable place to live. For these reasons, the Tobatí school is probably better than average.

The teachers are usually young women, particularly in the rural schools. The director of the school in Compañía Typychatý is in the fifth category, and she has one assistant, in the seventh category. She told us that, owing to the political unrest (five changes of government had occurred in less than a year), the teachers had not been paid for the last six months. Other problems faced by the rural teachers are the difficulties in getting equipment and in compelling attendance and enforcing discipline. Parents are quick to withdraw their children from school if they disapprove of the teacher. The director also explained that it is hard to teach the children very much in the two years available because of the necessity for teaching in Spanish. The children usually do not know any Spanish when they come to school, and outside school they continue to use Guaraní among themselves and at home, which makes the acquisition of Spanish very slow.

Overcrowding is a great problem in the rural schools. At Colonia 21 de Julio there is a small two-room schoolhouse, each room designed for twenty students. There are nearly one hundred students in attendance, however, so that each class comes

TABLE 9

SCHOOLS IN THE *Compañías:* NUMBER OF STUDENTS AND TEACHERS

Compañía	GRADE I		GRADE II		No. OF TEACHERS
	Girls	Boys	Girls	Boys	
Aparypý................	20	30	....	....	1
Typychatý.............	30	36	15	21	2
Colonia 21 de Julio.....	30	45	11	14	1
Ensenada.............	25	35	....	....	1
Tacuatý..............	23	35	....	....	1
Colonia Mompox.......	33	30	....	....	1
Loma Verde...........	30	25	25	17	1
Isla Guazú............	20	28	....	....	1
Costa Alegre..........	30	20	10	10	1
Santa Rosa...........	25	33	....	....	1
Isla Florida...........	25	30	....	....	1
Total.............	291	347	61	62	12

on alternate days for only one-half day each time. All these children are taught by one teacher, the director, although she is entitled to an assistant.

There is no enforcement of the compulsory-education law, but most parents seem to desire schooling for their children. There are many people so poor, however, that they cannot afford the notebooks, pencils, and uniforms required. Sometimes a child is sent to school for one year, and then the next child takes his turn, using the same clothing. Table 9 shows that seven of the eleven rural schools do not have any second grade at all, and, in all the schools, 638 children attend the first grade but only 123 the second.

Many people state that it is desirable that both sexes attend school but that it is especially important for boys, as the ability to read and write is more important for them. Tables 9 and 10 show that in the rural areas boys in the first grade outnumber girls 347 to 291 but that in town the proportions are nearly equal. This would seem to indicate that when conditions are difficult and a choice must be made, boys will be sent to school instead of girls.

It is mentioned by Emma Reh in her diet study of Piribebuý that there is greater insecurity, poverty, and illness in homes headed by unmarried women and that the children must help in the household work at an earlier age.[6] We found in Tobatí,

TABLE 10

COMPOSITION OF THE SCHOOL OF THE PUEBLO OF TOBATÍ*

PLACE	GRADE I		GRADE II		GRADE III		GRADE IV		GRADE V		GRADE VI	
	Girls	Boys	Girls	Boys	Girls	Boys	Girls	Boys	Girls	Boys	Girls	Boys
Students from the pueblo..	120	100	30	40	46	35	38	39	12	17	14	10
Students from the compañías...............	25	50	20	10	9	15	8	5	3	3	2	2
Students from other towns.	6	10	3	2	1	5	....	....	....	1	....	....
Total.............	151	160	53	52	56	55	46	44	15	21	16	12
Number of teachers per grade.................	5		2		1		3		1		1	

* Average number of absences daily in school year 1948–49: 60; number of school days in 1948–49: 185.

however, that, while this is essentially true, these mothers make every effort to see that their children get at least two years of schooling. If the mother cannot make sufficient money through her own work to accomplish this, she tries to get work for the children in other households, so that they may complete their schooling.

We were told that about two generations ago the attitude was different. Some people did not want any of their children to go to school, and many others felt that schooling was for boys only. Thus a neighbor of ours, now in her sixties, lamented the fact that she could not talk Spanish and thus could converse with

6. *Paraguayan Rural Life: Survey of Food Problems* (Washington, D.C.: Institute of Inter-American Affairs, 1946), p. 24.

us only in a limited way, because her mother had not permitted her to go to school. On the other hand, our cook, a woman of a little over thirty, is the daughter of a single woman, but her mother had managed to send her through the first three grades, after which she worked as a *criada* until she completed the sixth grade. She is highly respected and attributes at least part of her success at educating her two children to the fact that she speaks Spanish well and knows arithmetic and writing. She is very anxious that her children go to school as long as possible. These two cases are illustrative of quite general differences between the two generations.

CHAPTER XVII

Lore and Magic

MUCH of the lore of the Paraguayan rural people is that of the general ideological system of Catholicism, in part actually taught by the church and in part traditionalized folk-Catholicism. But, as in most of southern South America, the official church has never been as strong, either in colonial times or at present, as in Mexico or Peru, so that up-to-date official church teachings have not been particularly influential. Spain never was very interested in its southern colonies, and there were no great concentrations of Indians to attract the attention of either the church or the state. After independence was won from Spain, Paraguay was largely self-sufficient religiously, and none of the dictatorships favored the church. Francia held the priesthood in contempt as ignorant, slovenly, and immoral.[1] During the regime of Carlos Antonio López an observer reported: "Paraguayans were steeped in religious ignorance and floundering in idolatry under a Bishop who believed that Cain and Abel were sons of Noah. The priests were ignorant and immoral, great cockfighters and gamblers, possessing vast influence over the women, a power which they turn to the basest of purposes."[2]

The Paraguayan Catholic church does have a complete monopoly over the people in religious matters, even though its influence seems weak. There are no Protestant cults or even spiritualistic groups outside Asunción, and even there they seem to be composed largely, if not entirely, of foreigners. There are no anticlerical groups as such but merely a widespread passivity

1. Harris G. Warren, *Paraguay: An Informal History* (Norman, Okla., 1949), pp. 174–75.
2. G. F. Masterman, quoted *ibid.*, p. 182.

or actual disdain of the church, especially on the part of men. Much of this feeling takes the form of contempt toward individual priests rather than a generalized anticlericalism. There is some difference in Tobatí between townsmen and peasants on this score: males in the town who are roughly the social equals of priests generally seem disrespectful; peasants, on the other hand, are respectful, as they must be, to all men of higher status. Among many peasants, mixed with the normal social respect, there seems to be the view that a priest is a sort of magician rather than a truly religious moral and ethical teacher. The ritual of the Mass, the prayers, candles, and incense, are meaningless except as magical formulas. We know of no significant formal attempts, on the part of either the church or lay groups, to teach any of the meanings of Catholic ritual to countrypeople.

In a social context the priest fills a role much like that of the old-fashioned country doctor in rural North America. In one sense, the peasants regard the priest as a healer, possessed of an occult "science," but he is also an educated man and is wise in human affairs—a good man from whom to seek advice. The more educated townsmen are suspicious of the use to which this power may be put and disrespect priests for their alleged lack of morality. The upper-class town women are less devout than peasant women, but church attendance is to them an important aspect of respectable social behavior.

A regular Sunday Mass in Tobatí is fairly well attended by women of all ages and by children. Few men attend, and fewer take Communion. Men often stand in the back of the church, where they can wander in and out easily. Others stand outside the church, some looking in on the services, others standing in small groups to chat. It is rare to see a man praying. Even members of the highly devout Cofradía del Carmen are required to confess and take Communion only once a year. Certainly the great majority of Paraguayans observe this duty much less frequently than that. During Holy Week or at other times when there are visiting priests, the people go in greater numbers to confession and Communion. Even at Easter only about fifty people took Communion in Tobatí, and, of that number, over forty were women.

Strict observation of fasting is not enforced in Paraguay. A papal bull during the early days of the colonization ruled that, because the mission Indians lived by the chase and by herding, they should be permitted to eat meat on all the Fridays of the year except during Lent. According to the priest, this ruling has been renewed from time to time, and the Paraguayans, still largely dependent on a meat diet, are not accustomed to the idea of fasting.[3] There is also a strong feeling in Paraguay that those who do heavy labor should not be concerned with fasting at any time.

There are few Jews in Paraguay, as they are excluded by immigration laws, so that most rural Paraguayans have never seen one; but all have been influenced by the anti-Semitic teachings of the church. This feature of Catholicism is emphasized during the Holy Week observances, especially in the Via Crucis processions, when Jews are excoriated for nailing Christ to the Cross and spitting in his face. The burning of the effigy of Judas on the night of Holy Saturday is referred to as "the burning of the Jew." The general impression is that Jesus and his true followers were not Jews but that somehow a Jew, apparently thought of in a racial sense, had gained their confidence and then betrayed them. Padre Martínez was genuinely astonished when we told him that the initials "I.N.R.I." on his cross stood for "Jesus of Nazareth, King of the Jews."

The church, with its dominant central position in the town and with its strong social power, is important in many ways in the daily life of the people. The bell, tolling the *doble* for the death of an adult, or the *repique* for the death of a child, or calling a Mass or fiesta, is a means of communication daily noted by those living in the village. In every bus and automobile there is a blessed picture of the Virgin or a saint in the front window to protect the occupants from harm. Men often wear religious medals or crucifixes on the wristbands of their watches, and women wear them suspended around the neck. Nearly every household maintains a small shrine.

Religious vows are often taken by women. They may, as in

3. Apparently, fasting rules are not so strictly observed in any part of Latin America as they are in Europe.

the fiesta of the Virgin of Caacupé, light a candle to the Virgin and remain kneeling in prayer until the candle goes out. They may vow to go on foot to a certain fiesta every year or to burn four candles to the Virgin every *víspera* before a saint's day. Occasionally men may make such vows when in extreme circumstances, but women do so much more often.

A type of folklore or superstition which may grow out of church beliefs is illustrated by the following story of a local "saint." Once a man was attempting to escape from enemies and hid in a tree. He made a vow that if he escaped with his life he would make an image from the wood of the tree in which he was hiding and would always keep the image in his family. He escaped and carved an image of a child in a coffin. This image is now occasionally removed from the coffin and placed on a cross, and candles are burned before it, for it is believed to have magical powers to grant favors. The *"santo"* is referred to as the "Angelito de 21 de Julio" (the name of the *colonia* where it is located). It has been kept through several generations of one family. Persons who come to the shrine to ask favors burn candles and pray to the "saint" and leave donations of money if they can afford it.

There are also superstitions connected with priests. There is a Guaraní expression, *ryé acú*, which, literally translated, means "hot belly" and figuratively means bad luck. Some persons are believed to have occult powers not possessed by ordinary men, and many people believe that priests are "bad luck" in this way. Thus, when a countryman meets a priest, he may grab his knife, his belt buckle, a key, or any other object of metal to ward off the evil effect of seeing a *ryé acú*. There is, incidentally, a similar custom in Sicily and probably in much of peasant Europe.[4]

It is a custom of the country to erect a simple shrine or cross on the spot where a person was killed. The cross may be from two to three feet high and always has a piece of white cloth linked around the upright and falling in front over the crossbar. The cloth is called a *curuzú paño*, an adornment or dress for the

4. Desiderius Erasmus said that the people (of the Netherlands, presumably) regarded meeting a monk as bad luck (*In Praise of Folly*, quoted in *Introduction to Contemporary Civilization in the West* [New York, 1946], I, 429). See also Carlo Levi, *Christ Stopped at Eboli* (New York, 1947).

cross, and the act of putting on the cloth is called "dressing the cross." The priest suggested that the custom might derive from the loincloth worn by Jesus on the Cross, but no one else could offer any explanation of its meaning.

There are many confused beliefs about the representations of the Virgin and the saints. It is believed by many that each representation of the Virgin is a distinct personality and that the Virgins of Caacupé, Tobatí, and Itatí in Argentina are three sisters. All are images of the Virgin of the Immaculate Conception, and this confusion arises, according to one informant, from references in church to *las tres Marías*. It is said that occasionally small spines are found in the dress of one or the other image, indicating that they travel back and forth to visit each other. Some informants believed that God and Jesus are the same person. Others said that God and San Juán are first cousins. Since *Dios* (Jesus) had no brothers, his first cousin was very important to him. It is for this reason that the relationship between first cousins is a very close one, and there should be much mutual respect. Marriage between first cousins is sinful, like marriage between brothers and sisters. In former times the countrypeople observed this prohibition strictly. Now first cousins sometimes marry, but severe disapproval by older relatives often causes at least a temporary family rift.

A great many superstitions surround the celebration of the fiesta of San Juán, many of them having to do with marriage and courtship. Young girls believe that they may find out whether they will marry a young man or an old one, a blond or a brunet, or may even find out the initials or occupation of a future husband by following the prescribed rituals. Most of the superstitions involve activities carried out on the eve of San Juán's day. A cross of laurel leaves placed under the pillow will bring a dream of a future sweetheart. Corn and beans may be planted on the eve of the saint's day. If the corn grows, the girl who planted it will marry a foreigner, since corn is blond; if the beans grow, it will be a Paraguayan, for beans are dark. If a shoe thrown over the house lands upside down, the thrower will not marry within the year. A green lime plucked from a tree by a blindfolded girl means marriage to a young husband;

a ripe lime indicates marriage to an old man. One old custom, still common in the country, is telling fortunes from the forms taken by molten lead or candle drippings dropped into a pan of water.

Nearly everyone in Tobatí goes at dawn on San Juán's day to bathe in the arroyo. This is believed to promote good health through the year and is a specific cure for *granos*. It is said that if the hair is cut on this day, it will grow better, particularly if the cuttings are thrown in the arroyo. At planting time, ears from which corn seed is taken should be thrown into the stream, so that the new crop will produce large ears.

There seems to be no other saint with whose fiesta so many superstitions are associated. Others seem to be dedicated to protection of certain groups of people; for example, San Ramón is the guardian of pregnant women and childbirth. A woman who is pregnant may commend herself to his care, burn candles to him, and ask help for an easy birth. She may make a vow to name the child after the saint and may request that he use his influence to insure that the child be of the desired sex.

It is believed that the possession of a secret prayer to Santa Elena may aid a woman to marry and that after marriage the prayer should be given to a single woman. Some women keep such private prayers written on scraps of notebook paper and claim that they bring protection against any danger. Secret prayers written in Guaraní are considered to be more potent than Spanish prayers.

Legends

Most of the folk legends commonly told to children are also taught in school. Probably the most current, and also one of the most ancient, is the story of *Yasyyateré*, a beautiful small blond child, who carries a golden cane. He comes at siesta time to lure restless children to his straw house deep in the woods by promising them his cane. His power lies in the cane, so a person endangered by him can be saved by tricking him into dropping it. Some of our informants claimed to know people who had seen *Yasyyateré*. One said that a small cousin had been carried away by the creature and was found two days later wandering *loco* in the woods. A second baptism was required to restore the child to normalcy. A bird which has a call sounding like the word *yasyyateré* is believed to be the boy witch masquerading as a bird. Supposedly aboriginal Guaraní in origin, the tales of *Yasyyateré* are much like some of the middle-European stories of the Midday Witch.

Another common legendary or mythical character is the *pora*. There is great disagreement as to the attributes of this spirit, but it is usually believed to be a spirit which stays in dark wooded places, particularly to guard spots where treasure is hidden.[5] On passing a very thick, dark patch of woods, for example, one of our friends told us that many *poras* lived in there and that there must be some treasure buried near by. Some informants felt that the *pora* was the spirit of the original owner of the gold or treasure and that he might be there for the purpose of leading the proper person to the gold.[6] Others say that the spirit may take any form, man, woman, or even animal, but that it will do no harm if one does not speak to it.

In spite of the expressed conception that this is a benevolent spirit, it is clear that there is considerable fear of it. One informant told of a report some years back by a number of frightened people that they had seen such a spirit under a big tree near the arroyo. Our informant, together with the priest, went one night to investigate, guided by one of the persons who had seen it. The guide pointed from a distance and ran away. The priest called, "If there is some lost soul here that needs help, let him speak, that I may help!" Nothing happened, but the next day they found a large hole near the tree and concluded that someone had previously been guided there by the spirit and had taken the treasure, thus freeing the spirit from his bondage. A child told us seriously that one must not stay in the house alone at night, because "some *pora* might come and frighten you." Another four-year-old child was frightened of her great-grandfather and would not go near him. He had white hair and a white beard, and she declared that he was a *pora*.

5. *Pora* is described by Natalicio González as a sort of Guaraní Diana, but we did not discover this conception in Tobatí (*Proceso y formación de la cultura guaraní* [Buenos Aires, 1938], pp. 307–9). The Paraguayan *pora*, as described by some informants, seems to be similar to the *caipora* of southern Brazil.

6. Juán F. Bazán, *Del surco guaraní* (Buenos Aires, [n.d.]), pp. 246–52.

The *pombero*, another spirit of the night, is said to be known only by the noise it makes, since it is never seen. It is particularly noisy when rain threatens. It is described as very small. The spirit is often pictured as resting under a toadstool, which is called a *sombrero de pombero*. The *pombero* frightens people by the small animal noises or whistles it makes, and it is useless to search for it, for it is a ventriloquist. Women, particularly, are very much afraid of the *pombero*, and, if a woman is out of doors when she hears its call, she goes inside as rapidly as possible.

One must not call it *pombero* or it gets angry; it should be addressed as "Caraí" ("Señor"), or "Mi amigo," to placate it, and one should ask its permission to continue on one's way. During the season when the maize blossoms, it is the custom to put black tobacco in the patio every night for the *pombero*. It is said that then he will not eat the blossoms and that the next day he will return bringing cane syrup or manioc. One must be more than careful never to neglect the offering to the *pombero*, for fear of incurring his wrath, nor should one ever insult him or make fun of him, for he will sense it immediately.

Witchcraft

The most usual conception of malicious witchcraft is that of the *payé*, who can harm another person by putting secret herbal concoctions in a drink, cigars, or food. *Payé* (a Guaraní word) literally means "enchanted," but the word is also used to refer to the concoction or to the witch himself. All Paraguayans know of the concept of *payé*, and seemingly most people believe in it and can name specific individuals who practice the art. It seems that these individuals possess no evil power intrinsic in their persons but only a knowledge of secret formulas, which are usually referred to as *remedios*. It is believed that very few people know these formulas. A person bewitched by *payé* can be cured only by a stronger *payé*, but so few know the cures that many people die of these enchantments.

The *payé* or element which causes enchantment is prepared in a decoction from weeds, flowers, the blood of an iguana or of some other lizard, or menstrual blood of a woman. Prayers and incantations are not used during the preparations. The cure must be made of certain weeds and given in the same way in which the evil medicine was taken, i.e., in a drink, cigar, or food.

Old women are more likely to be *payés* than others, though it is said that a man or woman, old or young, could be one. Women, too, are generally more fearful of *payé* than men. An insane old woman named Jovita who died during our stay in the pueblo was considered a *payé*. A graduate of the *colegio* in Asunción said that in her youth in Tobatí people were afraid of Jovita and were sure she was a witch. This informant said that she had earlier believed that Jovita actually was a *payé* but that now she does not believe in bewitchments. Nevertheless, she is careful, because one never knows when someone will put something in one's food or drink which could cause illness.

Another informant, a relatively well-educated and progressive man, told of a boy in Compañía Rosado who had taken a *remedio* by mistake and had lost his reason. This informant firmly stated that some people have the ability to make *remedios* which can make a person love or hate another person, or can make him ill or insane. He also stated that the commonest conception seems to be that *payé* leads to a madness characterized by the desire to walk for great distances without rest. Another usual conception is that a certain illness, characterized by convulsions, is caused by worms (of a different type than those involved in *susto;* see chap. xviii) in the blood of animals used in the *payé*. These worms may cause insanity, illness, convulsions, or even death. The informant's brother was once working in Villa Hayes and was living with a girl there. He took a drink in an *almacén*, the owner of which was his rival for the girl, though he did not know this. The rival secretly put a *remedio* in the drink, which caused our informant's brother to become very drunk and later quite ill. He was taken to a doctor in Asunción. He had hallucinations and convulsions, and finally died because the doctor could not help him at all, not understanding *payé*.

A remedy for the *payé* caused by menstrual blood consists of boiling a small root of the *calabasito* (a gourd plant) in water to which seven drops of holy water has been added. The infusion should be taken in a drink like *caña* or wine and may also be applied to the head of the patient with a cloth. This is believed to make the *payé* go down from the head and leave the body.

Love potions may be prepared by taking a drop of blood from the end of the little finger and putting it in the food or drink of the person whose affection is desired. This is so powerful a *payé* that a man may be made to leave a woman he cares for and come to the one who made the *payé*. A friend of ours who was brought up on a large ranch in Uruguay described a similar conception in his country. He was always cautioned when he rode about the country never to accept refreshments in a country house for fear that some sort of love potion had been introduced into the food, drink, or cigars. In his case this was not for fear of *payé*, in which he did not believe, but for fear of falling ill from some foreign substance.

There seems to be a fairly prevalent conception of witches which mixes the old European "broomstick" type with the *payé* enchantress. Many informants told us that people used to think that certain old peasant women who looked *muy india* could fly by night. Such a witch, unable to fly in the daylight, might be caught near a house at dawn and thus be forced to remain there throughout the day in human form. One informant stated that most of the peasants still believe today that there are night-flying old women, who also concoct *payé*, but that most towns-people, especially men, no longer accept this belief. But it is clear from all information that everyone believes in, or has considerable uneasiness about, the concept of *payé*.

In spite of the fear surrounding the idea of *payé*, it does not play so consistent a role in daily life as does the conception of *oyeharú*, or "evil eye." *Oyeharú* has no secret maliciousness associated with it in the way that *payé* has; hence we had no difficulty in getting information about it. Everyone seems to believe in it completely, and there is great uniformity in the content of the beliefs.

Any person, man or woman, may have the power of *oyeharú* without knowing it, and the same person may have it one day and not another. Thus such persons might have a harmful influence only at times and therefore never find it out. Because they are innocent of intent to harm, they are never blamed or punished. A menstruating woman is somewhat more apt to have an evil eye than another person, but otherwise there is not likely to be any evidence that a person has it, except through experience with the results of his influence. For example, if a baby cries all day from illness, special attention is given to the time of day it began to cry; then it is recalled what person last saw the child at that particular time. Another possible means of identifying a person with an evil eye is that, when a person with *mal de ojos* (trachoma) is in the presence of an evil eye, his own eyes start to hurt. But if several persons are present, there is no way of knowing who is responsible, as this evidence is very subtly sensed and is not related to degree of nearness of the evil-eyed person. When a person is suspected of an evil eye, he is apprised of it. Mothers keep babies away from him, sick or weak people avoid him, and he tries to co-operate in the avoidance. Strangers are more feared than familiars, as their records are not known, but even a relative, including the father of a child (but never the mother), may be the cause of an evil-eye illness.

Babies, especially if newborn or in a weak condition, are particularly susceptible to the evil eye. Until a child has been baptized, one must be very cautious and, especially, keep it away from strangers. If a person with an evil eye looks at a baby, the baby may begin to get fretful and later become quite ill or even die. To a lesser extent, any person in a delicate condition may be harmed. Newly planted crops may not grow well. Delicate milk and egg dishes may curdle in cooking, or *dulce de leche* may sugar. Baking pottery may crack. The feeling is that the evil eye adds somewhat to the possibility of "bad luck" in such cases.

There are several ways in which an illness resulting from an evil eye can be treated. If the mother of a sick child can identify the offender, she gets some of his hair and burns it in a fire made of blessed palm leaves, at the same time throwing a little holy water in the fire. Then the child is passed through the smoke of the fire several times in the sign of the Cross. Sometimes a sock belonging to the father is made into a stocking cap to be worn by the baby until it is well. As soon as a child is born, it is a good idea to put a gold necklace, bracelet, ring, or medal on it, as gold offers even better protection than being blessed by a priest. Baptism is important, however, especially if the child is not only baptized with holy water but also anointed with oil.

Nature Lore

There are many beliefs about natural phenomena and explanations of their origins. Old women say that San Jerónimo makes the thunder and lightning in his anger and that, if one is afraid, he should commend himself to San Jerónimo to escape the danger of being hit by a bolt. Eclipses are feared, and the old people spend the time in prayer. They say that the sun and the moon are fighting and that, if one loses, it will never come up again. An eclipse is not believed to have any particular effect on children or on pregnant women but is generally feared. Any prayer is adequate for alleviating the danger.

The rainbow (*arco iris;* also called *arco de Noé* because of confusion with the story of Noah's ark) is said to be drinking water out of the Piribebuý River or the arroyo of Tobatí, and children are very frightened, for they believe that it is likely to suck them up. In drinking the water, which later falls as rain, it also sucks up fish and frogs, which explains why they sometimes are found in the fields after a rain.

Perhaps the most consistent and universal beliefs about natural phenomena have to do with the moon. During the time of the new moon nothing should be planted, nothing new undertaken, because the growing moon makes everything weak. This belief is associated with the menstrual period of women, which is referred to as *iyasý ra'y,* meaning "with the new moon." A person's blood is weak during the time of the waxing moon, and so are all the plants. Wood should not be cut or animals castrated. All planting and the training of horses and oxen should be begun during the time of the waning moon.

Falling stars are said to mean that "God is showing a traveler the right road." There is fear of the night, and people pray to protect themselves against the spirits of the night. Night air is considered dangerous, very much as in rural Europe and Latin America in general, but the people do not practice many safeguards against it. In summer many sleep out of doors or work in the fields before dawn or travel all night without overt signs of fear.

There are no magical means of predicting the weather; it is done by means of known natural phenomena and also by Bristol's almanac, which is equally respected by the most ignorant and the most sophisticated farmers. There are many superstitions, but they are not taken very seriously. When a cat washes its face a great deal, it will rain within three days. When the monkeys howl in the woods, rain will fall very soon. When the birds sing an unusual amount, and especially when the *carayá* and the macaco cry, rain is indicated. A red sun at morning forecasts a *sequía* (dry spell).

There is a saying that the cold south wind came and said, "I find only an old woman in the kitchen crying!" The north wind, which brings warm weather, came and boasted, "I find many lovely girls bathing in the stream!" There are two kinds of north wind, the *suave*, which the people prefer to all winds, and the *norte guaycurú*, a strong, steady north wind, blowing night and day, which makes one sleepy all the time. It is called *guaycurú* because it is "very ugly." The south, southeast, and east winds are feared, for they bring cold and illness. The *viento poniente*, or west wind, causes severe storms, particularly during the month of October.

It is believed that roosters crow regularly at ten or eleven o'clock at night. The second crowing will be at about two o'clock in the morning. The third cry will occur just before dawn. From that time on, the roosters will continue to crow sporadically. But it is thought that one can tell time during the night by the crowing, and, if the roosters crow at an off hour, rain is predicted.

There is a legend about a bird called a *chochi*, which God has punished by causing it to sing all day and all night without rest. The *chochi* singing near by brings dry spells, crop ruin, and other bad luck. The hooting of an owl in the patio is a sign of impending bad luck. A small yellow bird with a black breast, the *pitogué*, sings near a house where there is a pregnant woman.

Snakes are greatly feared and are associated with bad luck and disaster. A snake entering a house brings bad luck; dreaming of a snake indicates unfaithfulness of lover, wife, or friends. There is a very strong belief in a snake which lives in a hole in the floor of the house and comes out only at night. If a woman is nursing a child, the snake gives its tail to the child and itself sucks from the mother's breast. A woman who has a nursing child is always wary of this, and when the child gets weak or thin it is regarded as a sign that a snake has taken the milk. The snake will also take milk from a cow.

There are a few beliefs concerning dates and seasons. It is felt that the first Monday in August is a day of great danger. Only the lightest and most necessary labor should be carried out, and no travel should be undertaken. It is thought that this is the day on which Cain killed Abel, and one hour of the day is dangerous, but, since it cannot be known which is the perilous hour, the entire day is treated as a day of danger. On that day in Tobatí school was in session, but the factory was closed. The busses did not run to Asunción, and the town was very quiet. The day before, in a *compañía* where some road work was in progress, a speech was made urging the men to come to work in spite of the taboo, but there was little hope that many people would cooperate.

The entire month of August, which marks the end of winter and is often cold and rainy, is regarded as a period when health is poor and the blood is thin. No laxatives should be taken, and the hair should not be washed. More people are said to be ill in August than at any other time of year. Since pneumonia, bronchitis, and respiratory ailments are primary causes of death, this may be true.

October is a month of food scarcity. On the first of October, beans or *locro* should be eaten, and balls of *typyratý* should be secreted under the eaves of the house or ramada, so that the misery of starvation will not come to the household. October is represented pictorially as an old man with a huge straw hat. Any very old man wearing a straw hat may be referred to as "Caraí Octubre."

Miscellaneous Signs and Portents

Dreams are interpreted, but apparently more in fun than seriousness. Women who are *payés* and other old wise women are supposed to be particularly clever at reading dreams, but men pay little attention to dreams. The dream interpretations seem standardized and fairly common, and often come from books. A white horse means good luck; a dream of blond humans means good news will come. To dream of dark people or dark things is bad luck; dreaming of a child or of broken eggs is bad luck. Dreaming of a drunken person is good luck; wild or ferocious animals indicate bad luck, but to dream of a dog means that a good friend is thinking of you. One of the most interesting interpretations is that a fight with firearms, or any fight resulting in bloodshed, means good luck. A dream of a priest is *yeta* ("bad luck"). To dream of a burro, *un animal mal*, means that someone is gossiping about you. In telling of dreams, everyone is good humored and not at all serious, and there is no attempt to keep dreams secret.

A woman who whistles is said to be looking for a man. A tic in the left eye is bad luck, and a tic in the right eye is good news or good luck. A burning ear on the left means bad gossip; on the right, praise. In general, left is bad, and right is good. If a knife (*cuchillo*) or spoon (*cuchara*) falls, someone is thinking of you whose name begins with *C*, if a fork (*tenedor*), someone whose name begins with *T*; and so on.

It is bad luck to shake hands across another handshake. When a moth comes into the house to stay for the day, it may bring money, a desired visitor, or letters. If you spill oil in the house, it is bad luck; if you spill salt, it means happiness and visitors. Milk spilled in the house is good luck, for it indicates abundance. If a glass container is broken in the house, water should be sprinkled over the pieces in the sign of the Cross to avoid bad fortune.

Amulets are carried against *yeta*. They consist of such objects as tiger teeth, snake rattles, dog's toenails—anything of personal fancy or anything indicated by some experience to be valuable. These seem to be carried not against specific misfortunes but against general bad luck.

If a fox crosses one's path going to the left, it is bad luck. One informant claimed this belief to be so strong that, should this happen, a man would go home rather than go on about whatever business he had in mind. If the fox goes to the right or straight ahead, it is of no significance. If a horse is tied, and the rope is across your path, you must lift the rope and pass under it; never step over the rope, as it is bad luck. One can imagine how it might actually be dangerous, should the horse be startled, but this seems not to be the conscious motive of the superstition.

CHAPTER XVIII

Medical Beliefs

ALTHOUGH Paraguayans generally seem to be a reasonably energetic and vigorous people, they are much preoccupied with illness, and there is a great deal of mixed ancient and modern lore
concerned with the diagnosis and treatment of it. Contagion and
infection are recognized by some people as causes of at least a
few illnesses, but there is a greater tendency to think of illness
in terms of a generalized weakness of the body or "thinness"
of the blood which makes one subject to the influences of natural
phenomena. When contagion is fairly obvious, as during an
epidemic, it is blamed on *mal aire*. For example, the meaning of
malaria in Paraguay is not the mosquito-carried disease with recurrent fever and chills (which is called *paludismo*) but is an
epidemic of any disease. The belief is that the bad air carries the
sickness, and, as a result, many individuals fall ill at the same time.
The actual disease may be malaria, scarlet fever, yellow fever, or
any other which causes an epidemic.

The cold *mal aire* is probably the single most important cause
of illness. The night air is the most dangerous because it is colder;
one must guard against breathing it into the lungs, or risk getting
a cold or a more serious illness. A "cold" in the neck, shoulder,
or back or any unexplained muscular or neuralgic pain in any
part of the body is usually considered to be the result of a *golpe
de aire*, or draft. Infirmities are especially numerous when the
south winds bring cold air from the Argentine pampas. At such
times one should not bathe the body, and it is well to avoid
washing even the hands and face. July and August are the most
dangerous months, particularly the latter, for the winter is nearly
over, and the weather may be warm for a time and then ex-

tremely cold. The north wind, generally felt to be benevolent, is regarded as prejudicial in August, when it is called *viento guay-curú*.

Artificial heat in the house is considered bad for the health, and so is woolen clothing. Except for the wool *rebozo* or poncho, used as an outer garment, all clothing should be of cotton. Shoes are worn only on the coldest days by most of the lower-class population and immediately after childbirth by women. These beliefs all concern scarce items, not within reach of most of the population, so they may be rationalizations of an economic situation rather than actual medical beliefs.

The most common summer infirmities are believed to be caused by the sun. Adults wear hats or cover their heads with *rebozos*, and they make constant efforts to keep children out of the sun. When the north wind is blowing in summer, there is less chance of catching cold than in the winter, and a summer cold rarely develops into a real illness. During the summer, water should be taken as a *refresco* with parsley or lime. This prevents the desire to drink too much water, which is believed to dilate the stomach, to cause excess fat, and to increase perspiration.

Foods are divided into categories of "hot" and "cold" which bear no relation to actual temperature of the food item; in general, "hot" foods are good for "cold" illnesses, and "cold" foods are used to reduce fever. These foods, if mixed in certain ways or eaten at certain times, may cause discomfort or actual illness. Thus most foods should be eaten in a prescribed order and only at certain times of day, and water should be drunk only after eating, never before or during meals. The elaborate beliefs about food and its role in the prevention and treatment of illness are discussed in Appendix IV. Here we might say, however, that "hot" and "cold" relate to food consumption much as to other matters. Illness can result from exposure to a sudden change in air or water temperature, and so can one's internal organs suffer if they are subjected to rapid changes by mixing the wrong foods.

Cleanliness of body, hair, and clothing is recognized as related to good health, although asepsis is not understood. The people bathe frequently, often daily in the summer months, and clothing is washed regularly and changed frequently, except in the brief cold spells during the winter. The hair is washed and brushed regularly during the summer, and there is no superstition about disposal of combings.[1] Fingernails should be kept short and clean, according to instruction given in the schools. Older beliefs, now dying out, prescribed that nails must not be cut on any day which has an *R* in it, as the nails might become brittle and break. Monday was said to be the best day, and, as the nails were cut, a prayer was recited for the repose of the souls in purgatory. A few people still burn the nails.

Houses are swept out daily and dusted with feather dusters. Refuse is thrown out, where the dogs and chickens quickly dispose of it. House yards are kept clean, and bedding is aired in the sun. Nevertheless, occasionally in homes, and nearly always in such places as military barracks, infestations of fleas, bedbugs, and lice occur. Unironed clothes may carry a type of body lice called *sarna*, particularly if the clothes have been washed in the arroyo along with the clothing of many other families. In hot weather anyone may be troubled by fleas and by a small chigger-like, burrowing flea called *pique*. The latter causes particular distress by burrowing beneath the skin and laying its eggs, which later develop into the larval stage under the skin.

The people generally, and townsmen in particular, have been careful in disposing of human feces since the antihookworm campaigns initiated in the 1920's under the auspices of the Rockefeller Foundation. Nearly all homes have some sort of outdoor privy, and children are taught in school the consequences of carelessness. Intestinal worms, in general, are regarded as common causes of illness.[2] One of the most curious beliefs in Paraguay is the association of worms with the illness called *susto* ("fright" or "shock").

In some respects *susto* is similar to the general rural Latin-American conception. It is thought of as the general cause of fainting, fits, hysteria, and otherwise unexplained chills or fever. Children are especially susceptible to such fright, as are adults

1. In olden times, it is said, hair combings were always burned or buried, because it was believed that hair was sacred from the time of baptism on.

2. Some treatments for the various types of illness believed to be caused by worms, and superstitions concerning them, are described in Appendix V.

who are weak and nervous, as when convalescing from some other illness. Miscarriage may be caused by *susto*. The conditions which are believed to give rise to *susto*, however, are a little different in Paraguay from those in Meso-America and the Andes. We found no evidence, for example, that jealousy or anger can result in *susto*; usually fright arising from some impersonal or supernatural situation is blamed. And, so far as we can determine, no other Latin Americans explain the manifestations of *susto* in terms of the activity of worms. Too many worms in a child's body may make him weak and therefore more susceptible to fright, and fainting or hysteria results from the consequent agitation of the worms, which mount to the head.[3]

In most cases, when a child has an unexplained fever, it is said to be caused by worms. While worms are usually thought to infest the stomach or bowels, they may also lodge in the head— an itching nose is a symptom. When a child has a blue vein showing in his forehead, it is said to be a sign of the *sevo'i* ("worm") which is there. Leaves of the saltwort are used as a vermifuge, both internally in the form of a tea and externally as a paste.

Treatment of Illnesses

There are no trained doctors in Tobatí, but there are three licensed midwives who act as nurses, and there is a government *puesto sanitario*, administered by a young man who is equipped to pull teeth, give injections, and render first aid. There is a small hospital with professional personnel in the neighboring town of Caacupé. People who desire modern medical care and who can afford it go either to Caacupé or to Asunción. There is a drugstore in Tobatí, well stocked with herbal remedies, cough medicines, and various types of sulfa drugs and penicillin. The druggist is interested in modern pharmaceutical practice and is well informed; hence he is often consulted for medical advice. In addition, there are *curanderas*, who also function as unlicensed midwives, and a few male *curanderos*. The *curanderas* are generally older women who have had long experience in the administration of folk remedies. Diagnosis is made by questioning the

3. We discovered no evidence of the belief in soul loss as a consequence of *susto*, which is common in Guatemalan "Indian" communities.

patient about his symptoms, by palpating, and by examination of the urine. If the urine is a reddish color, it is believed that there is "fire" within the stomach or intestine. Remedies are prepared very carefully, according to exact measurements. Children are given smaller doses of the same medicines prescribed for adults. An outstanding *curandera* may have a reputation in a fairly large region and may travel from town to town to treat her patients.

One male curer, called *medico-ý* ("water-doctor"), moved from Arroyos y Esteros to Tobatí during our stay. He described his curing as dependent in large part on faith. Although he diagnosed illnesses by questioning about symptoms, by examining the eyes and mouth of the patient, and by the color of the urine, he also relied on grasping the patient's hands, presumably to discover the symptoms by transference. In cases of very grave diseases, he prescribed pomades for massages, or herbal medicines, but usually he cured by the use of water and prayer. The water, which he sold at 50 cents a liter, was dipped from a large jar which he kept in his house. Informants differed in their descriptions of this cantaro. Some claimed that it contained a human skull; others said that above it there was a representation of the Crucifixion, from which was suspended a small cross which was submerged in the water within the jar. There were many figures of saints in his house and many candles. His claim was that the water would cure all those who had faith, and he had gained fame over a wide region by his methods.

Apparently faith cures are fairly common in Paraguay. We were told of a woman named Epifania, who lived during the 1920's in Sapucay. She was called the "Señorita de Cerro Verde." The belief was that she had died and returned to life with power to make cures and to predict the future. She built a small *oratorio* and began to preach for a more sincere and moral observance of Catholicism. Soon her fame spread, and people began to make pilgrimages to her. For some years these pilgrimages to Epifania attracted as many people as the pilgrimage to Caacupé for the fiesta of the Virgin of the Immaculate Conception does today. It was not until after her death that it was discovered that she had had a business manager and had made a great deal of money.

Many of the home remedies are supplemented by supernatural

practices of one sort or another, but these practices usually are felt to be more efficacious in prevention rather than cure of illness, inasmuch as their function is largely to add to a person's good luck. Most of them involve secret prayers, in Spanish or in Guaraní. The prayers which are used in curing rather than prevention are essentially magical formulas rather than pleas to a saint for aid. For example, snakebite may be cured by taking a piece of straw and making a single overhand knot to form a loop about an inch in diameter, through which one should peer at the wound, silently reciting the appropriate prayer. A way to cure worms in animals is to recite a prayer while holding aloft a little cross made out of three plants of the *typychá'hu*. After the prayer is said, the cross is hung in the smoke above the kitchen fire until the worms come out. The belief is undoubtedly reinforced by the fact that these *ura*, or worms, are actually maggots of fly eggs, and they do leave the wound when they pass to the fly stage of development.

The greatest faith is in herb medicines.[4] Just as "air" and "winds" and various foods are classified as "hot" or "cold" with respect to their effect on health, so are the herbal remedies. Herbs which are *caliente* are felt to be stimulating, and those which are *fresca* ("cool") are soothing.

Rubbing alcohol is highly regarded as a cure for any ache, pain, or headache and is particularly good for grippe. Many of the old *curanderas* in the country have learned that patients in hospitals are rubbed with alcohol regularly, and they believe that therefore it must have curative powers. This indicates a certain respect for modern medical practice, but this respect is often mingled with fear and uncertainty or with stronger belief in the old-fashioned medicines. The most common purchases in the pharmacy illustrate the confusion: mercury ointment, zinc oxide salve, mentholatum, alcohol, castor oil, kerosene (to be used to stop toothache or as a disinfectant), leaves of senna and of *rosa mosqueta*, and a great many other herbs. In nearly all households one or more of the common herbal remedies will be tried before any medical help is asked. This is true even in Asunción, where

4. A number of specific herbal medicines for particular diseases are given in Appendix V.

the women at the city market do a large business in herbs which they bring in from the country for sale. There is tremendous interest in common remedies which may be prepared from readily available weeds, and a subject of unceasing interest in conversation is a comparison of recipes for medicines. Pills, drugs, and vaccinations are regarded with suspicion, and surgery is considered extremely dangerous. Injections, on the other hand, are much more acceptable, as they seem to be in much of rural Latin America.

Every effort is made to care for the sick at home. If one should fall ill while working in another city, it is desirable to go home for curing, if possible, and certainly for recuperation. When patients go to the hospitals in Asunción for examination and consultation, hospitalization may be recommended, but the patients often refuse to stay. They return to the country, instead, and often even refuse to use anything but the household medicines. One often hears of cases in which medical treatment in the cities failed and the patient was subsequently treated successfully by a relative or a country *curandera*. People feel, too, that the country environment and air are more beneficial than the city.

Menstruation

A menstruating woman is said to be "with the new moon." This is the literal meaning of the Guaraní expression and is also the Spanish phrasing when menstruation is referred to indirectly. This is associated with the belief that the waxing of the new moon weakens all nature in general, since it draws nourishment from human blood and from plants and animals. But a woman in this condition is also unintentionally dangerous; she has the power of the "evil eye" on occasion and in general is apt to have a harmful influence. For example, should she touch a rose, it dies. A woman should never be allowed to ride a horse when she is menstruating, and, in fact, care should always be taken for fear that she may have hidden her condition or does not know that she has begun to menstruate. Thus a woman is usually given a mare to ride, as mares are considered to be inferior mounts. Sex relations should be suspended, at least for the first three days, for reason of the "danger" and also because hemorrhage may result. For at least these three days, a woman should avoid heavy work and should not bathe.

There is a variety of food taboos associated with menstruation. The woman cannot prepare delicate foods, because they will curdle or spoil. For the sake of her own health she should not eat "cold" or acid things, especially *so'o yosopý*, salads, fruits, and pickles. Even many doctors and nurses in Asunción feel that these food taboos should be observed.

A menstruating woman is not particularly secluded. Her "dangerous condition" causes her to practice certain specific taboos, but men do not feel personally threatened or disgusted. Although they do not have sex relations at this time, the husband and wife continue to sleep in the same bed. There is, however, a belief that evil can be perpetrated with a woman's blood by a sorcerer; thus great care is taken that the menstrual clothing is carefully destroyed or washed.

There are many *remedios* associated with menstruation; some are taken to start or stop the period, others to increase the flow. Tea of *ruda* ("rue") may be taken to aid the flow if it is scanty or painful. *Ruda* and tea of *salvia*, sometimes combined with the application of heat, are believed to start the period. *Caña* is felt to be beneficial and is often taken along with *ruda*. To stop the period or to reduce the flow, tea of grape leaves is drunk. Tea of avocado leaves is used to correct irregularity, and tea of *doradilla*, which may be taken for any intestinal pains, is used in case of difficult menstruation. Scanty menstruation is taken to be a symptom of too little blood in the body, or of bad blood, which are common causes of ill-health.

Birth Control

Nearly all women and most men desire children, and a woman who is barren is regarded as unfortunate and incomplete. She may be called a *cuñá mburicá*, meaning "woman-mule," or *vaca machorra*, "cow without calf." These terms are used jokingly in direct address among close friends and relatives; used in reference, they express contempt. Women who desire children and fail to conceive take tea of *salvia* after each meal. This is a "hot" remedy and helps overcome the condition of "coldness" which may be the cause of failure to conceive. The treatment is continued for some weeks and may be supplemented by the use of bees' honey, which is also considered "hot." Such remedies are said to cleanse the uterus by stimulating the menstrual flow and may also be taken to start the menstrual period when an undesired pregnancy is suspected.

Childlessness is more usually regarded as the man's fault; it is blamed on his bad health, particularly on venereal disease. Remedies for male impotence include raw eggs or toasted peanuts mixed with bees' honey. These are the most commonly used medicines, although some informants claimed that bulls' testicles are useful for this purpose.

Informants stated that in the country a family of seven, eight, or even ten children is fairly common, because countrywomen do not know ways of preventing conception or inducing abortions. In the town, families are somewhat smaller. Countrywomen do not desire such large families but accept them as "God's will," whereas town women learn how to limit the size of their families. It does seem to be generally true that women, both in the country and in towns, do not want too many children, but perhaps a larger family is more advantageous in the country. Many townspeople regard two, three, or four children as a sufficiently large family.

A number of informants suggested that infanticide might be fairly common in the more remote country regions. Stillbirths are not reported to the authorities, and it would certainly be easy to bury a child immediately after birth. It is said that, before a child makes his first cry, he is not yet alive, whereas after he has uttered a sound he is alive, and interment would amount to murder. It is reasonable to assume that there are poor women with large families who might be tempted to permit an unwanted baby to die. There seems to be no reason to suspect that female infanticide is more common than male infanticide.

Several medicines are believed to cause abortion. Most of these should be taken just before the menstrual period is due if there is reason to expect pregnancy. The root of either esparto or *mil hombres* is used to make a tea which is taken in large doses to start menstruation. Repeated statements of informants that countrywomen do not know these remedies seems unjustified in view of the fact that we collected them frequently from *curanderas* whose advice would be available to the country population.

Dissemination of information about birth control is against the law in Paraguay, but it is reported that contraceptives are available to those who have enough money to pay for them. One informant had heard of withdrawal as a technique of preventing conception but did not think it would be very useful, "because men are so selfish." No informants had heard of the use of rhythms as a method for controlling conception. The druggist in Tobatí confirmed that the taking of abortive remedies is common practice and stated that, if he were able to obtain contraceptive devices for women, he could sell great quantities of them to the wealthier people in Tobatí.

Informants of all classes agreed that after two or three months of pregnancy no medicine would cause abortion. Abortions must then be performed by professional midwives or doctors in Asunción. Most informants said that midwives in Tobatí would not perform the operation.

Causes of Death

Deaths in Tobatí are supposed to be reported to the justice of the peace, as are births, but the statistics are unreliable because of rather casual reporting from the rural areas. It would be impossible to compute either the birth rate or the death rate, furthermore, because there is no accurate count of the total population of the *partido*. Statistics on the causes of death would be most instructive, but they are also unreliable because the diagnosis reported on the form used by the justice is nearly always made by an untrained person. Fortunately, those causes of death which seem to be the most common are those which are so obvious and well known that it seems unlikely that many errors were made: gunshot and knife wounds, pulmonary diseases, and syphilis. Other causes of death which appear in the reports, however, are useless for any precise purpose, as they are merely folk catchalls, such as "fever" and "liver."

Of the various causes of death listed in the public records of the *partido* of Tobatí for 1944, 1945, and 1948 (1946–47 were omitted because of the civil war), "pulmonary" was the most common; 33 deaths of out a total of 192 were reported for the three years. "Pulmonary" means, in this case, tuberculosis predominantly, along with bronchitis and pneumonia. The next most common (31 deaths) was a category variously called *sifilis, luez*,[5] or *hereditario* (which refers to infant death due to congenital syphilis). Heart disease claimed 25 and "wounds" 13.

Classifying the deaths by age groups reveals that all the syphilis deaths were of infants under one year, while 9 of the "pulmonary" deaths were of infants, out of a total of reported infant deaths of 66. In the age group from one to eighteen there were 9 deaths from "pulmonary" diseases and 6 from dysentery, out of 33 deaths. From eighteen to sixty years of age, "pulmonary" was again the most common, causing 10 deaths (7 of them specified as tuberculosis), and "wounds" accounted for 9, out of a total of 46 deaths. For the age group of sixty years and over, "heart disease" was far and away the most common, with "ulcer" and tuberculosis next.

In the town of Piribebuý Emma Reh found the same discrepancies in registrations of births and deaths, which made statistical analyses unreliable. However, she secured information on causes of death in 69 cases which were diagnosed by trained physicians.[6] Of these, 10 deaths were caused by pneumonia and 2 by respiratory tuberculosis. Ten others were caused by heart disease, and 7 by cancer and other malignant tumors. Homicide and accidents accounted for 6 more. The Paraguayan government's *Informe anual bioestadístico* for the year 1946 listed pneumonia and bronchopneumonia as the primary causes of death, with 13 per cent; tuberculosis was second, with 7.6 per cent. It is clear that respiratory diseases (including pneumonia and tuberculosis) were the chief causes of death, except for newborn infants and possibly the very aged. This is not surprising. The winter weather in

5. *Luez* in Spanish usage means "infection" but in Tobatí seems to have been used as synonymous with syphilis.

6. *Paraguayan Rural Life: Survey of Food Problems* (Washington, D.C.: Institute of Inter-American Affairs, Food Supply Division, 1946), p. 112.

Paraguay is extremely changeable, varying between warm sunny days and brief spells of near-freezing temperature. Houses are not heated, and warm clothing and blankets are very scarce among the rural population. Everyone is very uncomfortable at this time of year, and it seemed to us that many people, and especially children, suffered from colds most of the time. Grippe and influenza are also very frequent in winter. It is no wonder that "cold" illnesses are a major preoccupation of the people and that a large amount of preventative medicinal lore is concerned with them.

CHAPTER XIX

Behavior at the Life-Crises: Birth, Marriage, Death

As MIGHT be expected in a community with different levels of education, there is a great variety of beliefs and practices related to pregnancy and childbirth. Many people, including nearly all the peasants, accept only the traditional folk beliefs and have very little understanding of even the simplest of modern scientific methods of care. There are also certain members of the town aristocracy who are quite sophisticated; in a few cases women of this class have even gone away to a hospital for delivery, and others may have at least a professional doctor's advice during pregnancy and a licensed midwife at the delivery.

There are two midwives in town who have had some modern training and have a "sense of hygiene," and there are also four others who are licensed but are not considered very up to date. There are many *parteras clandestinas*, unlicensed midwives without training of any kind. Often a woman is attended only by her husband and an older female relative or neighbor.

One of the best trained of the local midwives told us that she had had nineteen years of nursing experience in clinics and hospitals. Her most emphatic criticisms of local customs were concerned with lack of sanitation, lack of medical equipment, and the use of force to expel the child. She charges 10 guaranis for all deliveries except the first, for which she charges 15, because it usually lasts longer and is more difficult. These fees also cover advance consultation and postnatal care. The people generally pay her, but often in driblets over a long period of time. She charges wealthy people 50 guaranis and often gets a tip in addition, but in these cases she cares for the mother and child for fifteen to twenty-two days after the birth, instead of the usual eight days given the poor. Her patients usually come to her for consultation and treatment after four or five months of pregnancy. She prescribes a diet which is light in meat, because meat causes the bones of the fetus to harden and makes a difficult birth. She advises an active life, but, particularly in the last three months of pregnancy, the patient should do no heavy lifting.

Children, "but not too many," are desired by nearly all women, even many unmarried ones. Children of either sex are equally welcomed. Some mothers prefer their first child to be a boy, because this is supposed to bring good luck. Girls are easier to manage than boys and are more help around the house, but boys are more of an economic asset later, when they can help in the fields. Twins are not desired because it is too hard for the mother to take care of them. There are, however, no beliefs concerned with the causes of multiple births, and we heard of no cases of infanticide connected with the birth of twins. We discovered no feeling that a child born at a certain time of year or on a certain day is luckier or healthier or that the birth is easier at some times than at others. The important thing is that the pregnancy should last for nine months. An eight months' birth, for example, is considered dangerous, and the child "wants to die." No explanation for such beliefs is given.

The four midwives interviewed all preferred a supine position for delivery, but most of the patients prefer a half-seated position, with the husband holding the woman by the shoulders and exerting force with his knees against the sides of the upper abdomen. Many patients also want to be on the floor for the delivery, but modern midwives are strongly opposed to this. In nearly all cases the father of the child is present at the delivery. A few informants expressed embarrassment at this custom, but all thought it was a good thing for the father "to see what the woman suffers."

No anesthetics are used, for the mother should be fully conscious at the time of birth in order to assist. If pain is severe, a little camphorated oil or *caña* may be given every two or three hours. It is reported that unlicensed midwives prescribe a tea made of cotton seeds to speed delivery and an infusion of burned ostrich plumes in water to ease the pain. Sometimes in case of difficult delivery the father's hat is put on the mother's head as an aid. Another common remedy used is a soft-boiled egg heavily salted, which is also supposed to help discharge the placenta. Tea of *doradilla* is frequently given after the birth to ease the pain. "Hot" remedies are beneficial, but all informants agreed that heat must not be used during the delivery.

Many people do not have access to midwives of the sophisticated sort, nor do they believe in them. If a licensed midwife is not in attendance, modern sanitary measures are not taken. A very important cause of death among infants is infection of the umbilicus. The people know that this is dangerous but cannot grasp the importance of asepsis. They do bathe the newborn child, of course, but thereafter they go by the folk customs. Immediately after bathing, the child is dressed in an old shirt of the father or a garment made of the shirt, so he will not "have fear." This is especially important for boys, but it is also done for girls. The water from the first bath should be thrown to the west, where the sun sets, so that the child will be laughing and happy all the time. One woman told us that she did not do this at the birth of her first child, a grave boy now eight years old, but that she did for her sprightly daughter and that this explains the difference in their temperaments.

The placenta is buried in the house or in the yard, and a fire is built over the spot so that the mother will not get "cold inside." The placenta is believed to be a "part of the mother" and should not be buried far away from her. It is also believed that the placenta is "part of the child" and should be kept near him to insure his well-being. There is a similar belief that miscarriages and stillbirths also should be buried near the house.

Two or three days after delivery the mother may get up and move about a little, but only inside the house. She must keep calm, must never get angry or upset, and must do no work. If the weather is fine, she may go outside a little on the seventh or eighth day. Among the peasants these rules may be violated through pressure of circumstances, but they are accepted as correct. Menstruation may last eight to fifteen days after birth, and some midwives say that the woman should not be bathed during that time. The great majority of the people, however, believe firmly that one should not bathe for forty days; some say that the hands and face should not be washed or even the tips of the fingers. A few of the most sophisticated of the upper-class town women profess not to believe in this taboo; others observed the forty-day restriction carefully.[1] A few people still believe that a mother should actually remain in bed for forty days, and nearly everyone believes that the forty days is a dangerous period and that no heavy work should be done. One should not have sex relations for fear of immediate conception, nor should a woman do any sewing or needlework in this period. The taboo against "touching the needle" is very strong, and the fear seems to be that, unless the prohibition is observed, the child's umbilicus will not heal properly. There are no taboos against the father's activity; he can eat and work as usual. A great deal of questioning discovered no survivals whatsoever of a couvade.

It is believed that the seventh day after birth is very dangerous for the child. The child's bed is adorned with a red cloth or ribbon to guard against death of *la mal de siete días*. It is possible that fear is associated with the seventh day because it is about this time that infantile tetanus ordinarily becomes serious enough to cause death.

After the umbilicus falls, it should be safeguarded in some place in the house. If it is lost the child will be stubborn or forgetful. When the child reaches the age of fourteen or so, the cord is buried in a corner of the house so that the child will stay close to the family. This practice is not consciously connected with the onset of puberty.

Most mothers want to nurse the child as long as possible, as it is believed that women are less likely to conceive during lactation. They supplement the breast feeding quite early but may allow the child to keep nursing until it stops of its own accord. If the mother becomes pregnant, she weans the child abruptly, for the milk has changed and is bad for the child. If the small baby seems to need supplementary food, a friend or *comadre* may help nurse it, or cow's milk may be given. Another common food is *candial*, a mixture of manioc flour with sugar or molasses and water. Rice water, cooked until quite thick, is also given.

1. The forty-day prohibition is quite general in Latin America and in the Mediterranean area. Forty is an important pattern number among Semites.

Paraguayans eat a lot of fruit, especially oranges, but mothers eat very little of it because the people think that fruit will sour the milk.

Weaning is considered a very delicate period. A child is given light foods and sometimes a small piece of roast meat to suck on. Various weaning methods are used. Sometimes mothers paint their breasts with a bitter or bad-smelling substance. A few people send the child away to a relative until it is completely weaned. After a child is weaned, it is generally fed whenever it wants to eat and is allowed to have as much as it desires.

The concept of "cold" is very important in child care, and the ideas about it are universal in the community. When babies are young, bed-wetting is dangerous, because it may wet the abdominal band, causing the child's intestines to get chilled. Umbilical hernia may also result. If the chest gets cold, it may cause bronchitis. Night wetting is also a *result* of cold. Cooking oil rubbed on the abdomen is supposed to be warming and to keep the child from wetting more than once in the night. Harm may also come to the child because of the "coldness" of the mother, who, perhaps, did not dress warmly enough while pregnant or was cold when the child was born. A child may also get cold from the usual causes, such as drafts or changes in temperature, especially in winter. The night is more dangerous than the day because it is colder and damper and the body less resistant.

Courtship

Since girls are so closely watched by their families from about the age of twelve or thirteen, even among the rural families, all formal courtship tends to take place under the eyes of others. A boy may dance with the girl of his choice and talk during the dancing; a couple may walk home from the dance, lagging a short distance behind their chaperones; or they may sit a little apart from the family at the girl's home. Thus, although real privacy is rare, semiprivacy can allow some more or less intimate romantic interchanges.

The ideal pattern of courtship requires that the youth make some opportunity to declare himself to the girl and ask if she will accept his courtship. If she accepts, he calls on her at her home, in the presence of her family, as often as he can. The formal request for the girl's hand may be made by the boy himself, but he should be accompanied by a responsible member of his family or by a mutual friend of the two families, who will complete the arrangements. If the proposal is accepted, the representatives of the two families usually have a drink of *caña* together. Often there is no other formality. There is no gift exchange and no dowry, but the parents of either the boy or the girl may give some help in establishing a home for the young couple.

Elopements, or "marriage by capture," are common when the couple do not intend to marry legally, as the girl's family often will not consent to a union in such cases. After the "capture," the girl's family is angry with the man, not with the girl, although the girl actually helps to plan the elopement. These elopements are called "captures," however, and the girl is considered a helpless victim.

Marriage by capture is said to be much more common in the country than in the towns. When a man wants a girl, he courts her for a time, to gain the confidence of the girl and her parents, and then secretly takes her from her father's house to the house of relatives or friends of his. In the town middle and upper classes, courtship is more likely to be close to the ideal pattern.

Wedding Ceremonies

When a courtship has resulted in an understanding between the lovers and the parents' approval has been given, the banns are posted at the *justicia*. Then the time of the ceremony is set, the choice of the *padrino* and *madrina* of marriage is made, and the guest list and arrangements for the fiesta are planned. Godparents are not selected according to any set rule. They may or may not be relatives of either of the couple; they may be older or of approximately the same age as the couple; and, while they are usually married, this is not a rule.[2] It is said that ordinarily the bride selects the *madrina* and the groom the *padrino* (as a maid of honor and best man are selected in North America), but the

2. Church records of 101 marriages between April, 1944, and August, 1948, show that 87 of the couples had married couples as *padrinos*.

preponderance of married couples among the godparents indicates that the bride and groom do not choose independently of each other.

The expense of the fiesta varies considerably with the financial status of the families involved, but the festivities must be as elaborate and costly as possible—any stinginess in this matter would be severely criticized. There is no rule as to whether the family of the bride or that of the groom should bear more of the expense; this depends on the relative economic status of the two families. It seems most customary, however, for the man's family to contribute the most money, inasmuch as the event is celebrated at the bride's home, and all the work is done by her relatives. But individual circumstances, rather than custom, determine most of the arrangements.

One large wedding took place while we were living in Tobatí. The local police commissioner, a man about thirty, married a girl who had been a schoolteacher in Tobatí for many years. There was a good deal of joking about the age of the bride. It is common for women to lie about their ages, particularly when, as in this case, their husbands are younger.

The wedding was set for a Thursday evening, and on the preceding Monday a list was circulated about town by a young policeman. At the top of the list appeared the invitation in handwriting: "Señor and Señora Gilberto Quirós invite you to attend the marriage of their daughter, Epifania, on Thursday, August 9." Below appeared a list of one hundred and thirty-one people, each of whom was to sign opposite his name to signify acceptance of the invitation. The list was said to include the entire *sociedad* of Tobatí and many other friends of the couple who were of doubtful social status.

On Tuesday before the wedding another list was circulated for the collection of contributions for a dance for the engaged couple. By older custom, the men should celebrate with the groom on the evening before the wedding, and the friends of the bride should give a small party for her. More often now a dance is given in honor of both, paid for by contributions from all invited guests.

On the day before the wedding and on the day of the wedding, the bride and all her women friends and relatives worked to prepare food for the party. Two long tables, covered with white cloths, were laden with dishes of small meat croquettes, chicken legs, salads, puddings, sweet *pasteles*, and the traditional dish which must be served at all weddings to insure good fortune, *sopa paraguaya*. Beverages served included *caña*, vermouth, beer, and fruit punch.

Gifts of food, drinks, or household items are customarily sent by messenger on the day of the wedding. They are wrapped in white tissue, decorated with flowers and ribbons, and accompanied by sentimental messages of felicitation, written by hand on note paper or calling cards. Gifts of food and beverages are used for the wedding feast, and other gifts, with the notes of congratulation, are displayed on long tables at the time of the wedding party. Relatives may on such an occasion properly give gifts of money to be used for purchasing furniture for the new household.

The civil marriage was completed without ceremony in the afternoon. As the hour for the church wedding approached, groups of people collected around the home of the bride. The bride, dressed in a long white satin dress, with a long veil, and the groom, dressed in a dark blue suit, came out with their parents and the wedding godparents and walked to the church, followed by the guests. The wedding party entered the church first and walked to the altar, and the invited guests took seats in the front pews of the church. The church was decorated with many candles and with a canopy of white ribbons tied from the center beam to the corners of the pews. The extent to which the church is decorated is an index of the wealth of the families concerned and is an important status indication.

After the ceremony, everyone returned to the home of the bride. The guests wandered about, conversing and enjoying the refreshments, and the orchestra played dance music, but space was so constricted that few people were able to dance. Many onlookers collected outside, as they do at any such occasion, and watched the festivities going on inside the house. A few of them came in briefly to speak to the bride and groom and to wish them well. Dancing and visiting continued until about midnight.

At a wedding of a lower-middle-class couple which took place a few days later, the bride was dressed in a short white satin suit and wore a white lace mantilla. The groom wore a brown wool suit, ill-fitting and uncomfortable-looking. At all times, as at the other wedding, the bride and groom were stiff, unsmiling, and embarrassed. The composition of the group of guests was socially mixed on this occasion, including both poor people and a few guests from among the *sociedad* who were friends of the two families. The house where the festivities were held was an *almacén*-bar, belonging to the bride, and drinks were sold to the guests. A large paved patio served as an outdoor dance floor, where the newlywed couple danced the first dance alone. The dancing continued outside, while a dinner for the young couple and the members of the wedding party was served inside the house. Later many uninvited people arrived, and much liquor was sold and consumed. The dance was eventually broken up because some drunken soldiers got into a fight.

Most of the marriages of people from the *compañías* take place in town. The priest charges a large fee for going to the house or chapel in the country to perform the ceremony, so the bride and groom ride into town, accompanied by their friends and relatives. The groom wears his best clothing, and the bride often wears a long white dress with a veil or a white mantilla; in this attire they ride the whole distance. After the ceremony is performed, usually in the morning, the group returns to the home of the girl's parents or relatives to have a fiesta dinner. All the friends and relatives for miles around are invited. The expense involved is considerable, but some of it is shared by the guests, who bring gifts of food and drinks. There is always a dance and much drinking of *caña*. We did not have the opportunity to attend any wedding celebrations in the *compañías*, but we were told that they were much like a birthday celebration we shared. On the latter occasion the guests arrived in the morning and chatted and danced until dinner was served at about one in the afternoon. After the meal, dancing was resumed until the party broke up about four o'clock. There was a great deal of drinking and some drunkenness, good-natured joking, and much less formality than at comparable affairs in town.

Old Age and Death

There are no individuals now living in Tobatí who claim to be exceptionally old. Our census figures for the town show that, out of a total population of 1,368 (609 males and 659 females), 26 gave their ages as over seventy years of age, 4 over eighty, 2 over ninety, and none over a hundred. Of persons over sixty, females outnumbered males 66 to 29.

A few cases of dead relatives who had lived to be very old were mentioned by informants, but little reliability can be attached to such statements, since most old people do not know their exact ages. It is sometimes possible to check within a few years from memories of their youth. Some remember events that occurred during their childhood during the great war of the 1870's. Women apparently begin to lie about their ages comparatively early and probably eventually become confused about their actual ages. After the age of forty-five or fifty, individuals may claim to be older than they actually are because a certain respect is due the aged as having much experience and wisdom. Some informants felt that the aged perhaps enjoy less respect than in former times. However, old people are generally well treated by their children or relatives.

When an aged person dies, the occasion is not marked by such extreme manifestations of grief as in the case of a younger person whose death was unexpected. The closest relatives customarily prepare the body for burial. The body is washed and dressed, usually in the wedding costume. Sometimes a woman is buried in the costume of the Virgin of Dolores, a black cloak over the wedding petticoat, skirt, and blouse, all embroidered in the old style. The brown robe and white manta of the Virgin of Carmen is also used as a burial garment for women, and the brown robe of San Francisco may be used for men. If special burial clothes are financially impossible, the best clothes available are used. If there are no "decent" clothes, the body is wrapped in a clean sheet. The dead who have no relatives are buried by the municipality or by contributions from their neighbors and friends.

When a child dies, the body is dressed in white and placed on a small table, surrounded with flowers and candles. Pennies are placed on the eyes, and the hands are fixed in a position of prayer, clasping a small flag or bouquet of flowers. The women relatives gather to mourn and wail all night, and the next day visitors are received. Visitors commonly bring flowers, food, or money to contribute to the family of the deceased.

Interment takes place as soon as possible, for the climate is hot and damp much of the year, and there is no embalming outside Asunción. Novenas are held after the death, again after six months, and at the end of one year. After this, it is desirable to have a Mass sung every year, but few people can afford it. A poor family may have to perform the burial without ceremony, postponing the funeral Mass until funds are available.

Mourning is worn for varying lengths of time, depending on the closeness of the relationship to the deceased. For a father, mother, or spouse two years is usual, though some widows wear mourning dress for life. For a child one year of mourning is proper; for grandparents and uncles or aunts the mourning period was formerly two years but is now usually less.

PART V

Conclusions

CHAPTER XX

General Remarks

LATIN AMERICA presents a bewildering variety of geographic conditions, differing racial strains in the populations, variations in cultural mixture, class differences, and great contrasts between rural backwardness and modern urban sophistication. Accepting these differences, which often are manifested within one locality or nation, there is nevertheless a common distinctiveness which sets off the area as a whole from Anglo-America. Probably most responsible for this difference is the fact that, so far, the great industrial revolution of modern times has affected most of Latin America relatively little. Many habits, attitudes, sentiments, and also structural aspects of Latin America's social, economic, and political organization remain old Spanish and fundamentally agrarian. In other words, in Latin America in general, we find a stronger survival of a relatively homogeneous, European-de-rived colonial culture than in Anglo-America, where there remains very little which is reminiscent of the sixteenth century. A nation like Paraguay is much more like southern Ireland than it is like the United States of America. And in many important respects it is more like any of the "underdeveloped" nations of the world than it is like the complex, highly industrialized nations with whom these are associated in a relation of dependency with respect to international economics (if not to politics).

If one thinks of differences among the various Latin-American nations today, one of the factors useful in assessing these differences is again the degree of survival of an earlier agricultural economy. Some nations have participated more fully than others in commercial and industrial development, which is the basic

282 TOBATÍ: PARAGUAYAN TOWN

cause of the modifications of the older cultural patterns. Paraguay, without question, remains strikingly "old-fashioned" in this sense, isolated as it has been from most modern economic trends.[1]

Paraguay has been consistently described by historians, however, as not only having preserved more colonial patterns than other Latin-American nations but also as having been profoundly influenced by the culture of the native Guaraní Indians. H. G. Warren recently summed up the current view by concluding that "the Guaranís practically overwhelmed the Europeans racially and had a profound cultural effect upon them."[2] Anthropologists, too, have been led to accept Paraguay as the only area in Latin America where the culture of unfederated, stateless, seminomadic forest Indians had been mixed with Spanish colonial traits and finally synthesized as a national culture.[3]

Paraguay's colonial culture was in some ways distinctive in Latin America, but our investigations into the history of its consolidation show that its character was due to certain historical and circumstantial factors rather than to the survival of Guaraní culture. The colonial culture, in short, was not similar to that of Meso-America and the Andean region, where certain Indian influences remain, but was more like that of the Río de la Plata area of Argentina, Uruguay, and even interior southern Brazil, where the Indian was culturally relatively unimportant— this in spite of the fact that biologically and linguistically the aboriginal heritage is stronger in Paraguay than it is in these adjacent countries.

1. Of the South American republics, Paraguay had (in 1938) by far the least amount of exports—$8,000,000—and the least imports—$8,100,000. This was only 0.4 per cent of total Latin-American exports and 0.5 per cent of imports (see George Wythe, *An Outline of Latin American Economic Development* [New York, 1946], p. 250, Table 13).

2. Harris G. Warren, *Paraguay: An Informal History* (Norman, Okla., 1949), p. 33.

3. Both Ralph Beals and John Gillin have included Paraguay with the Andean and Mexican *"indio"* and *"mestizo"* areas of Latin America in recent publications. See Ralph L. Beals, "Social Stratification in Latin America," *American Journal of Sociology*, XVIII, No. 4 (January, 1953), 329; and John Gillin, "Mestizo America," in Ralph Linton (ed.), *Most of the World* (New York, 1949), p. 161.

Despite the slowness of change since the colonial period, we find that in rural Paraguay today there are virtually no Guaraní culture traits surviving, other than language. There are, to be sure, certain native foods and perhaps a few culinary customs still in existence, but native items of this sort survived everywhere to some extent, even in North America. There is no Guaraní art, music, or dance, today, of course, because the aboriginal culture was not highly developed in such matters, nor was there an arts-and-crafts technology of much utility or interest to the Europeans. But a careful analysis of even such things as mythology, folklore, superstitions, and folk medicine failed to reveal anything of certain Guaraní origin. In fact, most of the common Paraguayan customs of this order can be quite easily traced to Europe or to a later general Latin-American provenience.

As tests of this generalization, we might mention again a few categories of traits which, in the areas of strong aboriginal influence, have been seen as derived from, or affected somehow by, Indian culture and which would be of the sort most likely to retain some evidence of a Guaraní heritage. One prominent cultural feature of this sort in Latin America is the institution of *compadrazgo*. In Moche, Peru, for example, not all the rites are related to Roman Catholic ritual, but some, according to John Gillin, "bear marks of being derived from an aboriginal or 'pagan' context." Thus, in addition to the relations established at baptism, confirmation, and marriage, *compadrazgo* may be established at rites of haircutting, ear-piercing, and nail-cutting.[4] In Mexico and Guatemala, too, certain aspects of *compadrazgo* are seen as influenced by aboriginal culture.[5] But in Paraguay

4. John Gillin, *Moche: A Peruvian Coastal Community* ("Publications of the Smithsonian Institution, Institute of Social Anthropology," No. 3 [Washington, D.C., 1945]), p. 105.

5. Francisco Rojas Gonzales, "La Institución del compadrazgo entre las indígenas de México," *Revista mexicana de sociología*, V (1943), 201–14; Benjamin D. Paul, "Ritual Kinship, with Special Reference to Godparenthood in Middle America" (unpublished Ph.D. thesis, University of Chicago, 1942); Robert Redfield and Alfonso Villa Rojas, *Chan Kom: A Maya Village* ("Carnegie Institution of Washington Publications," No. 448 [Washington, D.C., 1934]), pp. 373–74; Elsie Clews Parsons, *Mitla: Town of the Souls* (Chicago, 1936), pp. 525–26; Sol Tax (ed.), *Heritage of Conquest* (Glencoe, Ill., 1952), pp. 111–12.

the institution is purely Roman Catholic in all its ritual, and the crisis occasions themselves are solely those of the church—baptism, confirmation, and marriage. Paraguayan *compadrazgo* is more similar to the southern Brazilian version[6] than it is to the kinds practiced in areas where aboriginal influence has been strong.

Personal names, especially surnames, might be expected to reveal something of the aboriginal heritage, particularly in a country where the retention of the language is so strong. The complete census of the town revealed no Guaraní names, however, and, of the many collected in the rural areas, none were discovered except one, "Arepocó," which may or may not be Guaraní. The kinship terminological categories were Spanish even in the most remote rural areas, and, where actual Guaraní terms for these categories were retained, they were equivalent to Spanish usage, except in distinguishing older from younger siblings, which is, of course, of functional utility in any agrarian context. It is also worthy of note that certain Guaraní terms for kinship categories which were crucial in aboriginal Guaraní usage are now lost.[7]

Guaraní culture should also have influenced folk medicine, but here, too, we find no certain evidence, and, in fact, some traits which are considered aboriginal in other areas are missing here. The idea of psychosomatic causation (*susto*) arising from social situations like sibling rivalry or jealousy and anger, which is so common in Mexico, Guatemala, and Peru, seems completely foreign to Paraguay. The greatest folk-medicinal emphasis in Paraguay has to do with powers residing in various herbs. A few of the plant species used may be peculiar to Paraguay, but the

6. See Emilio Willems, *Cunha: Tradição e transição em uma cultura rural do Brasil* (São Paulo, 1948); Emilio Willems and Gioconda Mussolini, *Buzios Island: A Caicara Community in Southern Brazil* ("Monographs of the American Ethnological Society," Vol. XX [New York, 1952]); Emilio Willems, "Caboclo Cultures of Southern Brazil," in Sol Tax (ed.), *Acculturation in the Americas: Proceedings and Selected Papers of the XXIXth Congress of Americanists* (Chicago, 1952), pp. 231–43; Donald Pierson, *Cruz das Almas: A Brazilian Village* ("Publications of the Smithsonian Institution, Institute of Social Anthropology," No. 12 [Washington, D.C., 1951]), pp. 142–43.

7. The Guaraní had a "Dakota" system. Parallel cousins were lumped with siblings and cross-cousins distinguished. Similar distinctions occurred in the parents' generation.

conception is typically European. And, as a matter of fact, most of the actual recipes have long been in use in rural Uruguay and Argentina.

Some culture traits which are in some measure Indian are found in Paraguay, but they are part of the colonial culture complex which spread all over Spanish America and even to Spain itself. They cannot be said to be peculiarly Guaraní or Paraguayan. Some of these are the mortar and pestle, the poncho, adobe bricks, the reed mat, and straw roofs.[8] *Mate*-drinking was certainly early in the La Plata area, but it is not known whether or not it was borrowed from the aborigines.

In sum, we find little that is Indian in Paraguayan rural culture. To be sure, we had suspected on the basis of the documentary study of the colonial history that the Guaraní cultural component had been overemphasized in the later literature, but we were rather surprised to find so little of Guaraní origin. Another unexpected feature in rural Paraguay is that the people are not so Indian in physical appearance as we had expected. The prevalent anthropological conception in North America is that Paraguay should be rated as practically 100 per cent mestizo, with the Caucasian element in the mixture comparatively smaller than the Indian.[9] Our general observations led us to a different opinion as to the relative weight of the Indian and European components. Most of the population is mixed to some degree, it would seem, but we feel that it is the Indian element which is comparatively small. Our impression is supported by an earlier one reported by Emma Reh, who worked among Indians in the southwestern United States and in Mexico. On the basis of two years of intimate study of Paraguayan rural people, she observed: "In Paraguay although the lower class is somewhat darker than the upper, and country people somewhat browner than those of the city, few true Indian types are to be found. The 'native' coming out of the thatched hut in the country area and speaking *Guaraní* may be blond and blue-eyed."[10]

8. Most of these items apparently had an independent origin in the Old World as well, but it seems likely that their widespread use in the New World in colonial times was due to their earlier use by the Indians.

9. John Gillin, "Mestizo America," p. 161.

10. *Paraguayan Rural Life: Survey of Food Problems* (Washington, D.C.: Institute of Inter-American Affairs, Food Supply Division, 1946), p. 8.

Considering the history of Paraguay, it would certainly be unexpected if the purely Indian component were very large in the
present population. The nucleus of the nation developed during
the first hundred years of the colony in the vicinity of Asunción.
The growing population consisted largely of mestizos who were
products of the original Spaniards and their Guaraní concubines.
But the encomienda villages of pure Guaraní (the *mitayo* villages) never were large and by 1620 had largely become mixed
villages or had disappeared. It is possible that, at that time, although the population was almost entirely mixed, the genetic
predominance favored the Indian element. But from then on,
Indian groups were not being incorporated into the nation. Few
additions of any sort, Indian or European, were made to the population during the remainder of the colonial period, but those
few seem to have been European. And it should be remembered
that the Paraguayan population has always been small and relatively concentrated; it would not require many immigrants to
make their influence felt. J. P. and W. P. Robertson described
the people of Asunción in 1811–12 as follows: "The great bulk
of the population was of a breed between Spaniards and Indians,
so attenuated as regards any appearance of the latter caste, as to
give the natives the air and appearance of descendants from
Europeans."[11] Since 1870, Spaniards, Italians, and Argentines
have mixed with the population, considerably reducing the Indian genetic proportion, especially in the towns.

It seems to be the nearly universal use of the Guaraní language
in Paraguay which has misled writers to exaggerate the proportion of the Guaraní genetic strain and to assume that indigenous
culture has had an important effect. This retention of the language is, certainly, unusual. In Bolivia, Peru, Ecuador, Mexico,
and Middle America much of the population is pure Indian, and
some still speak an Indian language; but many large groups of
them do not. In Paraguay virtually the whole population speaks
Guaraní, but few or none are purely Indian genetically. The
historical concomitance of race and language is broken in one
direction in the former areas and in the opposite way in Paraguay.

11. *Four Years in Paraguay* (2 vols.; Philadelphia, 1838), I, 187. This comment is perhaps somewhat overdrawn. Even the modern population characteristically shows some traces of Indian mixture.

It is distinctive of Paraguay that the native language is in use not only among the peasantry but also among the middle and upper classes as well. As we have noted, however, the native middle and upper classes are very small. Possibly the use of Guaraní among them is due in some part to certain features of Paraguayan history, which included the concubinage of Guaraní women and the relative autonomy from Spain and later the defeat and devastation caused by the War of the Triple Alliance and the subsequent continuity of isolation and backwardness. The nation's lack of economic development and its low status compared with Argentina and Brazil probably have also had the effect of supercharging nationalistic emotions. Paraguayans in general, and the middle and upper classes in particular, remain intensely nationalistic, and much of this emotion seems to be concentrated in feelings about their language.

We should like to emphasize, however, that the influence of a native population on an emergent colonial culture cannot be measured simply by enumeration of the surviving indigenous traits. The many indirect functional consequences, especially economic ones, which set apart the areas of strong Indian influence from other regions are much more important. Some aspects of the cultures of rural Meso-America and the Andes are distinctive in their retention of particular indigenous culture traits, to be sure, and in blending certain Indian and Spanish traits. But there are also very striking differences in social and economic patterns which distinguish southern South America from "mestizo America," and these are directly and indirectly related to the presence of a large settled labor force in the latter areas.

Spanish colonization in southern South America was more truly a settlement, in the literal sense of the term, than the colonization in the regions where exploitation of large sedentary Indian populations was possible, where the Spaniards remained a leisured ruling class, distinct and foreign from the exploited population. In the south the encomienda and the *repartimiento* of Indians were of little economic importance. The scarcity of Indians and the lack of mineral wealth reduced the Spanish colonists to a subsistence way of life, and the few Indians they were able to control were most typically *yanaconas*,[12] household drudges and concubines, rather than a truly economically productive labor force. To some extent the Indians left their imprint on the physical characteristics of the developing population and on the household economy. Their role in the larger economy was so unimportant, however, that the agricultural hacienda never was possible. Also, in contrast to certain other regions, such as the Spanish West Indies and the coastal portions of Brazil, Venezuela, and Colombia, no plantation system based on either local or imported labor was ever developed.

Mestizos and creoles were all poor, and, as modified class divisions arose, they were not associated with racial or cultural distinctions—Hispanicized mixed-breeds could be found at any level of the society. The true Indians who were still tribally organized lived in the hinterlands, wandering and raiding. Even the missionized Guaraní of the Alto Paraná region largely retreated to the forests after the Jesuits were expelled in 1767. There never were any sizable groups of "republican Indians"—Spanish-acculturated Indian groups who had lost the old tribal organization yet had not become fully involved in the national life.

As a matter of fact, Paraguay has never had a complete tribe-to-city continuum of the sort so often found in the Andes and in Meso-America. In those regions one may place communities along a scale of national-cultural participation ranging from isolated tribal societies through republican Indian communities, peasant villages, and market towns to the urban center. Within the boundaries of Paraguay there are tribal Indians, chiefly in the Chaco wilderness and scattered thinly in the great forests of northeastern Paraguay, but there are no intermediate stages between tribal life and full involvement in Paraguayan national culture. Those Indians are not *becoming* Paraguayans; they are only retreating or becoming extinct. Paraguayans are culturally integrated in the fullest sense of nationalization; the state has not had the problem of assimilating tribally organized groups since the early days of the colonization. The quickly formed small nucleus of the nation developed into the modern nation through internal population

12. Usually called *originarios* in Paraguay.

growth. Cultural differences in the nation today are the differences between social classes and economic occupations of the sort implicit in the purely European cultural organization. The nation is "backward" from the point of view of modern international commercial and industrial development; it is essentially a peasant society. But from the point of view of internal cultural unity it is very advanced.

There are many other functional consequences related to the lack of a productive Indian labor force in southern South America. One is conscious especially of three of these which have made for important cultural distinctiveness in the colonial heritage. They are (1) lack of Spanish capital investment in the region after the original exploration and the consequent lack of continuing Spanish control; (2) the lack of interest and influence on the part of the official church; and (3), perhaps most striking of all, the failure of southern South America, until quite recently, to develop planned towns and agricultural haciendas.

Spanish Crown control by various kinds of administrators was never strong in southern South America. Creole revolts (*comunero* revolts) against Spanish authority occurred successfully very early in the colonial period. The region of La Plata was virtually self-governing from the beginning, and general Spanish economic and political influence became steadily less effective.[13] The official church, too, was a more important governing force in the Andean and Meso-American regions than in the La Plata territory. The church in the latter area was never strong politically or influential culturally, and it is not to this day. There were no extensive campaigns against "idolatry," for there were no native state religions competing with Catholicism, and the Holy Inquisition touched the La Plata people hardly at all. Except for the isolated mission area, neither church nor state created large planned towns (*reducciones*) of Indians which lasted long enough to be of consequence. The agriculturalists were more or less scattered, according to their convenience. The towns grew

13. As an illustration of this point, we may note that Spanish shipping to the La Plata region was actually prohibited by the Crown during the colonial period. All the Spanish trade was directed to the Caribbean because of the much greater wealth from Mexico and Peru and in order to muster force against the English raids on the shipping.

up slowly and naturally and tended to be made up of individual houses on large plots of ground, except on the central plaza. In the Andean and Meso-American areas a striking feature of the colonial history was the continuing influence of the farsighted and meticulously planned policy of the Spanish administration. Southern South America, on the other hand, had a more nearly autonomous, unplanned local growth and adaptation to circumstances.

Today a representative Paraguayan rural area such as Tobatí seems very much like other relatively isolated agricultural zones in Argentina, Uruguay, and southern Brazil. The basic occupation is subsistence agriculture, and the majority of the people live on their somewhat scattered *chacras*. There is only a slight tendency toward congregation of the peasants into hamlets. Villages and towns are business and administrative centers almost exclusively and account for only a small proportion of the population. There are enough differences between town and country, however, both in regard to presence or absence of particular traits and in emphasis of shared traits, that the distinctions may be considered subcultural.

The peasant families tend to be larger, and family ties are considered more important, than in town, but in actuality the family members tend to be scattered and disunited, and the functional unit is normally the nuclear family rather than the extended family. The only large effective families are those of the wealthiest townsmen. The town middle class tends to have a small effective family. A wealthy townsman has many *compadres*, but he is often on the giving, not the receiving, end of the relationship. The town middle-class people have few *compadres*, and the relations tend to be reciprocal. The town poor and the peasants have few *compadres* and seek to acquire some of them from among the wealthy in order to be the recipients of aid. With respect to marriage, the peasants place a high value on it but rarely can achieve that kind of social eminence. A civil marriage is not valued at all. The townsman of upper social standing is often married in the church, and the remaining townsmen are more likely than are the peasants to have a civil marriage.

Peasants are not interested in politics, but townsmen are inclined to intense factionalism and are more likely to have their economic interests involved in personal political loyalties. Townsmen are more orthodox with respect to religious beliefs, and the women, at least, attend church for social reasons. Peasants may be more devout, or more credulous, but participation is more often limited to saints' cults and profane "games." In many other matters, such as etiquette, folk versus modern beliefs, and use of language, the peasants practice older forms of behavior. Other trait differences are purely technological.

We feel that it would be inaccurate, or at least a misplacing of emphasis, however, to think of the subcultural differences between peasants and townsmen as being due to the peasants' isolation or lack of communication, although in a sense, of course, sophistication does grow with communication. It could be said that certain traits of international, or modern, culture come to the capital city first. These may pass from the city to the towns and thence to the peasant. The peasant receives them last, if at all, because he is more isolated. But most of these modern items are such trivial things as fads in dress style, ephemeral popular songs, and various gadgets.

The most basic traits which characterize the peasant's subculture are functionally a part of his way of life and are most typically those which are related to agrarian self-sufficiency, as opposed to commercialism. More ideological traits, such as knowledge of and faith in modern medicine, and formal education pertain more to town life than they do to peasant life because more townsmen have money to pay for such services and thus are enabled to learn of their value. These differences, as well as those in general values and aspirations, are best seen as merely the subjective aspects of occupational and wealth distinctions between peasants and townsmen. We cannot regard the peasant's way of life as being due to his isolation or to his ignorance of other ways. There is very little of importance in the townsman's culture that the peasant is not acquainted with, for the two have been in close contact for a long, long time. But the peasant cannot aspire to participate in this culture. He is forced to continue to live by the customs which work for him under the particular economic circumstances that he is unable to change. There seems to be little likelihood that even the unusual commercial boom now occurring in Tobatí because of the road-building will be of enough consequence to affect the peasants. The road is changing the town in certain obvious ways, but commercial townsmen participate more fully in the resulting economic advances than the peasants do.

Paraguay is relatively removed from the major world economic influences, so that the general economic expansion has not had all the effects that can be seen in some other Latin-American countries; but the few changes in Tobatí are suggestive of the influence of increased market participation. In general, most of the townsmen are merely sellers, rather than investors in productive enterprises, except for the medieval-like "cottage industries"— household handicraft producers typified in Tobatí by the brickmaking families. The few enterprises of the modern sort are the small cash-crop rice plantations. The opening of a truck route to Caacupé and Asunción has had the effect of stimulating the development of these plantations and, derivatively, of stimulating business in the town.

If prosperity is maintained and trucking increased, one might expect a continuing increase in the number of stores and distributing enterprises, added prosperity for some of them, and a correlated increase in the town population. Such an increase would create an added demand for farm produce, so we might expect to see two kinds of demographic changes in the rural areas. First, the rural population of the *partido* might increase as peasants previously outside the town's economic orbit are drawn into it; produce from *compañías* which lie between Tobatí and other towns could then be marketed more advantageously in Tobatí. Second, the nomadism of subsistence agriculturalists should diminish as the sale of produce becomes more profitable and as credit facilities increase. With added capital, some of the peasants, at least, might be able to improve their agricultural technology and take more interest in permanent ownership of a plot of land.

In town the most striking effect of the recent prosperity is an increase in wealth differences. Townsmen profit much more directly from commerce than do peasants, of course, but among townsmen, those who are already established in business profit more greatly than do the others. The growing wealth differences are obviously being translated into an increased gulf in status between the *sociedad* and those just below them. Another manifestation of added wealth is the emphasis on new bungalow-style houses. An increase in prosperity anywhere seems always to give an impetus to the building trades, but in Paraguay they provide an especially sensitive index, for people (rightly) have no faith in the stability of their currency and hasten to put any spare cash into permanent assets. There is not much profit in agricultural land, nor does ownership of it have the connotation of security that it has in other parts of Latin America; hence cash is more readily put into buildings.

The recent improvements in communication are clearly correlated with the relative prosperity of various towns; the normal Paraguayan view is that roads are directly responsible for economic progress. Each town within the nation needs communication with Asunción in order to compete with other towns. At bottom, therefore, Tobatí is progressing only relatively to other towns and, in a sense, at their expense. Ultimately, of course, it is foreign markets that Paraguayans need as a nation, if all the towns are to prosper. It seems unlikely, actually, that the changes which are incipient in Tobatí will actually reach fulfilment. The present boom is highly artificial and only local, because Tobatí beat neighboring towns to the road-building.

Another characteristic of the increase in prosperity in Tobatí is the highly speculative nature of the use of capital. We found the beginning of capital investment in equipment and in the hiring of labor exemplified most importantly and most typically in the several small rice plantations. We have preferred to call these entrepreneurs "farmers," to distinguish them from peasants. The peasant is an independent producer looking mainly to his subsistence needs. Thus he grows a round of diversified crops each year regardless of market conditions. The farmer, who is also an independent producer (even if he has borrowed his capital), produces mainly or entirely for the market in order to acquire money, and, according to the logic of commercial competition, he tends to become increasingly a specialist and thus ever more dependent on the market. The farmer, therefore, must have confidence in a stable and secure market, *or* he must have sufficient capital to risk a gamble if the market is not stable. It seems that the great predominance of peasant agriculture over farming in Paraguay is basically due to that very lack of a secure market, for the few farmers whom we encountered were essentially specialists gambling their capital on supplying a crop which was temporarily in great demand. Consequently, these entrepreneurs are farmers of a special sort, essentially speculators who are often involved in other commercial enterprises, such as cattle ranching, as well.

Farmers of the classic North American type, market-oriented, independent landholders who are not primarily speculators, depend on market stability for diversified cash-cropping. They have been typically the strong support of the conservative middle-class political forms. But no such farmers exist in Paraguay. And the only interest in politics is the direct one of immediate reward; this interest tends to be speculative, just as it is in the realm of economic investment. The purposes of the Paraguayan farmers are akin to those of the more important capitalists of the city. In any country whose foreign trade is based on an undiversified, purely extractive economy, as is pre-eminently the case with Paraguay, the economic fortunes of the nation's capitalists fluctuate wildly. The rapid boom-and-bust cycles imbue all of them with a speculative philosophy. All this is in some measure typical of any Latin-American nation, but Paraguay seemed to us an extreme case. The increase in farming, then, is an increase in the amount of speculative investment by town businessmen. It seems unlikely that many peasants could become farmers under such circumstances.

The Paraguayan peasant society clearly deviates from certain of the expectations suggested by several anthropological studies of Latin-American communities. We wish to mention one especially striking feature which was unexpected. In contrast to the considerable degree of family communalism so often attributed to rural Latin America, we found the Paraguayan rural family to be nucleated and unstable, the extended family to be nonfunctional economically and consequently unimportant in much of general social life. Production and exchange were highly individualized, although not depersonalized, as they might be in an urban-commercial milieu. And the land-tenure pattern of the Paraguayan peasants seemed anomalous in important respects. Land tenure is in so many ways closely related to other aspects of rural social and economic life and is so revealing of the general economic predicament of the nation that it deserves further discussion here.

Paraguayan peasants are typically very poor in terms of money income, producing little for the market and purchasing little from it. Also, the majority hold no title to the land they occupy. It is usually asserted, in studies of other "underdeveloped" areas of the world, that the economic problems of low productivity and extreme rural poverty are closely related to land scarcity and absentee landlordism. But, in contrast, Paraguay is a relatively underpopulated country. More than any other Latin-American nation, Paraguay has striven to encourage immigration, feeling that its poverty must be related to the low population density. And the political and economic problem of absentee landlordism, which has occasioned bitterness in some parts of Latin America, has not been of major consequence in Paraguay, especially since 1870, when most of the landholders lost their estates. About the only large landholders today are cattle ranchers, and their holdings are campo which would not ordinarily be used for agriculture.

To say that over three-fourths of the Paraguayan agriculturalists are landless is not to say the same thing that might be implied in a smiliar statement about other countries. The Paraguayan is often landless only in the sense that he holds no legal title to his plot; he usually has access to more land than he can cultivate with his primitive equipment. His problem is basically that of the whole nation; he is virtually without a market for his products and consequently is without capital. The internal market for agricultural produce is very small, as there are no large cities and the percentage of the nonargricultural population is the smallest in our hemisphere, except for Haiti. The foreign market is almost nonexistent, partly because the only egress is via the Argentine-dominated Paraguay River, where shipping costs are enormous. The cycle of sale of crops for cash, in order to invest in equipment or more land, in order to increase production for more profit, never received the necessary impetus to get it started and never can, until a sufficient market exists. For the Paraguayan peasant to hold title to the plot he occupies confers no economic benefit and might be actually a liability, in the sense that it would tend to tie him to increasingly less productive land, when, by moving, he could find a more fertile location.

A typical Paraguayan rural area such as Tobatí is not excessively primitive or poor, however, as compared with isolated rural areas in other Latin-American countries. What is striking is the fact that the whole nation is more backward than most other Latin-American nations. Poverty-stricken peasants are found in all these countries, but Paraguay is more overwhelmingly "peasant" in its general culture. The poverty of the rural agriculturalists clearly cannot be considered a "land problem," basically, but rather has to do with the situation of the whole country in its economic relations with the rest of the world. The *nation* of Paraguay is poor, and the plight of the peasant is merely the rural reflection of that fact. Such slogans as "Land for the landless" and "Break up the *latifundios*" have no meaning in Paraguay, and, in fact, we can think of no local political solution of any sort which could improve the peasants' condition permanently.

In most of Latin America there is a tendency for the governments to intervene bureaucratically in various enterprises and also to undertake or underwrite certain kinds of industries and many public works. But also, because of the general one-sidedness of foreign trade, the dependence on foreign capital, and the lack of internal savings, the governments tend to lack control over their currency and are thus especially prone to have extreme fiscal difficulties. In this matter, too, Paraguay has exaggerated problems.[14] The government, acting as a source of capital, cannot maintain projects which are undertaken for internal improve-

14. For example, all Latin-American countries have been struggling with inflation in recent years, especially with respect to dollar exchange, but Paraguay's inflation is phenomenal. The Paraguayan peso, which had been the basic monetary unit, became so worthless a few years ago that the guarani was created as a 100-peso unit. The *New York Times* on January 7, 1953 (p. 74), reported that the free exchange rate was 60 guaranis—6,000 pesos—to a dollar, and still rising!

ment, even when they are supported initially by foreign aid. Roads, schools, credit facilities, and public works in general are grandiose in plan but lag far behind in execution or fail completely.

Piecemeal economic aid of the sort offered by loans and technical assistance programs sponsored by the United States of America may lead to improvements in parts of the economy or at least may benefit certain individuals. Some advances in Paraguay are noticeable; farmers have been aided by loans and technical advice, interest has been stirred in a refurbished public health program, road-building has been stimulated by the influence of the partly completed asphalt Central Highway, and the intellectuals have become enthusiastic about the educational exchange fellowships. But the nation itself does not have the means to maintain the improvements now initiated, much less to continue further development. The roads built with foreign capital are falling into disrepair. Equipment is scarce, materials are expensive, and political turnovers often result in the abandoning of projects or at least in changes in their trained personnel. We feel that, while the foreign aids have resulted in notable achievements, they must be regarded as merely alleviations of certain symptoms of the economic problem, no more curative of a desperate illness than is aspirin.

In short, we view the immediate future of Paraguay with profound pessimism. Only a few natives benefit even indirectly from the extraction of natural resources, and such rewards are likely to be ephemeral. The agrarian bulk of the population in Paraguay will remain peasants until their produce can be sold in the external market or internally to a larger proportion of nonagriculturalists who are producing something else for the external market. We cannot see any possibility for a successful Paraguayan bootstrap operation.

Paraguay has been a true nation in the political sense for a long time now, but its internal economy is still basically garden subsistence. The majority of the Paraguayan people, as individuals, are economically independent. They are not bound as serfs or tenants in a hacienda or plantation system, and only a few are employed sporadically as wageworkers in extractive industries, in ranching, or in shipping. Paraguay's limited external economy is completely extractive, consisting almost entirely of the sale of a few raw materials. Nearly all these enterprises are foreign-owned. This modest economy, as a source of foreign exchange, is typically or even exaggeratedly a case of what is usually called "economic dependence." It is also an economy which cannot build on itself and become self-sufficient as a political entity, for Paraguay is not a natural economic unit in terms of what is required for modern industrialization and diversification of production. Paraguay seems destined to remain subordinate with respect to its relations with other nations. Perhaps in an economic and political union of Latin-American states Paraguay might contribute and share as a specialized region in a larger functional unit. But this is the idlest daydream from the point of view of living Paraguayans. It is sad not to be able to end this book on a note of hope, but what may sound like pessimism and hopelessness in this case seems to us to be actually realism.

Appendixes

Local Weights and Measures

The metric system is official and is taught in school, but among most of the people the following are often used instead:

Linear Measures

Vara (2.8 feet)
Vara cúbica (34 × 10 × 10 inches; used only as a timber measure)
Cuadra (100 varas)
Cuerda (82 varas; sometimes confused with cuadra)
Legua (5,000 varas, but oftener understood as 5 kilometers)

The old pulgada, pie, yarda, cuarta, and pieza have gone out of use, except in very specialized occupations such as carpentry and tailoring.

Weights and Liquid Measures

Arroba (originally 25.3 pounds, but normally understood in rural Paraguay as 10 kilograms)
Tonelada (1,000 kilograms; 100 arrobas)
Almud (24 liters; now used only in measuring oranges; often understood as 50 oranges)
Quintal (in Paraguay, 100 kilograms instead of the original 100 libras)

The old libra, onza, quartillo, fanega, and azumbra have gone out of use.

APPENDIX II

Family Names in the Town of Tobati

Name	No.	Name	No.	Name	No.
Acosta	3	Ferreira	7	Ortega	5
Agüero	5	Finestra	1	Ortigoza	1
Albarenga	1	Fleitas	2	Ortiz	8
Alcaraz	2	Florentín	2	Peralta	1
Alvárez	2	Franco	2	Piñánez	4
Arepocó	2	Fursi	1	Portillo	1
Arévalo	1	Galeano	4	Quiñones	7
Arias	4	Gamarra	3	Ramírez	3
Arzamendia	1	Garcete	1	Recalde	1
Ayala	6	García	1	Richer	1
Benega (Venegas)	1	Gómez	3	Rivas	6
Benjamín	2	González	8	Rodríquez	2
Berdejo	1	Irala	6	Rojas	1
Bernal	1	Jiménez	5	Rolón	1
Blanco	4	Lagraña	5	Romero	1
Bolaños	6	Ledesma	4	Ruíz	2
Brozón	3	Leite	1	Saldívar	5
Cabrera	1	Leivas	1	Salín	1
Cabriza	6	León	2	Salvioni	2
Cáceres	3	Limenza	2	Sanabria	1
Candia	3	Macchi	11	Sánchez	1
Cañete	6	Martínez	5	Santacruz	1
Cano	1	Melgarejo	1	Sarate	1
Castillo	2	Mena	1	Sarracho	10
Chena	3	Mernes	1	Soler	1
Coronel	2	Morales	7	Tanis	1
Delfino	1	Morínigo	3	Torales	1
Días	1	Morla	1	Valenzuela	1
Dionysis	1	Navarro	1	Vargas	1
Duarte	4	Noguera	2	Vera	3
Durañona	1	Núñez	17	Yegros	7
Enciso	2	Oreco	1	Zavala	1
Esquivel	13	Orrego	2		

Ceremonial Calendar

Date	Name	Description
January 1	Año Nuevo	A secular, unorganized, family celebration, marked by gift-giving; observed in all pueblos
January 6	Fiesta de los Tres Reyes	Religious and secular observance in all pueblos, with a primary emphasis on gifts to children; Mass and procession; *los negritos (cambá ra'angá)*; games
February 3	San Blas	Patron saint of Paraguay; a minor secular celebration in Tobatí, chiefly marked by appearance of *negritos*
Lent and Holy Week	Carnaval	Sunday, Monday, and Tuesday before Ash Wednesday; a pre-Lenten secular festival, including costume dances, clowning, etc.
	Miércoles de Ceniza	First day of Lent; Mass and fasting
	Día de Dolores	Mass and fasting; all images veiled
	Domingo de Ramos	Mass and procession with *santo* and sacred palms
	Lunes Santo	Mass; beginning of Via Crucis in evening
	Martes Santo	Mass; Via Crucis
	Miércoles Santo	Mass; Via Crucis; fasting
	Jueves Santo	High Mass; last ringing of church bells until Saturday; procession marking the anniversary of the Eucharist; cessation of work from noon until Saturday morning; last procession of Via Crucis in evening; a feast of meat is taken at noon
	Viernes Santo	Mass called by *matraca;* re-enactment of Crucifixion and funeral of Christ in afternoon; procession; fasting

Date	Name	Description
	Sábado de Gloria	High Mass, called by *matraca;* unveiling of images; blessing of holy water; lighting of candles; black altar curtain dropped; bells ring again; procession in afternoon; burning of Judas at night
	Domingo de Pascua	Mass, with Communion; procession; secular celebrations after Mass
May 24	María Auxiliadora	Patroness of the army; in Tobatí, patroness of one barrio; large fiesta, religious and secular
June 14	San Antonio	Patron of a barrio in Tobatí; Mass and procession
June 16	Corpus Christi	Mass; procession combined with fiesta of San Pedro, on June 29
June 20	Corazón de Jesús	Mass and procession; no secular fiesta
June 24	San Juán	Mass; no procession; many games: *cambá ra'angá, toro candil*, games with fire
June 29	San Pedro	Patron of Tobatí; Mass and procession; games, as for San Juán
July 16	Virgen del Carmen	Mass and proccession
July 20	Santa Librada	Mass and procession
August 15	Virgen de la Asunción	Mass and procession; big fiesta in Asunción, celebrating founding of the city
August 16	San Roque	Patron of dogs and workmen; sometimes a *novenario* and a procession; celebrated mainly in homes where he is patron
August 30	Santa Rosa	Fiesta and procession in Compañía Santa Rosa
August 31	San Ramón	Patron of women and of childbirth; women burn candles to him and ask for personal favors; no formal celebration
September 4	Santa Rosalía	Mass and procession in Compañía Santa Rosalía
September 24	Virgen de los Mercedes	Mass and procession in Compañía Typychatý; large fiesta attended by many people from town
September 29	San Miguel	Mass and procession
Last Sunday of October	Virgen de Rosario	Formerly celebrated by Mass and procession, but society now dissolved
November 1	Día de Todos los Santos	Mass; decoration of graves of children
November 2	Día de los Difuntos	Mass and prayers at the cemetery for the adult dead

Date	Name	Description
December 8	Día de la Virgen de la Concepción Inmaculada	Patroness of Tobatí; all *Tobateños* try to return to pueblo for this patronal fiesta; Mass; procession; fiesta; games
December 24	La Noche Buena	Midnight Mass ("Misa del Gallo"); making of crèches; visiting
December 25	La Navidad	Family reunions

Beliefs about Food and Common Recipes

The most pervasive beliefs about food are associated with the division of foods and beverages into "hot" and "cold" categories. These categories do not refer to the temperature of the food or to any single consistent characteristic, except that "hot" foods seem to be usually regarded as somewhat heavier, or more indigestible, than "cold" foods. Most generally, they refer to the presumed effect of certain foods on the state of the body, which itself may be "hot" (or feverish) or "cold" (chilled). Thus a "hot" food, such as beef, should not be eaten by a person who has a fever, whereas such "cold" foods as tea, fruit, or most vegetables, help to reduce a fever, even if served hot. Hot foods are considered to be best eaten in the winter, possibly because a person is more likely to be chilled then or to have a cold.

Under most conditions a judicious mixture of hot and cold foods at the same meal is considered ideal. Thus fruit or vegetables are said to "refresh" a meal which includes soup and beef. Too many cold items are considered prejudicial; one should not drink water (which is considered always to be exceptionally "cold") after eating watermelon. In fact, one should not even bathe shortly after eating watermelon. Pork, which is quite "hot," should not be followed with an alcoholic beverage, for all of them (except beer) are hot. It appears, too, that one should not shock the system with a good deal of heat and follow with something very cold. Tobacco is very hot, and one who has been working with tobacco should not bathe or wash for some hours afterward.

There is a definite belief that cold beverages, such as beer, cold water, or iced drinks, should be avoided when one is cold or when one has a cold. It is felt that there is a relationship between getting chilled or wet, drinking something cold, and then getting a cold, laryngitis, or earache. Fruits should not be eaten in cold weather and are never eaten before breakfast. Water is not drunk before breakfast or during meals. It is regarded as the end of a meal. If a person is offered anything more to eat, it will be refused with the remark, "No, now I have drunk water." Excessive drinking of water is avoided, even in hot weather, by taking *refrescantes* like *tereré* (cold *mate*), fruit-flavored water, or cold "mint tea." Milk or other beverages may be drunk, like water, after a meal is completed.

Foods and beverages considered "hot" and "cold" are listed below.

COLD	HOT
Squash	Soup
Oranges	Beef
Salads	Beans
All fruits	Milk
Fresh green corn (?)[1]	Butter and lard
Tomatoes	Macaroni
Rice	Peanuts
Honey (?)	Pork
Fish	Maize
Manioc (?)	Chicken and other fowl (?)
Potatoes	Peppers
Onions	Caña
Beer	Wine
Tea	Coffee
Tereré	Mate amargo

Eggs are believed to be aphrodisiacs and also to give strength. Chicken fat is aphrodisiac if rubbed on the lower abdomen. The chicken from which the fat is taken must be eaten to make the fat effective. Bulls' testicles, also believed to give sexual vigor, are skinned, boiled, split open, and broiled or fried. Most women do not eat them.

There are only a few tabooed foods. Lizards are never eaten, and informants profess horror of the Bolivian liking for them. Iguanas, however, may be eaten because they are said to live on chickens, eggs, and coconut husks, and the meat is much like chicken. Frogs and snakes are not used for food. Mushrooms are not gathered. It is said that Paraguayans do not know how to tell poisonous from nonpoisonous varieties.

There are two common superstitions associated with the preparation of food. Evil eye (oyeharú) has the power to curdle or spoil food, and there is also the fear that a herbal decoction (payé) might be put in food to enchant the eater (see chap. xvii).

Dishes Prepared with Maize

Two kinds of maize are utilized in cooking. One is the hard white variety, called maíz tupí. It is used primarily in locro, a meat stew in which the maize is prepared like hominy, and for masamorra, a sort of corn-meal mush which may be eaten with milk, sugar, honey, or salt, according to taste. The other, used for many different dishes, is maíz blanco, which is yellow in color and much softer. Either type may sometimes produce grains of various colors—white, yellow, red, dark blue. All colors are considered edible and good for seed, and they have no magical, curing, or religious significance. Maize is a staple food and is used in some form nearly every day throughout the year. It is especially favored as maíz choclo, or fresh green maize.

1. The question marks denote a difference of opinion among informants.

Maize is ground immediately before use in a large wooden mortar, but, for special festivals in which a large quantity will be needed, it may be ground and sifted in a straw *cedazo* a day in advance. An ordinary table knife laid in the meal in one direction, then lifted out and placed as the bar of a cross in the other direction, is left overnight. This is believed to prevent the grain from developing a strong odor and a bad taste. Maize is never ground earlier than the day before use.

Locro (prepared with *maíz tupí*).—The maize kernels are sprinkled with a little water, pounded in the mortar until the hard outer covering of the grain is loosened, and then sifted to separate the grains. These shucked grains are called *locro*, as is the soup which is prepared from it. The prepared maize is placed in an iron cooking pot with chunks of fresh meat or small bits of dried meat or both, and simmered. Sometimes cabbage chopped into small bits is placed to boil with it. Onions, small green peppers, and tomatoes are fried in beef fat and added to the soup. It should be stirred frequently, and, if an especially rich soup is desired, liver, blood sausage, or pork sausage may be added. Just before serving, a little dried oregano or fresh chopped parsley is sprinkled into the pot. Lemon or lime juice may be squeezed into the soup at the table. This dish is a favorite over the entire country. In the cattle country it is commonly made with dried meat, and liver and sausages are common ingredients. In the agricultural part of the country the dish is made usually of fresh meat. The favored cut of beef for the purpose is the brisket. *Locro*, like other soups, may be prepared for fast days without meat. More vegetables are used, milk is added just before serving, and fresh cheese is crumbled into the soup.

Locro is considered good to eat only in the middle of the day, for it is a heavy meal. *Locrillo* ("little locro"), however, may be eaten at the evening meal also and is considered a suitable food for invalids, while locro is not. The only difference is that for the *locrillo* the grains of corn are pounded until they are as small as grains of rice.

Masamorra.—Maíz tupí is pounded until peeled and is then put to cook in boiling water. It is stirred slightly from time to time. When the corn is soft, *lejía* (water in which ashes of wood or charcoal have been left overnight) is added to dye the mush yellow. This dish may be eaten hot or cold, with milk, sugar, honey, or salt. The *lejía* supposedly has medicinal properties which cure pains in the stomach or abdomen and which reduce fever.

*Maíz choclo.—*The fresh green ears are much prized for roasting and also for use in the preparation of a number of dishes.

*Maíz tostado.—*Toasted dried yellow maize, eaten plain or with a little salt, is especially favored by children.

Chipa de maíz or *chipa pyrú.—Chipa* is the name given to various types of breads, made of either maize or manioc flour. This one requires finely ground *maíz blanco*, salt, cheese, and lard or salad oil. It is mixed well and formed into round cakes. These may be baked and eaten hot or cold, or they may be cut open and toasted or used to prepare a *sopa blanca* (meatless soup, suitable for fast days).

Sopa paraguaya.—*Sopa paraguaya* is the national fiesta dish. It is essential for a wedding feast and is believed to bring good luck. It is used for all festival meals, formal or informal, by rich and poor, sophisticates and peasants, though its richness may vary considerably with the means and the ability of the cook. It is prepared for about ten people by grinding yellow corn rather fine, using about a kilogram of *maíz.* Two to four eggs, together with about one-fourth of a cup of olive oil, should be beaten very thoroughly by hand. (Paraguayans set great store by handwork and are reluctant to use grinders, egg beaters, or other utensils.) When this batter is very light, onions fried slightly in oil are added to taste, and one-half liter or more of milk, one-half kilogram or more of fresh cheese broken into small bits, and salt to taste are added. These ingredients and the corn meal are mixed thoroughly and placed in a pan lined with banana leaves on which cooking oil has been poured. The batter should be rather liquid for a rich *sopa.* It is baked in a beehive-shaped outdoor oven or in Dutch-oven style on a charcoal brazier. *Chipa guazú* is a variant of *sopa paraguaya,* made in the same way, but using fresh maize, raw and only slightly pounded. This forms a more liquid mass and a moister cake. *Sopa* batter is also used to make little cakes which are filled with a meat preparation. The meat is pounded fine, seasoned, and precooked.

Bori bori.—*Bori bori* are little corn-meal balls cooked in soup. They are particularly good in chicken soup but may also be cooked in a soup seasoned with onions, tomatoes, and peppers. A little crumbled cheese may be added to the soup at the last minute. The *bori bori* are prepared with corn meal, ground fine, one egg or two or three egg yolks, a little oil, and fresh cheese. Minced onion may be added if desired. These are salted to taste and mixed into a mass, then rolled into little balls and boiled in the soup for a few minutes.

Polenta.—Another common maize dish is *polenta,* which is used in all Latin America and in Spain and some other parts of Europe. Ribs of pork or beef are braised in hot fat and seasoned with salt, pepper, pimientoes, onions, parsley, and cumin seed. Then corn meal is added with a little water. It is cooked to the consistency of mush, deliciously flavored with the juice of the meat.

Leche endulzada or *cambý he'e.*—Milk, corn meal, molasses, and lemon leaf are boiled together until thick. This may be made with burnt sugar instead of cane syrup. It is like sweet corn-meal mush and is eaten as dessert.

Kiveve.—A calabash, called *andaí,* is used in a dish which serves as a meal or a dessert. The sweet squash is cut up and cooked with salt and water; corn meal is added, then milk, and, just before removing from the fire, sugar.

Corn meal is also used to mix with such dishes as *albóndigas* (see below) in place of manioc or wheat flour, to dust over fresh meat to keep off the flies when it is hung to keep through the day, and to put on beef which is being dried in the sun.

Dishes Prepared with Manioc

Manioc (*mandioca* or *mandió*) is a more important dish for the poor and for countrypeople than is maize. It is cheap and plentiful and keeps well in the ground until needed for use. It is simply boiled in salted water and used as bread at all meals. It is also used as a vegetable boiled in any stew. Many dishes are prepared of the flour. *Farinha*, as prepared in Brazil, is not so commonly used in Paraguay, but a fresh flour (which does not keep so well as *farinha*) is made rather frequently. Various types of bread are prepared of this flour, and it is also used for thickening sauces and soup.

Chipa de almidón.—This is certainly the most common bread made and eaten outside of Asunción. The recipe given makes about two dozen small loaves, but in the country a woman will often mix a quantity of dough in a wooden trough and bake a great amount at one time to sell in the country store or to her neighbors. The bread is often eaten as the only food at supper, with *mate cocido* or milk, and children nibble on it during the day. It is prepared according to the following directions: Using about half a kilogram of lard, work it until very light. Add eight or more eggs. Mix well, add a kilogram and a half of cheese, broken up fine. Add one liter or more of milk, and salt. Mix well, and add about two kilograms of manioc flour and a quarter-kilogram of finely ground corn meal. Season with seeds of anise; mix and work thoroughly. Separate into workable portions and knead very thoroughly until smooth; shape into small loaves and bake in a hot oven.

Chipa manduví, chipa con maní, or *chipa kandoi.*—This is a special *chipa*, made only during Holy Week, especially for Good Friday. It is prepared as follows: Toast and mash the peanuts, and mix with finely ground corn meal, using about a kilogram of meal and a kilogram of peanuts. Work about one quarter-kilogram of lard until light. Add, if desired, one quarter-kilogram or less of cheese. Add the peanuts and corn meal; mix well. Salt to taste and add a little hot water or milk. Work into a mass, roll, flatten, and shape into loaves. Bake on banana leaves in a hot oven. This amount makes about fifteen small loaves.

These breads may vary in richness according to the ingredients available. They are expensive to prepare, particularly during Holy Week, when eggs and cheese are in great demand. Less cheese, less eggs, or less milk may be used. A great deal of work is involved in shelling the peanuts, grinding the maize and nuts, and preparing the outdoor oven. Nevertheless, everyone tries to prepare this food for Holy Week.

Caburé.—This is a cake made of *typyratý*, pounded raw meat, onions, garlic, oregano, cumin seed, oil, salt, and pepper, which are mixed and formed into cakes and baked. A spicy cake with a texture something like *albóndiga* results. It is eaten hot as a bread substitute.

Lampreado.—Meat, manioc, and onions are boiled together, then pounded into small bits in a mortar, mixed with spices, formed into cakes, and fried in oil.

Mbeyú or *torta de almidón.*—Also called "bread of the poor," this is made of a paste of manioc flour and water, baked like pancakes in a

APPENDIX 311

greased pan. Corn meal may be added to make *mbeyú yopará* or *torta entreverada*. These cakes also may be made of *typyratỹ*, and cheese may be added. This is the most like Mexican *tortillas* of all Paraguayan breads.

Dishes Prepared with Beef

One of the most common of all Paraguayan dishes, rivaling the *locro* already described, is puchero, or stew. This is simply fresh meat boiled with whatever vegetables and seasonings are available, to form a stew or thick soup. Fat brisket of beef is favored for this as for *locro*. The soup should be started with cold water. If oil or beef fat is available, a few onions may be sautéed with tomato paste in the grease as a base for the stew.

So'o yosopy.—Raw meat is pounded and placed in an iron kettle with fried onions and garlic. Cold water is added and brought to a simmer, after which salt is added. This is a favorite dish, sometimes varied by the addition of rice or crumbled fresh cheese.

Bife pupú or *bife con caldo.*—This is a common late breakfast dish; it is simply a slice of beef tenderloin boiled in water and served with the broth.

Bife a caballo.—This consists of a slice of tenderloin broiled over charcoal and served with a poached or fried egg on top.

Guiso.—Fresh or dried beef, chopped or pounded, is browned in the iron olla. A little water is added, and macaroni or spaghetti is cooked in the same pot just before serving.

Asado en la olla.—Large chunks of *lomo* of beef are seared in the iron pot with a little fat and cooked with very little or no water until done. The meat is usually marinated in lemon juice, garlic, and salt and pepper before cooking.

Asado.—Chunks of beef or lamb are marinated in lemon juice, garlic, salt and pepper, and oil and are then broiled over charcoal. For large outdoor barbecues the same procedure is followed, except that huge broiling pits are dug in the ground and the meat is skewered onto large wooden poles and turned as it broils.

Milanesa.—A slice of beef tenderloin, pounded and rolled in egg, *galleta* crumbs or flour, salt, and pepper, is fried rapidly. Prepared with a batter of eggs, milk, and flour, it is called *bife forado*. The meat is usually marinated before cooking.

Chicharrón.—Fat ribs or fat strips of meat are cooked in a hot pan until all the fat is rendered. The crisp residue may be eaten plain or covered with toasted corn meal.

Albóndigas.—Beef is cut up fine and then pounded in the mortar with parsley. When it has been well pounded, salt, onions, pepper, and corn meal are added, and mixed well. It is then rolled into balls and dropped into boiling water, with rice or with *fideos*. The secret of light, tender *Albóndigas* is to pound the meat instead of grinding it.

Albóndigas enrellenadas.—This is made as follows: Pound the meat fine in a mortar with a garlic clove; mix with ground *galletas*, salt, and milk. Make into patties; pat a hollow in the center and fill with a sauce made of eggs, onions, garlic, oil, salt, and pepper; close and roll until smooth. Brown in oil, and drop into the kettle to boil in a sauce of oil, water, onions, garlic, tomato sauce, potatoes, etc. Simmer until the sauce is thick; flour may be added if needed to thicken the sauce. This may also be made in a large roll, like a stuffed meat loaf.

Dishes Prepared with Pork

Pork is slaughtered only in cool weather in the winter months and is valued first for the fat. Broiled or barbecued ribs of pork are a luxury, prepared by marinating in lemon juice, garlic, salt, pepper, and oil and baking in an oven or broiling over charcoal. Nearly all other cuts of pork are ground or spiced to make sausage. Some of these sausages keep well; others are only lightly spiced and must be used fairly soon. Pork is never smoked or dried.

Dishes Prepared with Fowl

Chicken is the most common fowl, although turkeys and guinea hens are also raised. Such wild fowl as partridge, grouse, and pheasant are also eaten when available, usually broiled. Young chickens are usually broiled, and older fowl are used for soups and stews. Stewed chicken is commonly cooled and made into salads. Chicken is prepared for broiling by flavoring with lemon juice and a little garlic and oil, as are other meats.

Dishes Prepared with Eggs

Eggs are used a great deal in the preparation of other foods and are also eaten poached, fried, soft-boiled, in omelets, or dropped into soup. A common egg dish is a cake, called a *tortilla*, made of one or two eggs and flour, well beaten and fried; this may be mixed with parsley, sausage, potatoes, or all three. A dessert is made of eggs by beating the desired number of whites, adding the yolks, and beating again very throughly for a long time. Then molasses or a mixture of sugar and water is placed in a frying pan and heated slightly, and the batter is cooked slowly. It may be allowed to rise as for an omelet, but it is usually broken as it rises and turned over in quarters to cook until all the foam is gone and the honey or sugar syrup is entirely soaked up. Then it is removed from the fire, cooled and served. Eggs are also used to make a toddy, beaten with hot or cold milk and *caña*, with cinnamon and anise for flavoring. Ostrich-egg yolks may be used in the preparation of *tortillas*, but the whites are not used, and the yolk is not used in other ways. Eggs of guinea hens and turkeys are used in the same way as hens' eggs. One of the commonest uses of eggs is to stir them with cheese into a soup at the last minute before serving.

Dishes Prepared with Cheese

In times of plentiful milk supply a great deal of cheese is made. It is added to soups, usually those called *sopa blanca*, which do not contain meat. It is used in the preparation of *chipa* and of *sopa paraguaya* and is eaten fresh as a dessert with molasses poured over it.

In the preparation of cheese, a milk-sourer is made of the large beef intestine. It is well washed and soaked in the juice of bitter oranges for at least three or four hours. Then it is stretched on sticks to dry in the sun. It may be used many times if washed carefully and redried after each use. Five liters of milk produce about three liters of cheese. In summer the sourer can be left in the milk only about an hour. In winter it is usually left from morning until late afternoon. The milk is filtered through a cloth bag to separate the curds from the whey. The curds are left to stand overnight and then packed into square wooden molds to set. The cheese is stored on high shelves in the shade, where air may circulate around it. The whey is fed to pigs or is used with sugar as a purgative.

Dishes Prepared with Vegetables

Vegetables such as lettuce, onions, tomatoes, squash (boiled and cooled), beans (lima beans and pea beans), and peas are used by townsmen in salads, combined with cold meats and hard-boiled eggs. Pea pods are used in *tortillas* as flavoring. Cabbage is used primarily in puchero and *locro*. Squash is a favored vegetable and is used in many ways.

Bomba de zapallo.—Squash is boiled until soft. Onions, garlic, small red peppers, tomato paste, salt, and bay leaf are mixed and sautéed in oil. Meat is boiled and then pounded fine in the mortar. The meat and seasonings are mixed. Wheat flour is mixed with the soft squash to form a paste, which is rolled into patties, filled with the meat mixture, closed, and rolled into balls. These are browned in hot fat and then dropped into the kettle with some of the sauce which was reserved for this purpose. A little oil and water may be added to the sauce at this time. The dish is boiled until hot, and the sauce thickened as desired.

Sopa de manteca.—Butter-bean soup is often served nearly dry rather than like a soup. Similar dishes are prepared with pea beans or black-eyed peas. The beans are cooked in water; cheese, eggs, onion, and salt are added, and ground meat is used when available.

Irish potatoes are little used, as they are imported from Argentina and are expensive. They are most commonly prepared as salad. Sweet potatoes are raised locally and are used a great deal, roasted in an oven or in the ashes.

Other vegetables, such as carrots, beets, turnips, string beans, *acelga* (a saltwort), and celery, are generally available only in the capital and are prepared according to European recipes.

Desserts

Fruits are eaten raw by both children and adults. The most common fruits so used are oranges, grapefruits, mangoes, papayas, guavas, bananas, grapes, and various small wild fruits which are similar to cherries and plums. Pineapple is eaten raw as a dessert, and so are cantaloupes and watermelons. Other fruits are cooked in various ways into thick pastes or jams to be eaten as desserts. *Dulce de guayaba* is the commonest dessert of this type. It may be prepared in a paste, a conserve, or a syrup. To prepare in syrup or as a jam, the largest ripe fruit is selected, peeled, seeded, and cooked in sugar syrup to the desired thickness. Or the fruit may be cooked in water, put through a strainer, and recooked with sugar until a thick paste is formed. Apricots and figs may also be prepared in this way. Papayas are commonly cooked in sugar syrup, which acts as a preservative. It is most delicious cooked very slightly in a thin syrup flavored with rum.

Dulce de la naranja ágria.—This is made as follows: Grate or cut into small pieces the skin of the bitter orange, and soak in cold water overnight. In the morning rinse the skins at least seven or eight times, until all bitterness is gone. Cook with water and honey or sugar, and throw off the juice. This should be repeated two or three times. Then the skin is cooked with molasses or sugar, until it is as dry as desired. The result is similar to candied orange peel, but perhaps a little more moist and more bitter.

Dulce de leche.—This is another common dessert, made either as a thick pudding or in cakes, like fudge. One and one-half liters of milk are brought to a boil and one kilogram of sugar is gradually added. The mixture is stirred constantly until thickened. A little vanilla is added, and the dessert is removed from the fire to cool. This amount takes about one and a half hours to cook. Once the sugar has been added, a person who has just gone to the toilet must not look at the mixture, or it will sugar. A menstruating woman should not cook this dessert, and the dessert may also be spoiled by the *oyeharú* ("evil eye").

Crema.—This is made in many ways, but a common one is to boil milk with sugar to taste and add yolk of egg and a little wheat or manioc flour. It must be stirred continuously until thick. It may be flavored with lemon skin or leaves and a little vanilla. When it is removed from the fire, it is covered with caramelized sugar or meringue or, less frequently, with chocolate sauce. This is similar to the dessert which the Spanish call *nata*, or *natilla*.

Arroz con leche or *cambý arroz.*—Another common Latin-American and Spanish dessert, this is made by cooking rice slowly in milk or by boiling rice first with sugared water and then adding milk. When the rice is tender, yolk of egg is added, and stirred until thickened. It is flavored with lemon leaf or vanilla, and a little cinnamon is shaken over the top.

Beverages

By far the most common beverage of the entire population is *mate*, which is drunk in three different ways, as described below. Oriental tea is expensive and is used primarily as a medicine. Fruit juices and tea of mint are favorite summer beverages, and fruit punch is served at dances with *empanadas* (small tarts filled with spiced meats or sweet custards). Coffee is used only in the middle and upper classes and is prepared as a strong essence and combined with hot milk or drunk very black after meals. Poor people toast and grind the seeds of *ca'aré* ("saltwort") and make a beverage known as "coffee of the poor."

Caña is the usual alcoholic beverage. Beer is made in Asunción, and some Argentine and local German-made wine is available, but these are used only by wealthier townsmen, and only rarely by them.

Tereré.—*Tereré* is a drink made in a glass or tin container or in a steer horn. The container is loosely filled with a large quantity of the *yerba mate* leaves, and cold water is poured over them and sipped through a *bombilla* (a hollow metal tube with a strainer at one end). *Tereré* is said to have been invented or to have become popular during the Chaco war, because the tea leaves acted as a filter for the muddy water. It is now a popular mid-morning or mid-afternoon drink in hot weather, but it is used more by men than by women.

Mate, mate amargo, or *amargo*.—*Mate* is always made in a gourd. The container, which is called the *mate*, is nearly filled with *yerba* leaves packed quite firmly. Boiling water is poured over the leaves, and the infusion is sipped through the *bombilla*. This is a strong bitter brew which can be made only in small quantities. Boiling water is added over and over again, until all the flavor is gone from the leaves. This is a drink for early morning all year round and is preferred to *tereré* in the winter.

Mate cocido.—This is a tea of *yerba* which is boiled with sugar. It is drunk with additional sugar stirred into it and frequently with milk. It is used for a second breakfast and for afternoon tea or evening supper and is especially favored by women. There are a few people who take *mate* only in this form, as they regard *tereré* and *amargo* drinking as a vice.

The social ritual surrounding *mate*-drinking seems to be an old one. It is a hospitable gesture to offer *mate*, and it is very nearly insulting to refuse to partake. In the case of the *tereré* and *mate amargo*, the same container is passed around the circle of drinkers, each taking his sips in turn. The guest or honored person is served first, and then the container passes around time after time, until the supply is exhausted. Occasionally in a large group more than one *mate* will be prepared, or a *mate* will be refilled and passed again. This custom of passing a common container has been extended to the drinking of alcoholic refreshments and is defended vigorously as a Paraguayan custom indicating friendship and confidence.

In social *mate*-drinking, each person drinks all the liquid from the *mate* gourd. This is only two or three swallows. The gourd is then refilled with water and passed on to the next person. Occasionally a jug of water or a kettle of hot water is placed near the drinkers. *Tereré*, which requires only cold water, is customarily made with more water than the hot *mate* and needs refilling less frequently. Ordinarily for hot *mate*, a servant, wife, or daughter will carry the gourd to the kitchen, fill it from the teakettle kept boiling there, and carry it back, standing by the drinker until he is finished and repeating the trip to the kitchen as often as necessary. *Mate* is drunk by the men wherever they happen to be at the moment, and it is the duty and supposedly the pleasure of the wife or daughter to serve the men, no matter how far from the kitchen they may be. Women less frequently are included in such gatherings but may participate if it is essentially a familial group.

It is estimated that an average man will use about one-quarter kilogram of *mate* per day during the summer, because *tereré* uses more of the leaves. In winter perhaps half that amount would be used.

Caña.—Men drink *caña* mainly on fiesta occasions. Drunkenness seems to be generally disapproved but viewed with tolerance when it occurs. There are few people in town who are considered drunkards. Women indulge in alcohol only rarely. They sometimes take a small glass of a sweet wine or cordial for sociability and politeness rather than for enjoyment.

Men do not buy themselves drinks but rather treat each other. That is, a man buys a glassful of *caña* and passes it around to all who are present, each in turn taking a sip. It is not polite to take too large a sip, for drinks are expensive, and the people have little money. Drinking is entirely social and toasts are common, in both Spanish and Guaraní. These toasts or drinking poems are called *pericones*, like the dance of that name in which participants are halted by a master of ceremonies to recite a short poem to the other dancers.

Folk Medicine

Although medicines prepared of herbs are by far the most common, other elements are used. The fat from around the stomach of chickens, carefully preserved with salt or lemon, is considered a good remedy for headache or for pain in any part of the body. The affected part is massaged with the dried fat. White of egg is used in bone-setting, and yolk of egg is given to build up strength during convalescence from an illness. Burned soil is used as a disinfectant and is applied as a compress to stop hemorrhage. Ground dog bones are used in making casts for broken bones, and dried dog excrement is used in combination with herbs to treat scarlet fever. Bees' honey is used in many ways: in cough syrups, as an abortive, to increase the flow of menstrual blood, and in treatment of tuberculosis. Mare's milk and the milk of burros are drunk for their medicinal value. Wood ashes and ash of burned alligator skin are used medicinally. Live toads are used as cataplasms to reduce swelling. Urine is used in the treatment of skin disorders.

Of various available commercial products, kerosene is used as a disinfectant and to eliminate head lice. Ink is used to treat burns, and alcohol is a general remedy for aches, pains, and rheumatism. Sulfa drugs and penicillin are known and may be purchased in nearly all small-town drugstores, but they are used only after treatment with herbal medicines has failed.

Like foods, herbal medicines are classified as "cold" or "hot"; remedies for fevers and swellings are "cold" to relieve the illness caused by excessive heat; remedies for colds and chills are "hot" to warm the patient. None of the remedies used appears to be aboriginal. The great majority are made of herbs used in European folk medicine.

In the accompanying table Guaraní names for plants are listed whenever possible. In nearly all cases the Guaraní name is a direct translation from Spanish. Identifications were made from the following sources: Moisés S. Bertoni, *Diccionario botánico* (Asunción, 1940); *Appleton's New English-Spanish and Spanish-English Dictionary* (3d ed.); *Webster's Collegiate Dictionary* (5th ed.); P. A. Guasch, *El Idioma guaraní* (Buenos Aires, 1948); *The Forest Resources of Paraguay* (Washington, D.C.: Institute of Inter-American Affairs, Food Supply Division, 1946).

317

Guaraní Name	Spanish Name	Latin Name	English Name	Use
	Achicoria	Achorium (Webster)	Chicory	The roots are used with *mate* as a purgative
Aguará ruguá'ý	Cola de zorra	Andropogen(?) (Bertoni)	Foxtail grass	Used in *mate* or mashed and prepared as a tea with no sugar, to cure diarrhea; only the roots are used
	Ajenjo	Artemesia (Webster)	Wormwood	The bitter leaves are prepared as a tea to treat colic
Ambaý sa'iyú		Cecropia or Ambaiba(?) (Bertoni)		The leaves are prepared as a tea to relieve coughing
Ambaý blanco				The leaves are prepared as a tea to relieve coughing
Ambaý guazú		Bumelia obtusifolia (Forest Resources)	Ginseng	Used as a cough remedy
	Berro	Roripa nasturtium-aquaticum (Webster)	Watercress	Prepared as an infusion for patients with "weak blood"
	Borraja	Borago officinalis (Webster)	Borage	The small blue flowers are cooked, and the resulting infusion is drunk to induce sweating; used usually in combination with other herbs
Ca'a	Yerba mate	Ilex paraguayensis (Forest Resources)		Prepared as a tea and used as a base to which medicinal ingredients are added
Ca'aré	Paico	Chenopodium (Bertoni)	Saltwort	Used as a tea, as an enema, and as a vermifuge; as a last resort, a paste may be made of the leaves and smeared on the patient from head to foot
	Calabacito		Calabash	The root is used to prepare remedies against *payé*
Capiúna			Similar in appearance to everlasting	The entire plant—leaves, roots, and stems—is used to prepare a tea for bronchitis or other severe chest coughs
Cavayú ruguaý	Cola de caballo	Equisetum (Bertoni)	Horsetail grass	The leaves and stems are prepared as a tea, drunk without sugar, to start menstrual flow; the plant is rubbed on a child's legs to make it walk at an early age
	Cedrón de España			Leaves are prepared in a tea to relieve colic or other stomach or intestinal pain; a "hot" remedy
	Culantrillo	Adiantum(?) (Webster)	Maidenhair fern	Used as a specific to stop hemorrhage
Curúguaý		Dioclea(?) (Bertoni)		The toasted seeds are used in a tea for treatment of *hígado;* the nut is carried in the pocket to relieve hemorrhoids
Curupica'ý		Sapium longifolium (Forest Resources)	Spurge	The gum is used to relieve the pain of spider bites, snakebite, and toothache; the gum also serves as glue and is used in trapping parrots

Guaraní Name	Spanish Name	Latin Name	English Name	Use
	Doradilla	*Adiantum* (Webster)		The roots are used to stop hemorrhage; it is a good remedy "for the blood" in many illnesses and gives vigor to old persons; the leaves are prepared in a tea to relieve neuralgia
(*Yriypica'ý*[?])	*Incienso*	*Myrocarpus frondosus* (*Forest Resources*)		The gum is used in setting broken bones
	Jazmín del Paraguay or *Jazmín de lluvia*			The small star-shaped white flowers of this bush are crushed and the juice put into water to make an eye wash for *mal de ojos*
Kokú		*Allophilus* or *Schmiedelia* (Bertoni)		Used to make a tea for the treatment of *hígado*
	Laurel de España, Laurel sa'iyú, Laurel canela, Laurel morotí	(Four species of *Ocotea* and *Nectandra* are listed in *Forest Resources*)	Laurel	A generally favored remedy, tea of laurel leaves is used in the treatment of many illnesses; leaves are also used in seasoning food
	Llanten		Plantain, rib grass	Used in combination with other plants to relieve digestive and intestinal upsets
	Lima purud		Lime	The juice is used as a tonic
	Luís Barbo			The juice of the root is squeezed out and used as a purgative and also to treat tuberculosis; a powder of the root is given as a tonic for anemic children
	Malva blanca	Malvaceae(?) (Webster)	White mallow(?)	A tea is made of the buds which is beneficial for a cough; this plant is also used to clean grease from pots and pans
	Manzanilla	*Anthemis*(?) (Webster)	Camomile	The strong-scented leaves are used as an antispasmodic and a diaphoretic
Mbaracayá nambí	*Oreja de gato*	*Hypericum*(?) (Bertoni)		May be used as a tea for *mal de boca* (mouth sores); mixed with salt and boiled for a long time, the infusion is used to bathe body sores; it is said to be effective as a cure for syphilis lesions
	Molle	Anacardiaceae (Bertoni)	A sumac or cashew	The roots are cooked to prepare a water for bathing *granos*
	Nardo	Valerianaceae, *Nardostachys jatamansi* (Webster)	Spikenard or nard	The flower, a tuberose, is dried and prepared in tea as a heart remedy or a sedative
	Pino		Pine	At the point where the leaf breaks off the stem, a juice is secured which is applied to an aching tooth; it is said the tooth will then rot and fall out

Guaraní Name	Spanish Name	Latin Name	English Name	Use
Piri rapó	*Esparto*		Matweed	The root is used as an abortive
	Poleo	*Hadeoma pulegioides*(?) (Webster)	Pennyroyal	An aromatic herb; the leaves are used as a tea for stomach ache and for improving the blood
	Rosa mosqueta	*Rosa moschata* (Appleton)	Musk rose	The flower is used to make a tea which acts as a purgative
	Ruda	Rutaceae (Webster)	Rue	The strong bitter leaves are used in treatment of erysipelas
	Salvia	Laminaceae(?) (Webster)	A sage(?)	An aromatic herb; considered a "hot" remedy, it is used in combination with other plants for rheumatism
	Santa Lucía	*Equisetum*(?)		The leaves and stem are prepared as an infusion and taken in *mate amargo* for intestinal pain
	Siemprevive	Carduaceae (Webster)	Everlasting	The purple flower is used as a tea for a heart remedy; the leaves are used in the treatment for erysipelas; often combined with cedron
Tapequé	*Abrojo*	*Richardsonia* (Bertoni)	A thistle	A small, creeping plant, it grows abundantly on abandoned roads; may be used as an infusion taken in *mate amargo* for diabetes; also used as a disinfectant for small wounds
Taperyguá		Anacardiaceae (Bertoni)	A sumac or cashew	The seeds are toasted and ground and prepared as coffee for pain in the lungs
	Tártago	*Euphorbia (Forest Resources)*	Castor	The castor bean is used as a purgative
	Tilo	Tilaceae (Webster)	Linden	Used as a sedative tea to calm heart palpitations
Typycha'hú	*Escobilla*	*Corchorus* or *Scoparia* (Bertoni)		Used to cure *ura* in cattle, in conjunction with secret prayers
	Verbena	*Verbena* (Webster)	Verbena	The leaves, moistened with *caña* and combined with leaves of everlasting and rue, are applied to reduce swelling
Yácaratía	*Papaya, papa'í*	*Didymopanax morototoni (Forest Resources)*	Papaw	The juice of the fruit is a purgative and vermifuge—the smaller and greener the fruit, the more effective the medicine; the flower of the male tree is also used; the leaf is used to remove stains from cloth
Yaguapetý	*Perdudilla negra*	*Solanum* (Bertoni)	A nightshade	Used in water to bathe milk leg
Yaguarundý		Piperaceae, *Artanthe* (Bertoni)		An aromatic pepper, used as a tea for cough
Yataý ca'a		*Butia*(?) (Bertoni)		Used as a cure for appendicitis
	Yerbabuena		Mint	Used as a cooling beverage, considered soothing to the nerves
Ysipó'peré	*Junco* or *mil hombres*	Juncaceae, *Cuphea* (Bertoni)		This may be used as an enema: a piece of stem 4–5 inches long is ground to a powder; may also be taken in *tereré;* also used to treat animals

Treatment for Specific Conditions

Anemia.—Yolk of egg, beaten and flavored with anise, wine, cinnamon, and sugar, is taken at night before retiring and during the night if the patient awakens. Pennyroyal is taken as a tea to improve the blood.

Appendicitis.—A common herb, *yatú ca'a,* is prepared as a tea and drunk regularly for a month to cure the inflammation so that the appendix cannot break. This herb may also be prepared as a syrup with burnt sugar and taken with lemon before each meal. Appendicitis is said to be very common in Paraguay.

Broken bones.—The bone is set with a mixture of burned dog bone, ashes, and crushed eggshells, mixed with molasses and gum of the *incienso* tree. Bees' honey or egg white may also be used as adhesives in such a mixture. Bruises, sprains, and dislocations are treated in the same way. The adhesive mixture is smeared on a cloth and wrapped around the break next to the skin. The bandage is wound tight and left for about forty days.

Burns.—Burns are treated with no understanding of the danger of infection. Most often, white of egg or ink is smeared on the burn immediately. A common cause of burns to women and children is upsetting of kettles boiling at the household fire.

Colic.—In children or babies colic is treated by giving a bitter medicine like tea of wormwood, camomile tea, or unsweetened black coffee. In adults colic is believed to result from heavy food, from eating pork and drinking water immediately afterward, from a chill if the stomach is not well covered, or from indulgence in sexual intercourse after a meal. A hot tea made of leaves of *cedrón de España* boiled with root of *ca'aré* and poured over manzanilla blossoms is taken. This is a purgative and is believed to cure the cause of colic. A tea of the leaves and stem of *Santa Lucía* is taken in *mate amargo.*

Diabetes.—Diabetes is treated by adding the dried leaves of *tapequé* or *abrojo* to the daily *mate amargo.*

Diarrhea.—Diarrhea often occurs as an epidemic and most frequently attacks children, though adults may suffer from it too. Children given a combination of laurel leaves, anise, and grass roots in black coffee. Tea of anise or oriental tea is also used. No food is given except *galletas,* and no water is given. Mashed roots of foxtail grass taken in *mate* or as a tea without sugar constitute another remedy.

Erysipelas.—Leaves of everlasting, rue, and verbena moistened with *caña* may be applied to reduce swelling. Common face powder alleviates the local fever. It is widely believed, even by schoolteachers and other educated people, that passing a toad over the inflamed area will cure the disease. The toad is believed to take up the fever, turn red, and die.

Fevers.—The same remedies are used for all fevers, no matter what the cause. The small flowers of borage are cooked and drunk as a tea to induce sweating. Often the flowers are mixed with parts of other plants. No food should be eaten, but tea of orange leaves or chicken soup may be drunk. A purgative of the musk rose is often given. As a last resort for a very high fever, a medicine made of squash seeds, melon seeds, grass roots, and petals of musk rose is prepared by smashing the ingredients and bringing them to the boiling point in water. Fresh milk is added, and the medicine is taken in the morning on an empty stomach. This is a very strong purgative and also induces sweating.

Chills and fever of unknown cause are called *acánundú-ro'y* in Guaraní and *chucho* in Spanish. The Guaraní term means "fever-chill," and the Spanish word means malaria. The name is applied to any high fever accompanied by chills. Quinine is often combined with squash seeds and other plants to prepare a remedy for such a fever.

Goiter.—Goiter is believed to result from poor food; it is treated by eating soft-boiled eggs beaten with vegetable oil and powdered sulfur.

"Granos."—Skin boils or pimples are most commonly treated by bathing in water in which the mashed root of *molle* has been boiled. A black soap made of zebu fat and ashes should be used in conjunction with this treatment.

Heart diseases.—Heart ailments are treated with tea of nard flowers or tea of everlasting combined with leaves of cedron. Tea of linden leaves is a sedative and may be given to stop palpitations.

Hemorrhage.—Roots of *doradilla* or *culantrillo* are used as a tea. The flower of the musk rose and roots of chicory, sweetened with bees' honey and drunk very hot, is said to stop hemmorhage rapidly. Burned soil is applied to wounds, particularly the dirt from inside an oven or from a brick factory. Nosebleeds are stopped by putting a cold key or cold water on the head or forehead or by tying the little finger of the left hand tight enough to stop circulation.

"Hígado."—Literally "liver," *hígado* seems to be a concept or a cause of sickness rather than an illness of a particular organ. Belching is caused by *hígado*, and so is a general feeling of illness. Remedies include tea of the *kokú* bush, coffee of toasted and shucked seeds of *curúguaý* taken daily, or soup made of cow's liver without salt. We heard many educated people speak of *hígado* as a cause of death, of general lack of energy, and of headaches, and it seems to be a common and fashionable illness.

Leprosy.—Although leprosy is generally believed to be incurable, one *curandera* insisted that she knew of a way to cure it with baths and teas but would not disclose her treatment.

"Mancha."—A disease characterized by swelling glands and fever. It is known as a highly contagious disease of cattle and horses which causes death of an animal within twenty-four hours, with great pain and convulsions. Humans may be infected by the animals or by other humans, and after burial of a victim the house and its residents should be washed thoroughly with water to which lemon juice is added. (See also "Scarlet fever.")

Menstruation.—An excellent regulator and pain remedy commonly used is leaf of avocado, prepared as tea. Root of *piri rapó* is used as an abortive, and so is horsetail grass, both prepared as a tea. *Doradilla* is used to remedy the condition of "weak blood" or "insufficient blood" if indicated by scant menstruation. (See chap. xviii for a general discussion of this topic.)

Piles.—The only treatment we heard of was to carry the nut of the *curúguaý* in the pocket.

Pregnancy.—Dry births and childbed fever are most feared. Milk leg is treated by bathing the patient in water with *yaguápetý*, a nightshade, and, after putting a tourniquet on the leg above the swelling, bathing the swollen part. Weak blood is the cause of milk leg and may also cause the mongoloid spot on the infant. (See chap. xix.)

Rabies.—Rabies is very much feared as incurable in humans. It is believed that dogs are more likely to become rabid during the waxing moon and reach the height of the disease at the full moon. Cutting a notch in both ears of the dog to cause bleeding may cure him.

Respiratory disorders.—Such disorders are a most common cause of illness and death. For colds the usual treatment is a tea of *yaguarundý* or *ambaý* and a cough syrup. One may eat as usual, except that "cold" foods must be avoided. Rubbing the temples and behind the ears with candle wax mixed with manzanilla flowers will heat the head. Good cough remedies are made of *ambaý blanco, ambaý saiyú, yaguarundý,* and *mil hombres. Capiuna* may be made into a tea as a remedy for bronchitis. All of these are "hot" medicines.

Smallpox; scarlet fever.—*Viruela negra* or *mbiru'á hu* (apparently smallpox) is nearly always fatal, especially to adults. *Viruela boba* or *loca, mbiru'á tavý* (probably chicken pox), is considered grave for adults but not so serious for children, though children are most susceptible. *Mancha,* a term commonly used to describe redness and swelling together, may sometimes refer to scarlet fever. A remedy prescribed for all types of *viruela* consists of dried dog excrement, pounded, burned, and strained through a clean cloth, and put in water in a cloth bag. This water should be drunk throughout the illness in place of pure water. Various herbal remedies may also be used, but usually in combination with the dog excrement, which is called *azúcar del campo.* Scars are treated with water in which *andaí* has been cooked.

"Susto"; worms.—It is believed that every child and adult has worms in his blood which may cause illness. A person is more likely to fall ill of *susto* if the circulation of blood is poor, if one has insufficient or "bad" blood, or "weak blood in the head," all of which allow the worms to attack. Children, being generally weaker than adults, are most susceptible. Contributing factors may be eating too many sweets, anemia, paleness, or nervousness. Any of these in combination with a frightening experience may bring on an attack of *susto.* The illness may be fatal, but there are many remedies, all of which depend on killing and eliminating the worms by purgatives. It seems to be generally agreed that *susto* or *espanto* activates the worms and causes them to rise to the head, causing convulsions, fits, fainting, hysteria, or death. In Guaraní *susto* is called *ñemondýi,* defined as an extreme fright in which the nerves are involved.

A common remedy is to rub the patient with leaves of *ca'aré,* or saltwort, and to take a tea made of the leaves. As a last resort, a paste may be made of the leaves and the patient smeared from head to foot with the mixture. Diagnosis of *susto* is by observation of general symptoms, aided by examination of the urine. When a child has fever, *susto* is suspected. Twitching in the sleep, particularly when combined with fever and poor appetite, is a definite sign of *susto.*

Since the Rockefeller antihookworm mission attempted an educational campaign in Paraguay, some preventive measures have been taken. The city and town laws require a privy as one of the household buildings. Children are taught the causes, symptoms, and prevention of hookworm in the schools and are encouraged to wear shoes. Nevertheless, it is still commonly believed that "everyone has worms, even those who appear to be healthy." Even animals may fall ill of *susto* caused by worms. A pig which has *susto* will not fatten.

Trachoma ("mal de ojos").—Trachoma is most common in children, though adults may be affected. Most commonly, it is treated with an eyewash made from the small star-shaped flower of the *jazmín del Paraguay*. The juice of the flower is pressed out and mixed with water. The cause of trachoma is believed to be heat and sun glare, and every effort is made to keep children in the shade during the hot summer months. Water in which the dried umbilicus of the child has been soaked is also believed to be an effective remedy. A person afflicted with trachoma is believed to be able to recognize a person who is *oyeharú* ("evil-eyed").

Tuberculosis.—Recognized as dangerous and contagious, tuberculosis is considered incurable. It is treated by giving tonics against anemia and by taking the juice of the root of *Luís Barbo* as a purgative. Seeds of *taperyguá* are toasted, ground, and made into a coffee as an alleviant for pain. Mare's milk, drunk immediately after milking, is considered helpful.

Whooping cough.—Burro's milk is poured over bees' honey immediately after milking and is given as a soothing syrup.

Rickets.—Goat's milk is given, if available, to children who have rickets.

Skin eruptions.—Various types of skin disorders are treated with urine. A woman who has a swollen or blotchy face during pregnancy or nursing uses the urine of the nursing child to cure the *mancha*. Adolescents use their own urine to cure acne. Infected eyes may be treated by washing the eye with one's own urine. (Sprains and rheumatism may also be treated by bathing the affected part with urine mixed with tobacco or salt; the mixture is very "hot" and reduces pain and swelling.)

Skin ulcers.—Skin ulcers are treated by application of ashes of burned alligator skin.

Syphilis.—Sores may be cured by application of water in which leaves of *oreja de gato* have been boiled for a long time. This may also be used as a mouthwash to cure mouth sores.

Umbilical hernia or "quebrado."—Believed to be caused by "cold." A woman may neglect her child, so that it becomes chilled. Failure to change diapers promptly or failure to use an abdominal band are common causes. "Hot" medicines are used, including hot infusions and putting "hot" remedies on the hernia and binding it.

Spider- and snakebites.—The sap of the *curupica'ý* is used to deaden the pain.

"Ura."—Juice of the *curupica'ý* is used to cure the *ura*, or maggots hatched from fly eggs deposited in open sores. The juice is placed on

the sore and causes the maggots to come out. This treatment may be used for animals and for adult humans, but the juice burns too much to be used on children. The maggots are squeezed out of the sore when children are treated. In animals they may also be cut out or may be exorcised by prayer.

Toothache.—Toothache is cured by placing the juice of *pino* on cotton and putting it on the aching tooth. The juice is secured from the point where the leaf breaks from the stem, and it is believed to cause the aching tooth to fall out. As a painkiller only, but not a cure, the sap of *curupica'ÿ* may be used.

Bibliography

Bibliography

Acosta, César R. "La Población rural del Paraguay," in *Materiales para el estudio de la clase media en la América Latina*, III, 95–106. Washington, D.C.: Unión Panamericana, 1950.

Arensberg, Conrad. *The Irish Countryman.* London: Macmillan & Co., Ltd., 1937.

Azara, Félix de. *Viajes por la América Meridional.* 2 vols. Madrid: Espasa-Calpe, 1923.

Bazán, Juán F. *Del surco guaraní.* Buenos Aires: The author, [n.d.].

Beals, Ralph L. *Cherán: A Sierra Tarascan Village.* ("Publications of the Smithsonian Institution, Institute of Social Anthropology," No. 2.) Washington, D.C.: Government Printing Office, 1946.

———. "Social Stratification in Latin America," *American Journal of Sociology*, LVIII, No. 4 (January, 1953), 327–39.

Bertoni, Moisés S. *Diccionario botánico.* Asunción: Editorial Guaraní, 1940.

Bourgade la Dardye, E. de. *Paraguay: The Land and the People, Natural Wealth and Commercial Capabilities.* London: Philip, 1892.

Brand, Donald D. *Quiroga: A Mexican Municipio.* ("Publications of the Smithsonian Institution, Institute of Social Anthropology," No. 11.) Washington, D.C.: Government Printing Office, 1951.

Brewer, Sam Pope. *New York Times*, January 7, 1953, p. 26.

Censo de agricultura del Paraguay. Prepared by the Servicio Técnico Interamericano de Cooperación Agrícola, 1942–44. Washington, D.C.: Bureau of the Census, 1948.

Christiansen, Asher N. *The Evolution of Latin American Government.* New York: Henry Holt & Co., 1951.

Dirección general de estadística del Paraguay. Asunción, 1946.

Dobrizhoffer, Martin. *An Account of the Abipones, an Equestrian People of Paraguay.* 3 vols. London: J. Murray, 1822.

Domínguez, Manuel. *El Alma de la raza.* Buenos Aires: Editorial Ayacucho, [n.d.].

Du Biscay, Acarete. *An Account of a Voyage up the River de la Plata, and Thence over Land to Peru. . . .* London: Buckley, 1698.

Firth, Raymond. *Elements of Social Organization.* London: Watts & Co., Ltd., 1951.

Forest Resources of Paraguay. Washington, D.C.: Institute of Inter-American Affairs, Food Supply Division, 1946.

Foster, George M. *Empire's Children: The People of Tzintzuntzan.*

("Publications of the Smithsonian Institution, Institute of Social Anthropology," No. 6.) Washington, D.C.: Government Printing Office, 1948.

FREYRE, GILBERTO. *Casa grande e senzala*. Rio de Janeiro: Schmidt, 1938.

GARAY, BLAS. *Colección de documentos relativos á la historia de América y particularmente á la historia del Paraguay*. Asunción: H. Kraus, 1899–1901.

GILLIN, JOHN. "Mestizo America," in RALPH LINTON (ed.), *Most of the World*, pp. 156–211. New York: Columbia University Press, 1949.

——. *Moche: A Peruvian Coastal Community*. ("Publications of the Smithsonian Institution, Institute of Social Anthropology," No. 3.) Washington, D.C.: Government Printing Office, 1945.

GONZÁLEZ, NATALICIO. *Proceso y formación de la cultura guaraní*. Asunción and Buenos Aires: Editorial Guarania, 1938.

GONZÁLEZ, NATALICIO, AND YNSFRAN, PABLO MAX. *El Paraguay contemporáneo*. Paris and Asunción: Editorial de Indias, 1929.

GONZÁLEZ, TEODOSIO. *Infortunios del Paraguay*. Asunción: Editorial Guarania, 1931.

GUASCH, P. ANTONIO. *El Idioma guaraní*. Buenos Aires: The author, 1948.

HARING, CLARENCE H. *Trade and Navigation between Spain and the Indies in the Time of the Hapsburgs*. Cambridge, Mass.: Harvard University Press, 1918.

HERNÁNDEZ, PABLO. *Organización social de las doctrinas guaraníes de la Compañía de Jesús*. 2 vols. Barcelona: G. Gili, 1913.

Introduction to Contemporary Civilization in the West. 2 vols. New York: Columbia University Press, 1946.

JAMES, PRESTON E. *Latin America*. New York: Odyssey Press, 1942.

LA FUENTE, JULIO DE. *Yalalag: Una Villa Zapoteca Serrana*. Mexico: Museo Nacional de Antropología, 1949.

LAFUENTE MACHAIN, R. DE. *El Gobernador Domingo Martínez de Irala*. Buenos Aires: Bernabé y cía., 1939.

LEHBURN, JAMES G. *The Haitian People*. New Haven, Conn.: Yale University Press, 1941.

LEVENE, RICARDO. *A History of Argentina*. Chapel Hill, N.C.: University of North Carolina Press, 1937.

LEVI, CARLO. *Christ Stopped at Eboli*. New York: Farrar, Straus & Co., 1947.

LEWIS, OSCAR. *Life in a Mexican Village: Tepoztlan Revisited*. Urbana, Ill.: University of Illinois Press, 1951.

LÓPEZ DE VELASCO, JUÁN. *Geografía y descripción universal de las Indias*. Madrid: Fortanet, 1894.

MALDONADO, SILVIO. *El Paraguay*. Mexico and Buenos Aires: *Fondo de la Cultura Económica*, 1952.

MECHAM, JOHN LLOYD. *Church and State in Latin America*. Chapel Hill, N.C.: University of North Carolina Press, 1934.

MÉTRAUX, ALFRED. "The Guaraní," in JULIAN H. STEWARD (ed.), *Handbook of South American Indians*, III (1948), 69–94. (Bureau of American Ethnology, Smithsonian Institution of Washington, Bull. 143.) 6 vols. Washington, D.C.: Government Printing Office, 1946–50.

MINTZ, SIDNEY W., AND WOLF, ERIC R. "An Analysis of Ritual Co-parent-hood (Compadrazgo)." *Southwestern Journal of Anthropology*, VI, No. 4 (winter, 1950), 341–68.

MOSES, BERNARD. *The Establishment of Spanish Rule in America.* New York: G. P. Putnam's Sons, 1892.

MOUSSY, V. MARTIN DE. *Mémoire historique sur le décadence et la ruine des missions des Jesuites.* ... Paris: C. Douniol, 1864.

NELSON, LOWRY. *Rural Cuba.* Minneapolis, Minn.: University of Minnesota Press, 1950.

PARSONS, ELSIE CLEWS. *Mitla: Town of the Souls.* Chicago: University of Chicago Press, 1936.

PAUL, BENJAMIN D. "Ritual Kinship, with Special Reference to God-parenthood in Middle America." Unpublished Ph.D. thesis, University of Chicago, 1942.

PENDLE, GEORGE. *Paraguay: A Riverside Nation.* London: Royal Institute of International Affairs, 1954.

PIERSON, DONALD. *Cruz das Almas: A Brazilian Village.* ("Publications of the Smithsonian Institution, Institute of Social Anthropology," No. 12.) Washington, D.C.: Government Printing Office, 1951.

REDFIELD, ROBERT, AND VILLA ROJAS, ALFONSO. *Chan Kom: A Maya Village.* ("Carnegie Institution of Washington Publications," No. 448.) Washington, D.C., 1934.

REH, EMMA. *Paraguayan Rural Life.* Washington, D.C.: Institute of Inter-American Affairs, Food Supply Division, 1946.

ROBERTSON, J. P. AND W. P. *Four Years in Paraguay: Comprising an Account of That Republic, under the Government of the Dictator Francia.* 2 vols. Philadelphia: E. L. Carey & A. Hart, 1838.

ROJAS GONZALES, FRANCISCO. "La Institución del compadrazgo entre las indígenas de México," *Revista mexicana de sociología*, V (1943), 201–14.

RUÍZ DE MONTOYA, ANTONIO. *Conquista espiritual hecha por los religiosos de la Compañía de Jesús en las provincias del Paraguay, Paraná, Uruguay, y Tapé.* Bilbao: Imprenta del Corazón de Jesús, 1892.

SERVICE, ELMAN R. "The Encomienda in Paraguay," *Hispanic American Historical Review*, XXXI, No. 2 (May, 1951), 230–51.

———. *Spanish-Guaraní Relations in Early Colonial Paraguay.* ("Anthropological Papers of the Museum of Anthropology, University of Michigan," No. 9.) Ann Arbor: University of Michigan Press, 1954.

STEWARD, JULIAN H. *Area Research: Theory and Practice.* (Social Science Research Council Bull. 63.) Washington, D.C., 1950.

———. "The Changing American Indian," in RALPH LINTON (ed.), *The Science of Man in the World Crisis*, pp. 282–305. New York: Columbia University Press, 1945.

———. *Handbook of South American Indians.* (Smithsonian Institution, Bureau of American Ethnology, Bull. 143.) Washington, D.C.: Government Printing Office, 1946–50.

TAX, SOL (ed.). *Heritage of Conquest.* Glencoe, Ill.: Free Press, 1952.

TAYLOR, CARL. *Rural Life in Argentina.* Baton Rouge, La.: Louisiana State University Press, 1948.

TECHO, NICOLÁS DEL. *Historia de la provincia del Paraguay y de la Compañía de Jesús.* Madrid: Librería y casa editorial A. de Uribe, 1897.
——. "The History of the Provinces of Paraguay, Tucumán, Río de la Plata, Paraná, Guairá, and Urvaica," in AWNSHAM CHURCHILL (comp.), *A Collection of Voyages and Travels,* Vol. IV. London: Printed by assignment from Messrs. Churchill, for H. Lintot, 1746.
WARREN, HARRIS G. *Paraguay: An Informal History.* Norman, Okla.: University of Oklahoma Press, 1949.
WASHBURN, CHARLES A. *The History of Paraguay.* 2 vols. Boston: Lee & Shepard, 1871.
WHETTEN, NATHAN L. *Rural Mexico.* Chicago: University of Chicago Press, 1948.
WILLEMS, EMILIO. "Caboclo Cultures of Southern Brazil," in SOL TAX (ed.), *Acculturation in the Americas: Proceedings and Selected Papers of the XXIXth Congress of Americanists,* pp. 231–43. Chicago: University of Chicago Press, 1952.
——. *Cunha: Tradição e transição em uma cultura rural do Brasil.* São Paulo: Secretaria de Agricultura do Estado de São Paolo, Directoria de Publicidade Agrícola, 1948.
WILLEMS, EMILIO, AND MUSSOLINI, GIOCONDA. *Buzios Island: A Caicara Community in Southern Brazil.* ("Monographs of the American Ethnological Society," Vol. XX.) New York: J. J. Augustin, 1952.
WYTHE, GEORGE. *An Outline of Latin American Economic Development.* New York: Barnes & Noble, 1947.

Index

333